The Radical Soldier's Tale

John Pearman, 1819–1908

Carolyn Steedman

Routledge
London and New York

First published in 1988 by
Routledge
11 New Fetter Lane, London EC4P 4EE
29 West 35th Street, New York, NY 10001

Set in Linotron Bembo
by Columns of Reading
and printed in Great Britain
by Biddles Ltd.,
Guildford and Kings Lynn

Library of Congress Cataloging in Publication Data
Steedman, Carolyn,
    The radical soldier's tale: John Pearman, 1819–1908/Carolyn
Steedman.
    p.   cm. — (History Workshop series)
"A transcript of 'Memos of late Sergeant John Pearman of H. Mgt.
3rd or Kings own Light Dragoons' ": p.
Bibliography: p.
Includes index.
1. Pearman, John, 1819–1908. 2. Great Britain. Army — Biography.
3. Soldiers — Great Britain — Biography. 4. Policemen — Great
Britain — Biography. 5. Radicalism — Great Britain — History —
19th century. 6. Sikh War, 1845–1846 — Personal narratives, British.
7. Sikh War, 1848–1849 — Personal narratives, British. 8. Laboring
class writings, English — History and criticism. 9. Autobiography.
10. Buckinghamshire — Social life and customs. I. Pearman, John,
1819–1908. Memos of late Sergeant John Pearman of H. Mgt. 3rd or
Kings own Light Dragoons. 1988. II. Title. III. Series.
DA68.22.P43S84 1988
941.081'092'4 — dc19   88–2382

British Library CIP Data also available

ISBN 0-415-00207-9

ERRATUM

For maps I and II on pages 9 and 10, please note that the captions should be reversed.

Documents are themselves historical realities that do not simply represent but also supplement the realities to which they refer.

Dominick LaCapra, *History and Criticism*, Cornell University Press, 1985, p. 62

The soldier's tale serves in some way to de-mythologize and hence de-narrativize history . . . to re-enchant the world, to invest the notion of heroism for instance, with new meanings that crack open the reified exterior with which its usage by the state has wrapped it in medals and decorations.

Mick Taussig, 'An Australian Hero', *History Workshop Journal*, 24 (Autumn 1987), p.113

Contents

Acknowledgments	*ix*
Introduction	*1*
Map I	*9*
Map II	*10*

Part One

1	Writers, Editors and Historians	13
2	A Working Life	25
3	Soldiers' Stories	34
4	'A Low Order of Men'	52
5	The Practice of Writing	62
6	The Propulsion of Experience	86
7	Public and Private	103

Part Two

Note on the Dating of John Pearman's 'Memoir'	109
Note on the Transcription of John Pearman's 'Memoir'	111
A Transcript of 'Memos of Late Sergeant John Pearman of H. Mgt 3rd or Kings Own Light Dragoons'	112
Notes to the Transcript	250
Notes	270
Bibliography	290
Working Class Military Autobiography	297
Index	299

Acknowledgments

Over the past seven years, a great many people have helped me by reading and talking to me about John Pearman's 'Memoir'. My first thanks must go to Philip Donnellan, for had he not made, and I not watched his 'Gone for a Soldier' on television in March 1980, I would never have encountered John Pearman at all. His continued interest in this project has been a great help to me. Peter and Betty Pearman have most generously provided me with permission to transcribe and publish the 'Memoir'. I am extremely grateful for all their kindness and support. I hope that they think the old man has had some kind of justice done.

Any attempt like this, to discover something of what someone living in the past read, thought and encountered as ideas in the course of a lifetime, has to be a collaborative effort, and I have thrust collaboration upon a great many people. I hope that these acknowledgments will show the extent of my gratitude for their generous interest and help. Librarians and archivists at the National Army Museum, Paul Quarry at Eton College Library and Andrew Cook at the India Office Library have offered help and information quite beyond the call of duty. I would especially like to thank Peter Boyden and Claire Wright of the National Army Museum, for bearing with my ignorance of matters military. Gordon Everson most generously gave me information about the recent history of the manuscript itself and shared with me his knowledge of John Pearman's life.

I have greatly benefited from talking to and corresponding with Raphael Samuel, Christopher Hill, Shula Marks, Ian Smith, Margaret Donaldson, Sheridan Gilley, John Stokes, Keith McCleland, Raymond South, Michael Ignatieff, Bill Livingstone and Ludmilla Jordanova. Philip Dodd's search for the sources of the 'Memoir' as a literary text has been the most enormous help: I said that my thanks would be fulsome; I hope they are.

At different stages, David Vincent, Barbara Taylor and Edward Royle provided me with crucial readings of John Pearman's manuscript and my own. Indeed, without Edward Royle's *Victorian Infidels*, and his *Radicals, Secularists and Republicans* it simply would not have been possible to pursue John Pearman this far. I am very grateful for his help. Barbara Taylor raised a necessary and restraining hand against the wilder reaches of my romance of historical sources, for which my gratitude. David Vincent's reading of the 'Memoir' allowed me to see in it things that I had hitherto ignored. The argument of the following pages owes a good deal to that reading.

Introduction

I first saw a photograph of John Pearman in March 1980 when I was watching the BBC television production 'Gone for a Soldier', a documentary history of the rank and file in the British army. Voice-over gave this extract from John Pearman's writing:

> my sincere impression is man was not made to Slaughter is Fellow man. for any other man or state although he may have ingaged himself as a hired assassin in my mind one man as as much right to the earth as another[1]

The man on the screen wore the uniform of a policeman. He had, it seemed, joined the Buckinghamshire Constabulary after his discharge from the army in 1857. Buckinghamshire was one of the two Midland counties in which I had collected detailed information for what was to become *Policing the Victorian Community*,[2] and John Pearman was a policeman of whose career I had a full account, taken from the Register of the Members of the Force ten years before, in the County Record Office at Aylesbury.

I telephoned the BBC at Pebble Mill in Birmingham the next day, and spoke to Philip Donnellan, the producer of 'Gone for a Soldier'. When he had been working on the programme in 1979, he had discovered the whereabouts of John Pearman's 'Memoir', part of which had been published in an edited version, in 1968.[3] Peter Pearman, a great-grandson of its author, brought it across the Atlantic with him on holiday from Washington DC, where he then lived; and Philip Donnellan had used several extracts from it in his production. On the telephone, we talked briefly about soldiers and policemen, the faint echoes in the writings of the rank and file, of a subterranean and radical analysis of society made by such men: recruited as body-servants of privilege and property they were given, as servants must be, access to privileged information, took away with them secrets, an understanding of how the social machinery was kept working, and often, miserably, an understanding of their own role in that process.

I was due to spend the year 1980–1 in the USA anyway; I went to Maryland, met the Pearmans; I transcribed the 'Memoir'[4] and I talked a great deal to John Pearman's remaining family. John Pearman died in 1908; but still, in family photographs and in the memories transmitted to his great-grandson he sits, levelling his

1

gaze at the onlooker and the reader, grimly, doggedly, determined to *work it out*.

The title that I have given to the following transcript of John
Pearman's 'Memoir', and to my Introduction to it, is deliberately
meant to evoke Margaret Atwood's *The Handmaid's Tale*.[5] This
analogy may be considered the kind of rhetorical usage that gives
women a bad name. But it is not an analogy that should push
anybody concerned with the labour movement, people's history,
or working-class autobiography to that condemnation. The
fictional narrator of *The Handmaid's Tale* lives in a United States
of the imagined future, in which Biblical fundamentalism and a
triumphant moral majority dictate the structure of social, political
and sexual life. In this nightmare future, the handmaid – Offred –
has been selected for breeding purposes, by literal reference to the
scriptures. Her resistances to the situation she finds herself in are
small, though she survives for long enough to make and leave
behind her a pile of tapes that tell her story. The transcript of
these tapes is what makes the narrative; so Margaret Atwood's
dystopia is, among other things, a novel that deals with the
transcription, editing and interpretation of historical documents.

Once, in her room in the General's house to which she has been
drafted to conceive and bear a child, Offred finds a tiny scratched
inscription in the cupboard, 'in the corner where the darkest
shadow fell'. It has been left behind by a former inhabitant of the
room, another handmaid, and it reads: *Nolite te bastardes
carborundorum*. One of Offred's purposes, and the novel's purposes, is to translate this message from its dog-Latin. It turns out
to say: 'don't let the bastards grind you down.'

To be resentful and angry in small and uninscribed ways is one
form of resistance, though the labour movement and socialism
have not given such strategies much more recognition than have
the official canons of bravery and honour. It means only that you
don't give in, that you stay alive and resentful until the end, no
matter what the exigencies of life prevent by way of action from
you. Margaret Atwood's novel gives literary substance to this
form of resistance; and John Pearman gave expression to it in the
account of his life that he wrote in 1881–2. John Pearman was a
good policeman, that is, he got by, kept his own counsel, did
well, got a pension. They can buy your labour, make you put on
their uniform; but they cannot purchase your mind. Through the
long life that Pearman subjected to analysis in his writing, he did a
lot of thinking, but he took nothing ready-made in terms of ideas.
In 1881–2 his experience and his thought were there, waiting for
him to work on them. Growing old does not necessarily mean
becoming less radical; getting by, doing the best you can with

what life hands out to you, is one form of resistance.

However, it is not often called resistance; its more common name is complaint, or, in Virginia Woolf's striking observation about the difference between women's writing and men's writing, 'special pleading'. 'In *Middlemarch* and *Jane Eyre*', she wrote,

> we are conscious of a woman's presence – of someone resenting the treatment of her sex and pleading for its rights. This brings into a woman's writing an element which is entirely absent from a man's, unless, indeed, he happens to be a working man [or] a Negro. . .[6]

She went on to argue that such special pleading 'introduces a distortion, and is frequently a cause of weakness' in writing. John Pearman was a working-class man, and one who understood the structural relationship of the position of his class with the exploited of Britain's imperial realm – with the third world – in a way that we, mid-twentieth-century inheritors of analyses of working-class imperialism and jingoism, may find difficult to believe at first. His writing suffers from the distortion that Woolf indicated because, as I hope my introduction to it will show, there is a difficulty in *being* resentful, in knowing that the world *is* obdurate and unfair. What has been described is a style of writing that is produced by being ill-at-ease in the world as it is; a distortion that matches the distortion of what it is that is observed and expressed in the writing. What a study of this radical soldier's and policeman's tale may suggest in the end, is that resistance to dominant ideas and dominant political forms will not always look heroic; and it may at the same time provide for the edgy realisation that our very notion of heroism is defined by what those dominant forms have said is a proper and fitting set of feelings for people in John Pearman's position to hold.

What is being dealt with here is not a military memoir, but a working-class autobiography, written at the end of a working life. To have called this book the *Radical Policeman's Tale* might have been the clearest way of signalling this, for John Pearman's reflection on his own life story and his political arguments with himself came at the end of, and I shall argue, were largely propelled by, his most immediate experience as a working-class man who had become a policeman. He was a policeman for 25 years, and served in the King's Own Light Dragoons for only 13. Yet more than half of his 'Memoir' is taken up with a description of his soldiering years, and he writes very little about actually being a policeman. It was memories of his time in the army that propelled the radical analysis of the 'Memoir's' second half, and my title emphasises that point.

Historians of the nineteenth-century British army will find the following material useful only in as far as they find a complete and literal transcription of John Pearman's account of his involvement in the Sikh Wars (1845–9) useful. I am not a military historian, and I can add very little to the account given of the wars and John Pearman's record of them, given by the Marquess of Anglesey in his edition of 1968.[7] But of course, the historical purpose of presenting a complete and literal transcription of a document is to allow it to function as a source for other historical accounts, other analyses. In this way then, military historians may find the following pages as useful as may historians of the police, of popular political culture and of working-class writing.

The central purpose in publishing John Pearman's writing in this way is to make it generally available to historians, cultural anthropologists, and to literary theorists interested in autobiographical writing, and for them to make connections and recognise sources that I have not. There are a small number of references in John Pearman's text that I have not been able to locate. These are indicated in the Notes to the 'Memoir', and I hope in a future edition to rectify these omissions. I should at this point, though, repeat the warning that I came to issue to myself in the course of editing this manuscript. My own obsession in the search for sources centres on John Pearman's use of the phrase 'animated nature'. ('Memoir', pp. 159, 162, 163, 182) I have made many phone calls about these words, fixed people with my glittering eye at parties. 'What', I have asked, 'does "animated nature" mean to you?' It took me some time to realise that combing Milton and diligently searching concordances was not going to answer the more proper question of what 'animated nature' meant to John Pearman.

This is not a quotation from Coleridge's 'Aeolian Harp', and thus John Pearman was not, I think, using the romantic transmutation of eighteenth-century materialist philosophy into the idea that this 'varied and eternal world' is animated and directed by a pervading spirit. This is not the Spirit of the Universe via 'Queen Mab' and Shelley's later learning from Wordsworth. Neither is it the freethinker's necessitarianism taken from the late eighteenth-century doctrine of philosophical necessity.[8] It was an organising principle for Pearman, this phrase; a usage, not a quotation. This is a point that is often elided by talking about a 'tradition' of thought (as in this case, one does want to talk about a Painite tradition). When John Pearman wrote of 'an animated nature all ruled by a certain law of its own', then the closest to a *definition* of this idea is to be found here:

All nature acts in conformity with universal laws; man forms an integral part of Nature, and must act in unison with his elements; the laws of Nature are beyond human controul, they are independent of men, unchangeable by any power less than the contriver; the Laws of Nature are neither arrested, interrupted, biassed, or controverted by venal, bigoted, fanatical Priests.[9]

John Pearman is likely to have read Richard Carlile's *Character of a Priest*, from which this quotation is taken (and his *Character of a Soldier* and *Character of a Peer*, through which the phrase 'animated nature' echoes), for Carlile was one of the most widely distributed and read of nineteenth-century freethinkers. But having noted this, what we need as readers of John Pearman's text is a sense of the complexity of knowing things, a sense of what inheriting a radical tradition as a working-class man in the mid-nineteenth century might actually mean: John Pearman made his own all the books he read, all the ideas he came across in a lifetime; and it is unlikely that he would have known where most of these ideas came from.[10]

In the course of my transcription and editing of this document, there was a point at which I decided not to present the first half of it, the half that contains the soldier's tale: I decided it was a tedious narrative, and that I could easily give the reader a flavour of it by extensive quotation in my introduction. Other people read my transcript, and expressed their fascination with it. It took very little appeal to the historian in me to agree that the reader needed the whole story in transcript to make sense of what it was I was going to say about it. I started then to read other working-class accounts of military life: a summer spent getting off the tube at Sloane Square, going down Royal Hospital Walk to the National Army Museum, past the machines for killing people and the small boys looking at the machines, to the harbours of the reading room and the small, mid-Victorian volumes that deliver up the soldier's tale. In many ways, these volumes laid before me the most familiar of territories: they were working-class autobiography, part of a larger genre on which much has been written over the last ten years.[11] In reading them, I took a particular pleasure in seeing the transparency with which nineteenth-century editors demonstrated what it was they wanted from these stories: they wanted simple virtue and simple honour from uncomplicated men. The editor of John Ryder's *Four Years' Service in India*, a military working-class autobiography of the 1850s, was gratified to find linguistic simplicity too:

The author having learned to read and write after he became a
soldier, his composition was necessarily very incorrect and
ungrammatical; but though incorrect and ungrammatical, the
bright ore gleamed through the rough vein of earth in which it
was encrusted. And, though the language will be found rugged
and plain, even to excess, it is the same kind of language that
has found its way to all hearts in the winning narrative of
Defoe, and in the world-known allegory of Bunyan – it is the
speech of rural England, which yet stubbornly refuses to
mingle with the Norman and classic elements that frequently
strive to blend with it – it is the almost uncontaminated speech
of our Saxon and Scandinavian forefathers, in the presence of
which every foreign word is, even to this day, recognised at
once as an intruder.[12]

This simple goodness has been sought out in working-class people
in many ways over the last century and a half: it is what Elizabeth
Gaskell wanted when she described the cosy littleness of the
Barton parlour; and why Richard Hoggart could celebrate a rag
rug, and all it represented of domestic virtue, in *The Uses of
Literacy*.[13] In a further example, closer to the central concerns of
this book, I had, in working on the policing of mid-Victorian
provincial communities, found the hope, among middle-class
ratepayers, philanthropists and managers of police, that simple
countrymen might become good and faithful servants of property
and propriety, when they turned policemen.[14]

I was quite familiar as well with the processes of identification
with the authors of these mid-Victorian volumes of working-class
autobiography. As a young woman in her early twenties, I
explored intensely personal questions of class transition and class
betrayal, using the figure of the mid-nineteenth-century rural
labourer become a policeman. I have never had any difficulty in
understanding that this is what I was doing at exactly the same
time as I produced a most conventional piece of historical
narrative. Later, when I became intimately acquainted with
children learning to read, I saw them on a daily and casual basis
employing such figures as a witch, a stepfather, the Black Bull of
Norroway, becoming now a prince, now a princess (no matter
what their gender actually was) as they read the fairy tales. No
reader of eight or nine can operate unless he or she performs this
simple act of transformation upon the text; and the circumstances
in which I observed it happening made it seem very ordinary, and
remarkably like what I had been doing with nineteenth-century
policemen a short while before. This brief excursion into
autobiography is by way of explaining that in the past, I have not

found it odd to read and write in this way: sitting in the National Army Museum, reading through the soldiers' little books, I was being the kind of reader that I was used to being.

What was unfamiliar, and quite shocking in its way, was my growing and intense interest in the content of the stories that these particular men imparted. It was not the set battle pieces that engaged me, the shots fired, nor the horrible wounding that held me; for I literally turned my eyes away from such detail (as I had hidden under the cinema seat when my father took me to see *The Dam Busters* in 1955). Certainly, it was the minute accounting of eating and drinking, and sleeping and shitting that appealed: it is rare, as an adult, that one is allowed to dwell on narratives constructed around the 'primary and compelling material processes'.[15] Soldiers' stories do bear a strong resemblance to those produced by children in the early stages of writing development. To point this out is not to diminish them, but rather to point to one factor in the universality of their appeal.[16]

But there was more to it than that. These other soldiers' tales were not written by political radicals (as John Pearman's was); or if they were, editors had seen to the disappearance of everything but simple valour and political conservatism. There was, however, a use that I was able to make of them, in the same way that I could of John Pearman's radicalism, and this is to do with the soldier's presentation of himself as a figure who is used in some way, by other people, or by social forces. (The world which frames character and action in children's stories is mysterious in something of the same way, beyond their cognitive reckoning.) My family has had practically nothing to do with the army or with military life; my father was of an age that meant that he fought in neither of the two world wars. My mother, though, sometimes talked about the death of her own father at the Somme. A weaver in one of the PALS regiments,[17] she remembered seeing him only once before he died. I have always somehow known, probably from her recounting, that the Battle of the Somme was disgusting, that they kept pouring in men and letting them be killed, because to them, all those small lives were cheap. I've always known, then, that the soldier's story is about *what they can make us do*; about *what they can do to us*. The terrible and sickening privations that those officially simple and valorous nineteenth-century soldiers told, were about what might happen to all of us, about what could happen to me. So from this perspective, the idea of being a soldier has not for me been to do with the horrors of masculinity;[18] it has been to do with powerlessness, and the situations that the powerless get into, those places where people can do things to you, and with you, as if you were not properly human.[19]

I read these stories, then, out of that understanding. I have mentioned another understanding, which is the grid of children's writing. I spent some years of my life teaching people how to read and write, and for me, quite irreducibly and despite everything else it is, John Pearman's manuscript is the product of someone who was learning to write. The linguistic framework that I employ in the following introduction is developmental and cognitive; that is, it is taken from an understanding of language learning and language development, in which literacy is understood to have particular psychological effects.[20] Readers who approach the text from the quite opposite direction of structural linguistics will perhaps be unfamiliar with the idea of writing as a psychological process. Indeed, these two linguistic frameworks have remarkably little to say to each other. But developmental linguistics has something to say to the historian: an approach from its direction allows the written word to yield up just a little more of its producer across the years – his way of thought, his frame of mind – than other analyses of content can.

Map I: *John Pearman's journey from Calcutta to the Punjab*

x — Site of battle

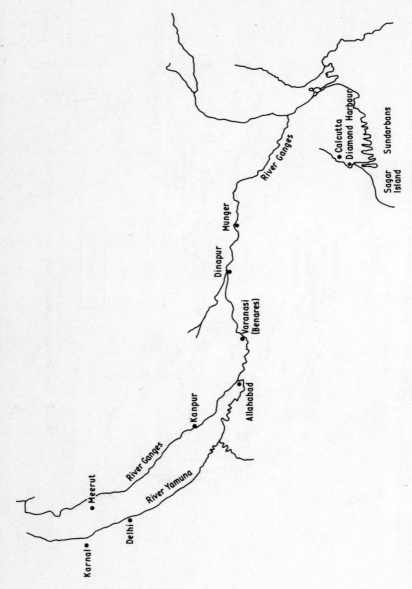

Map II: *Punjab – Land of the Five Rivers; places mentioned in John Pearman's 'Memoir', scene of the two Sikh wars*

Part One

1
Writers, Editors and Historians

John Pearman was a radical, republican, freethinking policeman who worked for the Buckinghamshire Constabulary from 1857 until 1881, and who was stationed at Eton, in the environs of Windsor Castle, from February 1864, until he retired. In the 18 months or so after his retirement, he wrote his memoirs, presenting in the 278-page notebook that is introduced here, his life as a soldier and a policeman, and an analysis of the ideologies that divided people from each other, in the societies he had known and those he had read about.

The 'Memos of Late Sergeant John Pearman of H. Mgt 3rd or Kings Own Light Dragoons' (hereafter, the 'Memoir') is worth dealing with in some detail, both because they make up a working-class autobiography that throws light on popular political thought in the mid-Victorian years, and because the notebook in which they were recorded shows very clearly a man using writing to further his political understanding, and his understanding of himself as someone shaped by the social and political world he was describing.

John Pearman has been published before. In 1967, the Marquess of Anglesey advertised in the national press for private diaries and memoirs of cavalry life in the nineteenth century, and he was contacted by George Pearman, the grandson of a man who had served in the King's Own Light Dragoons between 1843 and 1856. George Pearman had in his possession a manuscript written by his grandfather. The Marquess was interested, and 'Memos. of Late Sergeant John Pearman' was sent off to him. He considered that 'from the point of view of military history it has some importance. While not adding a great deal to our general knowledge of the campaigns [against the Sikhs], it does supply a number of new details.'[1] Responding to the description it offered, of the British Army in India before the end of East India Company rule, and Pearman's description of the wars in the Punjab against the Sikhs (1845–9) which preceded British annexation of the Punjab,[2] he published a part transcription of the 'Memoir', and a commentary on it in 1968, under the title of *Sergeant Pearman's Memoirs*.

The author of these memoirs was much misrepresented in this

13

publication. What Anglesey did, in fact, was to transcribe the first 152 pages of the notebook, which deal with Pearman's Indian years and the Sikh Wars, and to briefly summarise the remaining hundred or so pages, while presenting some fairly long auto-biographical extracts dealing with Pearman's police career, in Chapter 5 of his book. He did this for reasons that he thought would be obvious to his audience: 'Here,' he remarked, 'Pearman indulges in page after page of philosophical and social reflections, few of which are original or of particular interest. From these I have made no more than a representative selection.'[3] His editing of the manuscript also involved his correcting Pearman's spelling, tidying up his grammar, and sometimes, altering his sentence structure.

The 'Memoir' does in fact, fall into these two main parts, even though it was almost certainly all written within the space of 18 months or two years. (The argument for dating its composition as 1881–2 is presented throughout the following introduction; and the argument is summarised in 'A Note on the Dating of the "Memoir"'.) The pages that Anglesey was interested in, then, concern Pearman's time as a soldier. John Pearman's family believe that the 'Memoir' was based on a series of letters that he wrote home from India between 1843 and 1853, and Anglesey concurred in this belief,[4] reproducing in its entirety, and in facsimile, a letter dated February 24, 1849 that Pearman himself copied out into the last pages of his notebook. But it is doubtful that there were a great many more letters than this one. It was used at the time by its writer to describe two months of campaigning to his mother, and in it he mentioned twice difficulties in receiving and sending mail. ['Memoir', pp. 251–264] Yet his accuracy in dating events at a distance of more than thirty years, which is highlighted by his occasional haziness over dates, especially in the period 1850–1852, does suggest that he had some sort of written record of this time to refer to.

However, the one letter that we do know existed was greatly expanded – and changed – in the account of the same events that Pearman wrote in his 'Memoir'. ['Memoir', pp. 75–126] The letter of 1849, matched against the account of 1881–1882, shows that whilst he may have used the letter (or letters) as working notes, he transformed the original material by the analytic memory of later years. By cutting the narrative of the Indian years off from the political ideas that Pearman used to give meaning to his narrative, Anglesey was able to see Pearman as an atypical soldier of the 1840s, an odd-ball, whose condemnations of army life had some connection with the fact that he was 'considerably above the ordinary run of men in the army in the mid-nineteenth century', and whose 'resentment of the gap between officer and men' was an aspect of personality, rather than of political analysis.[5] What he really objected to in the last 120 pages of the 'Memoir' was that, as he put it, 'in old age Pearman became excessively class conscious.'[6] What his editorship did, in fact, was to prevent any presentation of the process by which Pearman used a developing political consciousness to recast the story of his life.

This introduction to the 'Memoir' is an attempt to find the groundwork of John Pearman's radicalism, to see the consciousness of his sixties forged not only of ideas newly received from secularism and freethought, and from the socialism that emerged in the land nationalisation and land reform movements of the late 1870s; nor just out of older ideas that he had access to, of Christianity as a vehicle of radical social analysis; but also out of his active reworking of his own experience, especially the experience of his Indian years.

John Pearman's struggle to understand, to achieve a written and radical social analysis, derived from three main sources: from his experience as a member of the uniformed working class (as railway worker, soldier and policeman); from talking and reading about a wide range of ideas through a long working life; and finally (and most clearly evidenced in what follows) from writing. It was in the act of writing, in the winter of 1881 and the spring, summer and autumn of 1882, that we have the first record of John Pearman attempting to wed his own experience to the world of ideas. Imperial events of the late 1870s, and of 1881–2 – British annexation of the Transvaal, and defeat of the Zulu nation at Ulundi in July 1879, the First Boer War of 1880–1, and British occupation of Egypt in the summer and autumn of 1882 – obviously all gave contemporary shape to John Pearman's past, to his memories of serving 'John Company' in India, of a time when 'if they were Thieves and stole the Country I must say they gave some of it to the Blood hounds (i.e. soldiers) who hunted down the rightful owners. . .'. ['Memoir', p. 192][7]

The situation and circumstance of writing clearly mattered, and much of this introduction is concerned with the attempt to uncover that situation and those circumstances, partly through the evidence of the text itself, which shows its author reading widely and reflecting on current political events. But not all the impulses were contemporary ones. We should listen also to John Pearman's assertion, that he had been thinking about these matters for 'the last 40 years'; ['Memoir', p. 169] that is, since he was a young man in his twenties. So rather than fixing the moment of analysis and revelation solely in the act of writing, or in the period of composition between 1881 and 1882, we should look as well to a situation in which a published and available language (in this case, the language and analytic framework of freethought) gave a clothing of words to what it was that someone knew already, from a life lived and from other books read, other ideas encountered, within it. What we cannot do is to assume a direct and simple link between the two, cannot just say that John Pearman read the freethought press (which he almost certainly did) and was 'influenced' by it, in the two years or so after his retirement.

Yet this introduction pays detailed attention to the text John Pearman produced in these years because writing allows access to its producers, allows us to see them as psychological and intellectual beings, who *learned* things as they progressed through life. The evidence for John Pearman's state of mind, for his political and emotional understanding, does lie in the text, in its shifts of topic, its use of other men's rhetoric, in the sudden and startling voice of dialogue inserted there. It lies in the words he placed upon the page, and the psychological processes that the placing involved – rather than in some direct line of influence from the books and newspapers he read, from outside to within him (though, of course, that line of transmission and reception did exist, and is of immense importance to the historian using the text). His writing worked over, shifted and altered what John Pearman had come to know, from a wide range of sources, during his lifetime.

Writing can act as a powerful synthesiser of belief and experience, of ideas and reality. But that synthesis did not occur in John Pearman's case. We can see the document introduced and transcribed here as a testing of the wisdom of popular freethought against a man's life story and its interpretation; and we can see that the two did not fit; the one only partly illuminated the other; something was not achieved. The 'Memoir' is a document of jagged dislocation; for the theories most readily available to Pearman, the new oppositional voices of secularism (and radicalism, and republicanism) could not clothe the meaning he gave to his life by the writing of it.

I think that we can see John Pearman's own recognition of this dislocation taking place at several levels throughout the text, and that a recognition of it of some sort on his part can be argued for in the following ways: in the narrative break that occurs just over half-way through the 'Memoir'; in its author's discordant and contradictory attitudes towards discipline that can be read in the manuscript; and in the syntactic structure he used when he was dealing with this contradiction. All these points will be dealt with in the section of this introduction that is concerned with writing;

here it is intended to introduce them for readers who prefer to proceed directly to a reading of the 'Memoir'.

The most obvious point of dislocation is at the place where the narrative shifts dramatically, around pages 153–6. Up to this point, John Pearman wrote a military memoir, an account of enlistment, journeying, travail and battle. We can read similarities in form between Pearman's account and other narratives of the Sikh Wars written by private soldiers; these, in their turn, link with working-class memoirs of the Peninsular and Crimean Wars.[8] The reader might note striking similarities between Pearman's accounts and others, written by similar men about the same experience: the sea-journey and its entertainments, the sharks caught and shot, the signs of human mortality read in their stomachs by fascinated soldiers.[9] There is no way of telling if John Pearman had read these published accounts before he set to write his much later one, though later in this introduction, it will be argued that in the first half of the 'Memoir' he used a narrative form that was quite conventionalised in the writings of the rank and file.[10]

In *The Face of Battle*, John Keegan explores a better-known narrative tradition of military history, with its 'typical "battle pieces" . . . its reduction of soldiers to pawns, its discontinuous rhythms, its conventional imagery, its selective incident and its high focus on leadership'.[11] He traces this formulaic presentation back to Caesar's *Commentaries* and contrasts it with the less-used but 'richer, more subtle, more psychological' Greek tradition of military history, of Herodotus and Thucydides, and their 'frank . . . treatment of how men behave in battle'.[12]

The writing of the rank and file can be expected to produce a clearer account of what military life is 'really like', how battles really are, and John Pearman's writing is revelatory in this way, especially in his willingness to present the confusion of the battlefield, and the incompetence of army administration. It is possible to set the writing of men like John Pearman against the highly conventional set-pieces of officers like D. H. McKinnon in *Military Service and Adventures in the Far East*[13] and to see the latter account of the wars in the Punjab as a schoolboy essay in two volumes. We should perhaps see McKinnon (and other officers writing in the same way) as actually constrained by the form they used, prevented from making their accounts 'psychological', in the terms of the distinction that John Keegan has drawn. Later, this introduction will suggest ways in which the form of working-class military autobiography, which bears some relation to the folk-fairy tale and to chapbook fiction, may in fact have allowed the expression of psychological complexity to some men using it.

Just over half-way through the notebook, this conventionalised narrative breaks down, and John Pearman's account becomes a written political argument, into which he inserts autobiographical detail at various points, usually for the purposes of illustration. It is difficult to know what to make of this fracture. One of the autobiographical traditions to which Pearman may have had access was that of the seventeenth century: the Puritan spiritual autobiography was an interpretative form, dealing with the understanding of events rather than with the narrating of them. [14] The legacy of this tradition meant that it was possible to accommodate a great deal of material that seems 'unautobiographical' to the twentieth-century eye: commentary, extemporisation, essays on various topics. What is more, many autobiographies produced by Victorian middle-class and professional men used the essay as a model, and their life stories often included poetry, political commentary, fiction and so on. As we do not know what John Pearman read by way of autobiography during his lifetime, and therefore do not know whether his models were working-class autobiographies within the Puritan tradition, or modern middle-class autobiographies (nor indeed, whether he read anything like this at all), we have to look at what it is within the text that seems to cause the striking break between the military memoir and the play of ideas that makes up the second half of the 'Memoir'.

What moved John Pearman away from narrative and towards interpretation was the end of his career as a soldier. He tried to revive this structure by going on to write about his career as a policeman (so that he might use a life spent in uniform as a framework); but that attempt did not last long. It was soldiering that brought forth a story, and the rest of life that produced explication. In his own experience then, there was something about being a soldier that allowed him to tell a tale.

This narrative fracture is connected to the tension that John Pearman came to see lying between and experience and explication. It is most clearly to be read in his attitude towards order and discipline. He wrote for instance, of the ordered beauty of a great army ready for battle; ['Memoir', p. 33] later he will demonstrate how clearly he sees the connection between that military panoply and the kingcraft and imperialism he is intent on condemning. He will write of his connection with the 'poor brotherhood', the outcasts of the earth, and he will trenchantly analyse a system that makes criminals of working people; then he will say 'But still I like Law and have always tried as a Soldier and a Policeman to maintain it and to keep up Disciplin'. ['Memoir', p. 245]

The two do not fit; these things cannot be put together; and this realisation is expressed in the particular syntactic structure that he used at moments of maximum contradiction. He links the contradictions together in a paratactic chain: he cannot make the connections between them, only present them, one after the other, with that unsatisfying, unsynthesising 'but':

> one man as as much right to the earth as another But I know we must have rulers But not as they now live in Luxury and riot. God made animated nature all ruled by a certain Law of its own But man as Prostituted that Law and made artificial Laws to suit his own purpose. . . Look at the pride of the Church the Bishops must have his Coach to go to church on Sundays. . . But we must highly respect the founders of many religions. . .
> ['Memoir', pp. 159–60]

John Pearman's difficult and unresolved attitude towards discipline points to another way in which the 'Memoir' is rare among nineteenth-century working-class autobiographies. John Pearman wrote – albeit briefly – about his wife and family, and put his own marriage on the agenda for self-analysis. The exploration is brief and oblique (and indeed, some of it was probably excised from the notebook), but nevertheless, his interest in this aspect of his self-formation allows the reader to make some exploration of working-class masculinity in this period.

John Pearman was not a simple man, and the ideas he worked upon in his writing were not simple either. To say this suggests that other people like him were uncomplicated, their understanding limited, the ideas they had access to second-rate; and I do not mean to imply that. A reading of John Pearman's 'Memoir' shows rather what simple and insubstantial interpretative devices there are available for seeing people like him, and the history they represent. He was a policeman – and a radical, a republican; he thought about and debated the tenets of socialism with himself; he used the language of the Levellers, and he knew beyond all doubt that he was one of 'the poor Brotherhood'. His writing is counter-evidence to accounts of soldiering and policing that assume that conservative convictions and conservative politics are the necessary and natural corollary of performing a conservative function in society.

Indeed, the officer class of the time were sometimes able to irritatedly deny that conventional assumption, as for instance, did a naval officer writing from retirement in Italy in 1881, supporting the campaign for Charles Bradlaugh to enter the House of Commons without swearing the oath of allegiance to the crown in a form that called on God's help in keeping it:

I am glad to see in the *National Reformer* subscription list for Mr Bradlaugh's support the names of officers of the army and navy. This proves that there are officers in both services who do not believe in the divinity of Toryism, or even its honesty.[15]

There was much less opportunity for the rank and file to make such a denial, particularly in the later part of the nineteenth century, when two factors mitigated against the expression of radicalism by enlisted men. There was an increased and general expectation that the private soldier would *personally* embrace the principles of imperial expansion, his political understanding and political stance become a kind of accoutrement and necessary, in a way alien to earlier thinking about the status and importance of the rank and file. A growing (though still small) literature of working-class military autobiography came increasingly to frame its narrative by this assumption,[16] and this body of literature came to influence men's understanding of and writing about the role of soldiering in their own socialisation.

But if we look at policing in this period (a function that the modern eye sees as akin to soldiering), then the wage demands, walkouts and periodic strikes of police in the mid-Victorian years should allow us to understand that (and this is not a contradictory point) even though their most ready self-definition was 'servant', some working-class men saw policing as a job of work, a passage in a working life, not a matter of political conviction.[17] Accounts that make the casual link between conservative function and conservative principle must be seen as reactionary accounts, suggesting that conservatism is seductive, irresistible, something *natural*, automatically embraced by those who take the king's shilling.[18] John Pearman's text offers quite straightforward evidence that this is not necessarily the case.

The stuff of the historian's working life is the written word, but the conventions that we possess for its interpretation are, as yet, extremely limited. Partly, this is a reflection of the relative neglect of writing within the fields of developmental psychology, developmental linguistics and – to a lesser extent – literacy studies, where reading has received far more detailed attention. It may be argued that the historian, by using the evidence of *oral* history on occasions, is absolved, by default, of ignoring the process of writing. But the fact that all *spoken* language is analysed through written language – through words transcribed – is one of the contradictions of their discipline that linguists have, in general, ignored.[19] The practice of oral history, by making spoken testimony available in written form, falls within this wider contradiction.

Linked to this general neglect of writing within their discip-
linary framework, there exists what Dominick LaCapra has isolated
as historians' lack of concern with 'critical reading and a sensitivity
to the problematic relationship between texts and contexts'.
Lacking a means of analysing this relationship, 'the great
temptation of historiography is to veer in the direction of over-
contextualisation'. He goes on to argue that historians are
completely at home with the idea of context as the reality to
which the text might lead, and to show that within this
framework historical understanding is frequently defined as a
function of contextualisation.[20] My argument in this introduction
to John Pearman's writing will be that no amount of contextualisation will reveal the complete meaning of what he wrote;
and that whilst contextualisation will certainly help us, as readers
of the text, to interpret it, the evidence that it presents lies as
much in the writer's organisation and presentation of its content
in written language, as it does in an account of republicanism and
radicalism in the 1870s, the concerns of the freethought press,
current British imperial exploits, and a narrative of the wars in the
Punjab. To use the document itself as historical evidence – not just
to use it as evidence of other events, other circumstances – as
evidence in its own right, we have to wed an analysis of written
language to an exposition of its contents.

The practice of oral history, and the support that it has given to
the rescue of working-class writing from the past and the study of
working-class autobiography, does not usually see its subjects, the
authors of those long-hidden narratives, as *intellectual* beings. The
son of toil holds a pencil clumsily in his hand, and the wonder of
it is is that it can be done at all – to have lived a working life and
to have recorded it in some way. But the point of analysing a
document like that of John Pearman's 'Memoir' is that it allows
the reader to follow the ebb and flow of a *mind*, to see an intellect
engaged with theoretical problems that connect directly with lived
experience. If we consider closely any user of a language system,
whether in a modern or a historical context, then we have to use
the implication of work done over the last 20 years within the
fields of language acquisition and the development of literacy: see
clearly the theoretical bias of the human mind. To learn to speak
is to construct theories about the relationship of sounds to entities
in the real world. In the process of learning to write, that is, in
learning to make the aural visible, this theoretical process is
elaborated, as the writer first makes hypotheses about the
relationship of the written symbol to spoken words, and then
about the direct relationship of the written symbol to the thing-in-
the-world that it represents.[21]

Making this kind of theoretical connection between idea and reality is an attribute of human psychology, and it is clear that it is no longer possible to characterise those people in the past, who devoured books, and who, 'the poorest of the poor', wrote them too, and changed other men's minds, as 'oddities', which is the characterisation that E. P. Thompson came up with some years ago to explain the writing and political thought of men like Tom Barclay and Tom Maguire.[22] We need rather to see their work as representative of the ordinary intellectual capacities of all people, which though often undeveloped, demonstrate a communality not only of the poor and of labour, but of intelligence too. But given the extremely simple psychology with which most of us as historians work, it is our bias to see theoretical analysis as a possession of the refined, and to hide from ourselves the intellectual achievements of a man like John Pearman by an indulgent smile at the quaintness of his spelling, and the oddity of his sentence construction.

It would be useful then, as a counterpoint to this bias, to be able to use John Pearman's writing to assess his capacities as a reader. It is possible to calculate the difficulties of texts by referring to various tables and formulae that show how average readers of a certain age cope with them.[23] Calculations like these are made by counting the number of words in sentences, or the number of syllables in words, and the formulae based on these calculations are widely used in modern schools, and in literacy programmes worldwide, to assess the *readability level* of texts, and by implication, the *reading age* that the reader of the text possesses. A good deal of criticism attaches to their use, for they embody an extremely simple model of the reading process, defining reading as a matter of decoding, and difficulty in terms of sentence length and polysyllability. In these circumstances however, they have some very limited use.

Using one particular formula (chosen only because it is relatively quick to apply) it is possible to calculate that anyone who read with ease and fluency the *Guardian* editorial of 25 March 1987 had a reading age of 11:6 years, that is to say a good average reader of eleven and a half would perform in the same way. The formula used here, and others, rest on the unit of written language that is the sentence. John Pearman did not always punctuate his text to show sentence boundaries, but those grammatical boundaries are there in the majority of what he wrote, in that it is possible to punctuate his text for him.[24] It is therefore possible to calculate what demands are made of readers of the 'Memoir', and what, by implication, was the reading ability of its writer. Writing ability almost always lags behind ability in reading:

people acquiring written English will find it easier to read material of a certain level of difficulty than to produce it themselves. So when the formula used above is applied to John Pearman's text, and we find that it has a readability level equivalent to that of the *Guardian* editorial, and by implication we say that its author had a reading age of 11:6, we are almost certainly underestimating his abilities.

For instance, it is probable that John Pearman read and was influenced by Henry George's *Progress and Poverty* (1881). George's sentences, which are made up of a series of clauses divided by semicolons, take calculations of readability off the edge of the scale. Yet the reader treats these clauses as if they were sentences, and they can be punctuated in this way for the main part. By doing this, George's prose presents a little more difficulty than does the *Guardian* editorial.[25] Anything that John Pearman wanted to read, he could probably cope with.

As a writer, John Pearman used an informal English (the term used in this book in place of 'non-standard English');[26] and he made mistakes. To the psychologist and the linguist, speech-errors and errors in writing are not mistakes in the social sense, but pieces of evidence that allow a reconstruction of the theory that went into their making. 'Error' is a neutral term, and that is how it is used throughout this introduction.

The facility of making a reconstruction of a state of mind from a century ago by using the written errors of a text is a useful historical tool; but what is reconstructed in this way may not always be very interesting historically. I spent several days looking at every spelling error that John Pearman made in writing the 'Memoir', got very close to him that way, would know him less well as a writer and a thinker if I had not performed this task; but in the end, there is very little to say about *John Pearman* as a result of this enterprise, a lot to say about the difficulties that written English presents to *all* its users, particularly the difficulty of distinguishing between the graphemes that are used to represent vowels in an alphabetic writing system.[27] John Pearman spelled many words from speech, and it is possible to reconstruct some of the spoken dialect he used from these spellings – a mildly interesting and antiquarian exercise. In his spelling errors there is also some evidence for the method by which, in the 1820s, he must anyway have been taught to read.[28] It is also possible to see in these spelling errors the way in which he learned the phonetic principles of the English language from experience – from reading – rather than from instruction.[29]

He did correct his own work, but not consistently. Had he proofread in a systematic manner, then he would probably have eliminated many more errors of omission and visual recall than the 'Memoir' shows him making. In the first half of the 'Memoir', the part that deals with his time as a soldier, he made 111 corrections (by addition, deletion and overwriting) in 152 pages. In the second part, in his religious and political dialogue with himself, he made only 34 corrections in 112 pages.[30] The second half of the document was written in a hurry, under the pressure of difficult and challenging ideas; it was not a matter of measured reflection.

Looking, at spelling errors in this way is only a preliminary stage in making a detailed description of the process of composition in writing. If such a description is to be at all useful historically, then it must help us see more clearly *how* people used the information – social, political, emotional – that they were presented with in the past, and *how* they went about thinking through ideas. So in this way, we should come to see a text not just as a literary object to be analysed in more or less conventional ways, but also as a place of mediation between a culture and an individual mind.

The following introduction will suggest that within the pages of the 'Memoir' lies evidence – linguistic evidence, and because linguistic, also historical evidence – of the intellectual achievement of a working-class man of the early 1880s. Within the pages of his notebook, John Pearman pursued justice and equity as ideas. He did this most clearly, as we shall see, through a contemplation of the possession and ownership of land. Here, his experience as a soldier and a policeman allowed him to take the rhetoric of natural law, and its modern use by the land reform movement, and make it momentarily his own. It was his welding of the idea of a natural law to a class analysis of the corruption that it exposed, that allowed his presentation of a life lived with great intelligence; with the dour and watchful irony of the good and faithful servant.

2
A Working Life

When John Pearman joined the Buckinghamshire Constabulary in 1857 he was 36, considerably older than the average recruit to rural police forces in this period. Across the country as a whole during the 1850s and 1860s, the most common experience was to join a county constabulary sometime between the age of 20 and 25.[1] Most policemen, then, had a considerable stretch of working life behind them, and John Pearman shared the perspective of this experience: 'I must be very thankful that I have never been out of employment or without a Shilling since I first took to Keep myself at Age 13 years and 9 months' he wrote, and the autobiographical sketch that he presented in the 'Memoir' was prompted by the reflection that

> as poor men we cannot find much to live for ours is a life of heavy toil to get a bare living and to amas money and Whealth for the great men of the day. . .should you be so unfortanate as to be out of work you and the Family have much to suffer. . .
> ['Memoir', p. 189]

Looking back from the vantage point of his sixties, the author of these words saw his history as both soldier and policeman, as chapters in a working life. But in fact, John Pearman worked as a policeman – and became a police officer – during a period when the officer class across the country succeeded in establishing in the public mind the idea of a police as separate and distinct from the social hierarchy in which it operated.

The officer class of English police forces bought its right to middle-class sympathy by consistently presenting themselves as a 'very patient long-suffering set of men'.[2] But in contrast with the officers, the vast, fluctuating army of the rank and file spent the years between 1850 and 1880 using police forces as local employment opportunities, a way of getting over a temporary difficulty in the labour market, of making the journey from country to city. In boroughs this understanding of police forces as part of a local labour market could be given dramatic and overt expression in the petitioning of watch committees for increased wages, or in strike action.[3] Police unionisation, the petitions, marches and lockouts of the early 1870s, were only a heightened demonstration of what every constable knew: that policing fitted into the pattern of some working–class men's lives. 'We have men join our force who have been farm labourers', a Northampton sergeant told a select committee in 1875. 'They leave and put themselves under a shoemaster. . .and bounce and tell us he [sic] can earn 5s a week more than I can. . .'.[4]

By way of contrast with borough constables, county policemen were forced to live a life of institutionalised passivity, and they were unable to express this kind of identity with the work situations that they had (usually only temporarily) left behind. But John Pearman's private delineation of a working life does give some substance to the anonymous identification with working men that county correspondents made in the policeman's newspaper, the *Police Service Advertiser*, in the 1860s and 1870s.[5]

When men joined county forces, their trade was recorded in the recruiting book, but few gave theirs as 'policeman'. Many of the rank and file consciously defined themselves in terms of their former work, even after many years in a police force; and on joining the Buckinghamshire Constabulary, John Pearman called himself a sawyer.[6] In recounting his passage from sawyer to railway guard, to soldier, to policeman as Pearman did in his 'Memoir' he placed all the work he had done in the context of labour:

> Working at my Trade (Sawyer) until I was 21 years I thought it time to give up such hard work which brought little more than a liveing for myself but much for my employers. The Railway started and Joined the Great Western and was employed as a Guard. . . ['Memoir', p. 190]

Twenty-one of John Pearman's fellow police recruits in 1857 had recently served in the Crimea and they, like him, had not been working at their trade before becoming policemen. Another eight recruits, men without army experience, had also spent several years working away from the trade they gave the recruiting sergeant. The railways had claimed half of these men, so in spite of his age, John Pearman's experience was a typical one.[7] He had stayed on the railways for two years, but then:

> not likeing London I was far from being settled although we made – good wages and not worked hard But I felt I should like to travel and see other Countries. Well one day I had a tiff with the Supperintendent and we got to word and my temper very hasty we got nearly to blows so I made up my mind to be a Soldier and enlisted at once and soon went to the east Indies ['Memoir', p. 190]

John Pearman's life was punctuated, as we shall see, by these moments of disgrace and difficulty, and by his rescue of himself. On this occasion in 1843, he used a well-established escape route: 'Traditionally, the regular army served as a refuge for men escaping from their domestic circumstances', comments Edward Spiers.

> All initiatives to improve the quality and quantity of the recruiting intake foundered upon the profound contempt with which the military career was viewed. . .'to have a member who had gone for a soldier was for many families a crowning disgrace'.[8]

But John Pearman loved soldiering:

> Now of all my life this was the most worth liveing for although We oftimes had to face Death in the worse form. But there is a pleasure in that for it places the great man and the poor on a footen. I have oftimes put my foot on a Dead officer. . .and said to myself were is your Rank now and then MR Officer was not the same *Tyrant* as in england ['Memoir', pp. 190–1][9]

It was India, and the contradictions of a soldier's life that first gave John Pearman the opportunity to worry at a problem, to make those leaps in understanding which are given by the placing together of two perspectives, and the tension between them. There was a particular tension between what public service took from him, the attributes that he sold when he took the queen's shilling, or signed the police recruiting book, and those parts of him that had to remain hidden, and it was the disjuncture between the two that helped him abstract meaning from circumstances. It was in this way that John Pearman came to know himself.

He recollected both freedom and friendship when he wrote of India; but when he joined the Buckinghamshire Constabulary in 1857, he went to a work situation of extreme curtailment and rigidity. What is more, over half of his fellow recruits were natives of Buckinghamshire or neighbouring counties, most of them having formerly worked the land. The officers who directed his work had nearly all been employed in the county before 1857, under the system of partial policing many quarter sessions had opted for before the compulsory legislation of 1856.[10] John Pearman, on the other hand, had been born in Kingston-upon-Thames, had spent six years in India, and had recently worked in Lancashire and at Sandhurst.

He was then, in March 1857, a stranger to both a place and to an administrative hierarchy – and he was at the bottom of that hierarchy, taking home in that first year something between 17s and 18s a week. He came as well to a work situation in which the social virtues – sobriety, punctuality, obedience, smartness – were enforced as a means of discipline, and in which the pattern of work was closely supervised and regulated.

Before the 1870s, police work – length of beat and hours on duty – was not at all standardised. During the 1860s, stretches of duty ranged from 10 to 15 hours in a seven-day week (though the concept of off-duty is a modern one anyway) and constables were liable to have quite random demands made on their time by officers and local magistrates. In Buckinghamshire in 1859, police constables spent about six hours a day walking. Meeting at conference points, reporting before and after duty, consultations with officers and magistrates, and the writing of reports and making entries in police journals measured out the rest of the working day. 'I worked hard,' recalled John Pearman, 'and was rewarded with Promotion and more money and another Change of Station to Great Marlow with rank of Inspector. . .' ['Memoir', p. 214] This was in January 1862. He continued to work hard and finally, two years later, was rewarded with what he wanted: 'the Rank of 1st Class Inspector. . .and I must say I was very much better off as my Pay was better & my Duty much lighter and nearly my own master and the people was a sort of persons that wanted but little looking after.' ['Memoir', pp. 214–15]

He had been rewarded with a relative freedom. A detailed account of his working day as a police inspector is not available, but the official journal of another county inspector, George Williamson of Northamptonshire, shows that in this other Midland county in 1865 an inspector worked from 8 to 13 hours a day in one average January week, occasionally putting in more hours when travelling was involved. The following entries from Williamson's diary indicate the sort of working day that Pearman led after 1864:

> Feb 2 1866 10 a.m.–1 p.m. called at the Bank for £31.17.1 to pay the men with 1.15–4.30 p.m. Paid the men examined their diaries and on duty at the station. . .
> April 5 1866 9 a.m.–5 p.m. On duty to Northampton with the weight and measure books & paid to the county treasurer 11s 8d the fees received for stamping during the past half year. . .
> June 4 1866 10 p.m.–2.30 a.m. Patrolled the Neighbourhood of Thrapston & Islip and attended a club feast at Islip all passed off quiet. . .[11]

A good deal of the working day in a county police force was spent like this, on the maintenance of its own organisation. In 1865 Inspector Williamson was visited by his divisional superintendent three times a day, on average; patrolled for about five miles with one or more of his constables, examined their journals once a week, and was himself examined by his chief constable once a month. Yet for long stretches of most days he was alone, his 'own master', as John Pearman said he was.

By 1864 then, Pearman had done exceptionally well. He had been a working-class recruit to the bottom of the hierarchy, yet he had risen through the ranks and was to stay on to achieve his ambition, which was a police pension. But this rise (which is discussed in more detail in the third section of this introduction) did not change his perception of himself as a working man:

> when I look back for only the past two generations of my
> Family what an amount of temptations we have to endure to
> avoid and to look at if what our parsons Calls sin to git a
> chance to live while our Queen and the Lords & Dukes fare of
> the best, the poor Children of this – Carrupt earth can get for
> them. . .there is one Law for the poor and another for the
> Rich. . . ['Memoir', pp. 239–40]

He was able to see his position, and indeed his success, as part of the pattern he described, by aligning himself with the enduring poor – 'the poor Children of this Carrupt earth' – that is, with those outside the gate, outside the bastions of power, influence, ownership and money. The images of the gate, the railings, the castle walls that cut the children off from their inheritance were probably, as we shall see, the vehicle of his radical realisation of 1867, the personal and political crisis of that year, which showed him exactly where he stood, as working man and policeman.

John Pearman articulated his connection with the community of the underprivileged and powerless, and other policemen did the same. It is likely that, stationed at Eton from 1864 onwards, he read the *Police Service Advertiser*, which was published in neighbouring Windsor, and so knew of other policemen whose past experiences, taken to the new job of policing, were expressed in its columns in the language of class. 'How preposterous it is,' wrote the anonymous policeman 'Justice' in 1867, 'for officers in the upper reaches of the police hierarchy, to "tell the world what men could do and what service they could be. . .".' 'Justice' was complaining about the appointment of a man with very little police experience to the position of deputy chief constable ('DCC'):

> Ask 'DCC' if he ever did five years police service as a
> constable? If he has he is a model. . .I suppose there is not to be
> found in all England three deputy chief constables that have,

and therefore. . .he. . .cannot say a word to ameliorate the
condition of the working man. . . If I stood before him I
should at once see before me a man I suppose of about thirty
who has by good friends been lifted to a very comfortable
position and has got as much feeling for the men under him as
a sweep has for his apprentice. . .[12]

'Justice' saw real relations of rank and privilege represented in the
police forces he worked for. It did not, for him, reflect the idea of
a separate order cut off from the social and political world that
some officers were already engaged in promoting in the late
1860s; and in the reflected and real social hierarchy that his police
force represented for him, 'Justice' knew that he was a working
man.

It was this understanding of himself as a working man that was
John Pearman's straightest route to self-knowledge. 'True self-
knowledge was impossible without a comprehension of the
structure and historical identity of the section of society in which
the personality was formed', remarks David Vincent of nineteenth-
century working-class autobiography. 'The search for such
knowledge was both a pre-condition and a result of the growth of
class-consciousness.'[13] The firm basis for John Pearman's class-
consciousness was what he knew of a family history throughout
which people had struggled to get by without breaking the law –
'to git a chance to live'. He saw this family history set within a
broader narrative. 'If we look to past history,' he commented, 'we
find the poor was always the same.' ['Memoir', p. 193]

> the temptation of Break the Law or what is called sin is very
> great with the poor. . . The cause are not been the same
> with. . .the Poor and yet they sin but very little Compared
> with the Rich. . . ['Memoir', p. 188]

Into this history of the world, fitted his own personal story:

> as poor men we cannot find much to live for ours is a life of
> heavy toil to get a bare living and to amas money and Whealth
> for the great men of the day. True we have some hours of rest
> from labour. But should you have a Family that is taken up for
> them – But should you be so unfortanate as to be out of work
> you and the Family have much to suffer. . . My own married
> life as been a life of much care haveing to raise eight Children
> out of Eleven borned. . . ['Memoir', pp. 189, 208]

There were many complaints in the *Police Service Advertiser*
from policemen writing about 'exercising their wits' to feed their
families, about rarely eating meat, about the impossibility of

making anything on the side (county police wives were forbidden to work), and about the cost of housing. 'Men with families paying £7–£10 a year in rent are poor, badly kept and a few years in the police unfits them for other labour. Then they become a sort of "come day, go day, God send pay day" men,' wrote a constable from the West Riding in 1866.[14]

In the 1870s there was to develop a specific understanding of policing as a kind of trade, a work situation that presented its own difficulties, and out of which developed particular sets of skills. This understanding was transmitted in the *Police Service Advertiser*, but more widely and generally in the publicity given to the findings of the Select Committee on Police Superannuation of 1875, and its delineation of policing as specialised work.[15] A campaign for police pension rights and the formation of a nation-wide insurance scheme by the officer class of local forces in the late 1860s and 1870s also served the same function, of outlining the particularity of police work.

To the eminent Victorian statistician who summed up the lives of 25,000 policemen for the Select Committee of 1875, a policeman was distinct from the general working population, the police mortality rate in 1876 being nearly half of what it was for the average working man. In both counties and boroughs though, life expectancy for policemen decreased as years of service were clocked up: policemen were, after all, chosen for the qualities of health and strength that made them such good risks in their first years of service. What policemen said of these statistics, and what they had been saying for years past, was that they were worked to the limit of their capacity, and then discarded.[16] Out of the thousand pensions that were granted to English and Welsh provincial policemen between the creation of their forces and 1874, only about one in eight was given for injuries received on duty. Rather, as Constable Chambers of Hertfordshire explained to the Select Committee on Police Superannuation, 'it is the inclemency of the weather that tells on you; you get one cold lodged upon the other until at last it affects the lungs. . .'.[17]

Neither James Chambers nor John Pearman drew on the evolving perception of policing that the officer class promoted in the 1870s. Constable Chambers described clearly what the work was like, tramping through 'a lonely, very hilly country', and what the job did to a man; and a feature of John Pearman's 'Memoir' is his assumption that being a policeman was simply a passage in a working life.

It is more difficult for us to read his understanding of the job of soldier in the 'Memoir', partly because the narrative form he uses to describe it obscures his attitude, and most of his commentary on soldiering as work was reserved for the second half of the notebook. It was, though, both a feature of his understanding and of the form of the tale he told that soldiering was partly a romance, an episode before life (and marriage, and children, and concerns about housing and pensions) began. As might be expected of a romance, it is not entirely truthful, and the particular evasion of the truth that the first half of the 'Memoir' involves can throw some light on Pearman's re-reading of his past as a working life, in the 18 or so months during which the document was written.

The recent researches of Gordon Everson in the muster rolls of the 3rd Light Dragoons show that John Pearman was not made a sergeant until February 1856, three years after leaving India. Three months after enlisting in August 1843, he deserted the Dragoons' depot at Maidstone.[18] He was absent for eight months, and court-martialled on his return to the regiment at the end of July 1846. He was imprisoned and sentenced to forfeit all service towards his pension. This period – two years between enlistment and embarkation for India – is not dealt with at all in the 'Memoir'. ['Memoir', p. 1] He was made a corporal in December 1850, and in 1852 his former service was restored to him, that is, allowed to count towards his pension.

The regiment sailed for home in February 1853, reaching Gravesend at the end of June. ['Memoir', p. 148] In August of that year Pearman was again absent without leave, for just four days this time. He was court-martialled for a second time, again reduced in rank and forfeited pension rights. These were restored in September 1854. He got back his corporal's stripes in September 1855, and was finally made a sergeant in February 1856. The title he gave to his notebook – 'Memos. of Late Sergeant Pearman' – involves a reading back of status into the Indian years. In the 'Memoir' itself (as his family remembered him being in life) he was vague about promotion, and told a lie about sergeantship on two occasions only, when he has General Thackwell call him 'Sergeant' before the Battle of Gujrat, ['Memoir', p. 113] and his friend Makepeace say to him of a stolen arab horse after the battle, 'you cant ride him Sergeant.' ['Memoir', p. 129]

This mild deceit has several sources. Simply, John Pearman believed he deserved his fictitious rank, deserved to rise. The rank of sergeant may also have added weight to his old soldier's tales. The apotheosis of this piece of story telling is to be found in his obituary notice in the *Windsor and Eton Express* in 1908, where he is immortalised as a sergeant, with his sergeant's tale, someone having told the reporter in question that 'being a good writer, an uncommon thing in those days (he) was soon promoted to

Sergeant'.[19] Until Gordon Everson told John Pearman's surviving grandsons, in 1975, what his searches in the muster rolls had revealed, they had believed this very firmly established story.

We can move beyond ascribing to John Pearman the simple motives of vanity, or resentment, or wish-fulfilment in his establishment of a fictional sergeanthood. We ought rather to consider what it is he actually tells us about his working life, and his understanding of the value of his own labour, in as much as these questions cluster around the question of promotion and what it entailed. For what Pearman hides by not telling the complete truth in the first half of the 'Memoir' is that at successive points in his army career his pension rights were removed from him (and that also, by buying himself out as he did in 1856, he forfeited them again). What he reveals in the second half of the 'Memoir', what he in fact presents as the culmination of his career, was the pension he was awarded at Buckinghamshire Michaelmas Quarter Sessions, in October 1881, of £69.6.8 per year, for life. He had got what he said he had always wanted – 'I always had in my mind the chance of geting a pension which I did & a very good one.' ['Memoir', p. 208]

Other policemen of Pearman's generation saw this sum of money as both a right, and a reward for a working life of service. I think that we can read this same understanding in John Pearman's expressed attitudes, and in what he hid about what earlier demotions in the army had actually cost him. In terms of his broader political understanding, the pension might be seen as the articulation of his belief in the rights to the earth of the poor brotherhood, a sum of money that was an assertion of his belief against a world in which all the community of labour struggled to 'git a chance to live'.

John Pearman actually lived for another 26 years after the bestowal made at Michaelmas Quarter Sessions in 1881, thereby costing the ratepayers of Buckinghamshire nearly £2,000, a calculation that must have afforded him the profoundest satisfaction.

3
Soldiers' Stories

In making the change from army to county police force, it is certain that John Pearman experienced an improvement in pay and working conditions. He had little to say in fact, about the working conditions of police life, but what little he does mention emphasises a relative degree of ease and comfort in the years after 1857 – the 'nice home &...good Garden' at Great Marlow ['Memoir', p. 157], the people who made few demands on his time at Eton. ['Memoir', pp. 214–15] He represented police work as an improvement in the material conditions of life.

He had worked as a soldier in a period when the pay, the living conditions and the health of the common soldier were subject to fluctuating and intermittent attention by army reformers.[1] He lived to tell his story in the post-Crimean period, when that attention had been transformed into a public outrage that both raised the status of the army in society and effected some improvement in the standard of living of the rank and file.[2] He wrote then, about his soldiering experiences at a distance of 30 years; and it is possible that his overt concern with food and supplies, cooking and eating arrangements, sleeping conditions and the particularly appalling experiences of soldiers on the march in very high temperatures, reflect the public debate over army reform in the 1850s and 1860s. Yet Pearman's letter to his mother, written from Camp Gujrat in February 1849, ['Memoir', pp. 251–64] deals in the same personal and domestic detail. John Spencer Cooper's *Rough Notes of Seven Campaigns* of 1869 was surely directed by mid-Victorian concerns when he remembered back to 1813 and the 'State of the Hospitals Where I Was';[3] yet other working-class autobiographies of the Sikh Wars, written in the 1850s, deal in the same physical detail as John Pearman's: John Ryder's *Four Years Service in India* of 1853, James Gilling's *The Life of a Lancer in the Wars of the Punjab* of 1855 and Joseph Donaldson's *Recollections of an Eventful Life* of 1856[4] were propelled by personal experience and by resentment, as well as by the Crimean War and its scandalous revelations.

The young officer who published *The Field of Ferozeshah in Two Cantos* in 1848 emphasised in his notes to his verse the same foul

34

living and fighting conditions that John Pearman was to dwell on years later:

> None but those persons who have suffered from want of water can know the value of it. I saw men drinking water from the wells, after the bodies of their comrades and the enemy had been precipitated into them, and the water was stained with blood. Nay, one man I even saw drank his own urine.[5]

J. W. Baldwin, in his *Narrative of Four Months Campaign in India* of 1853, was more circumspect − 'I witnessed truly disgusting scenes arising from want of water' − but physical frankness about the problems of ingestion and excretion is a certain feature of working-class military autobiography in this period. Though John Keegan performed an important historical function in restoring those actualities to the face of battle in his book of 1976, the evidence of men getting by on the battlefield had already been recorded by dozens of common soldiers of the nineteenth century.

Edward Spiers has shown that the mortality rate for men serving in the army in the years 1837–46 was 17.1 per cent, in a period when the death rate for men living in British urban centres was 11.9 per cent. The death rate for men serving in the cavalry, as John Pearman did, was 13.9 per cent. These are average figures, which mask the much higher mortality rate of active campaigning. Even so, the cavalry took 'the cream of the available recruits', provided them with a better working life than the infantry, and gave them marketable skills to take out of the service.[7]

Even on active service, it was the hazards of soldiering as a working life rather than wounds received in battle that provided its major threat to life. 'As late as the Second World War,' notes Richard Holmes in *Firing Line*, 'sickness caused more casualties than battle.'[8]

John Pearman wrote in some detail about an operation he underwent and four months he spent confined to bed in 1851 (incorrectly remembered as occurring in 1850); ['Memoir', pp. 139–43] but he does not mention other frequent stays in hospital. He was often ill during 1846, and spent the last three months of 1847 in hospital. After the Battle of Gujrat he was hospitalised again in February 1849 (for a wound-related illness), and the muster rolls show that he was incapacitated from May until August after the operation that he does describe in some detail.[9] Pearman had carried into military service the health of a young man, born in the early years of the century, from a semi-rural environment. He did not spend the majority of his years as a soldier confined to insanitary barracks, where respiratory diseases, the scourge of the wider society, were so rapidly spread.[10] In any case, wounding on the battlefield did not always bring with it the consequences of more modern warfare: wounds in this period were often 'single and simple: penetrations or perforations by lances or low-velocity bullets, or cuts by swords'. John Keegan suggests that 'if the bleeding were not too severe, if dirt was not carried into the wound or the intestines opened, the patient's chances of survival were better than we would expect';[11] even during the wars in the Punjab, where the design of Sikh swords and their owners' techniques of sword combat meant that the wounds received by the British were of a severity not encountered in European warfare of the nineteenth century.[12] John Pearman's survival, then, was by no means extraordinary, especially when we consider that the cavalry was actually very little used during the eight military actions that he experienced – very little used in fact in all of the 'six battles for India' that made up the Sikh Wars.[13]

Policemen of the 1860s and 1870s often presented their working life as one of extreme curtailment and rigidity, though few had army experience to compare it with. Making a more general comparison, Thomas Quinney, who had enlisted in the Indian Army in 1807, wrote in 1853 that he could not see how

> any man accustomed to labour can complain that the duties of
> soldiers are hard. If he would only balance the ten hours'
> labour with the three hours drill, he would soon see that he has
> no reason to complain. Besides, if he would consider how
> much cleaner he is obliged to keep himself than the labouring
> man. . .[14]

In the 1840s, the working day in the army stretched from 6.00 a.m. until 10.00 p.m., with a break of four hours in the early evening. Drill and fatigues measured out the working day, which was longer for cavalrymen, who were responsible for their horses.[15] John Pearman's story of his Indian years is punctuated by his concern for his horse, particularly its watering and feeding after a battle, a concern both intensely practical, and one that possibly allowed him to express a more general sympathy towards the human casualties of war.[16] As a later recruit to the police, his experience with horses was a considerable asset, for county police forces depended for their administration on horse patrol by officers. Pearman was in fact recruited as a groom as much as a constable, ['Memoir', p. 153] and his expertise probably overrode the objections that all police authorities articulated over the employment of ex-soldiers.[17]

Chief constables objected to ex-soldiers because they believed that military life had accustomed them to drunkenness, and that if a society were to be policed by the principles of decency and respectability (in theory, at least) then the public image of the soldier made him an unsuitable employee. Other comparisons between the army and the police force were made, by policemen themselves, and they often dwelt on the possibility of promotion and of rising through the ranks that constabularies held out as promises to their recruits.[18] Certainly, some policemen believed that police forces offered them what the army refused them, and John Pearman's hidden history, a slow rise to the position of corporal, de-ranking and an even slower rise to sergeant, shows the lack of promotional opportunities in the Victorian army. By way of contrast, his rise through the ranks of the constabulary was rapid (though the rarity of Pearman's police experience will be discussed later).

To go for a soldier was an uncommon experience for nineteenth-century working-class men: in the 1840s and 1850s only about 1 per cent of the male adult population was under arms. It was 'axiomatic that only a very small percentage of the total male population had any experience of army life'.[19] It has been argued that it was this cultural and physical remoteness from the parent society, and the alienation of the military from social life that lay at the root of the contempt in which soldiers were held in the first half of the nineteenth century. We should add to this a class condescension which dwelt consistently on the vices of the unskilled labouring poor, on their brutality, illiteracy and immorality, in making a composite picture of the early Victorian common soldier.[20]

It was an uncommon experience in statistical terms, and yet at the same time it was the most common metaphorical expression of a man's life, in Richard Holmes' striking phrase, that 'most passionate drama of all',[21] in different ways and in different historical periods, the very epitome of manhood. There are more autobiographies written by working-class men become soldiers than by those become miners, or agricultural workers, or weavers, though mining and farm labouring were vastly more common nineteenth-century experiences. There were more ballads to celebrate a statistically rare military life than ever there were songs of weaving and ploughing. Soldiering is at once an experience that is absolutely divisive sexually, and is at the same time the experience that we all know about, whether we be men or women.[22] The soldier's tale is a story that is more than the sum of its parts, but is rather a social myth, a drama of alienation, journeying and arrival; and of course, it is also a tale about the compulsion of conflict.

Within the genre of nineteenth-century working-class military autobiography, the reader notices a certain self-consciousness about form. Indeed, James Gilling, publican's son and hairdresser from Worksop, bound for the Punjab with the 9th Royal Lancers to fight in the wars against the Sikhs, understood quite clearly the narrative terms in which he was dealing:

> To an Englishman going to India, the long voyage he has to make is an excellent preparative. The temporary absence of ordinary scenes and employments produces a state of mind peculiarly fitted to receive new and vivid impressions. The vast space of water which separates the two countries is like a blank page in his existence. . . As I saw the last blue line of my native land fade away like a cloud on the horizon, it seemed as if I had closed one volume of the world and its concerns and had time for meditation ere I opened another.[23]

In Gilling's writing there is the same shock of surprise on landing that Pearman shows, the same magical journey up the Ganges (Gilling was reminded of his childhood reading of 'The Arabian Nights');[24] and there is the heat, the forced marching, the mosquitoes, the terrible thirst.[25]

In soldiers' writing from the nineteenth century, the magical river journey did not need the Ganges to make an appearance. John Spencer Cooper wrote in the same way of a journey in flat-bottomed boats up the Tagus, during the Peninsular Wars:

> We were conveyed in large, curiously built boats up the Tegus to Villa Franca. The scenery was beautiful; the countryside on both sides of the noble river being like a garden. Nothing but villas, vineyards, olive, lemon and orange groves could be seen down this mighty stream.[26]

Alexander Somerville recalled the broad panoply of life come out to watch the soldier's progress on a march from prosaic Brighton to prosaic Birmingham in 1832, in an account where it becomes impossible to tell who are the spectators – the marchers or those who watch them:

> I. . .can at will, sitting by the hearth, looking dreamily into the fire or vacantly upon a book, draw out the whole line of country before me: the villages, road-side inns, half-way houses where we halted to rest, swinging sign-boards, village greens, broad commons, cross-roads, finger posts, travellers journeying with us, telling us where a gibbet once was. . .[27]

The soldier progressed – along a road, up the Tagus, up the Ganges – through a landscape made magical and strange by his presence, and his gaze upon it.

There is no way of telling if John Pearman read these published

accounts before he set out to write his much later one. The
speculation is probably irrelevant anyway, for narrative similarity
is not to be entirely explained by the simple fact of one man
reading another's work, nor even by the content of the stories told
in those accounts. What we can look for here is the set of
expectations held of soldiers' stories, and the way in which the
soldier's tale is one of the few that poor and unimportant men
have been allowed to tell during our recent history – allowed in
the sense of audience expectation and audience desire; allowed in
the sense that the story of work, or of labour (the narrative of a
working life) is denied the structure of romance that the soldier's
story works within. The military autobiography was the only
consistently produced working-class account of the early and mid-
Victorian years. Pearman knew about the romance that it
embodied, for he described the way in which, in the 1860s, he
held the beer-house crowds of rural Buckinghamshire with what
he called 'many a soldiers tale of India'. ['Memoir', pp. 156–7]

When John Pearman's understanding of himself is explored,
then his understanding of soldiering, which was the central
emotional experience of his life, will have to be discussed in some
detail. What it is important to deal with at this juncture is the
nineteenth-century soldier's *recounting* of similar experiences, and
the meaning of their narratives for teller and audience. The
soldier's tale deals in the currency of violence and glamour; and it
is thus a profoundly sexy story, not just because it deals with
the heightened sexuality that accompanies dislocation and
violence,[28] and not just because in the figure of the soldier we may
choose to see an abstracted picture of masculinity; but rather
'sexy' in the American sense of 'meaningful'. John Keegan in *The
Face of Battle*, and Richard Holmes in *Firing Line* both deal with
the connection of soldiering and sexuality, and the general
interplay between sexual and military prowess in our common
stock of cultural referents.[29] If we only shrink in horror and
disgust from the brutal sexual imagination in men that is revealed
by Holmes in particular then we miss the point of the soldier's
tale, a point missed by Holmes himself: that the story has a power
that cuts across gender, and tells of life's struggles, in isolation and
far from home, the body and its needs carried through that dark
night, at the end of which it is not certain that death will be
evaded.[30]

It has been suggested that the beer-house crowd that listened
with such pleasure to John Pearman's story in the late 1850s may
have seen him as a more respectable figure than they might have
done ten years before. But we should consider the possibility that
the story of soldiering met with working-class interest in the pre-

Crimean period as well. Indeed, in his Preface to *A Narrative of Four Months Campaign* of 1850, J. W. Baldwin specifically addressed the question of a working-class audience's needs in military autobiography: cheapness, brevity, amusement and instruction.[31] Whatever contempt military life may have been held in, or however much soldiers may have been despised, the story they represented and sometimes imparted may have been received as a common story, the story of the poor: the epitome of struggle in an ungiving world.

It is the form used for the telling, and the analogies made by the soldier-narrator that must draw our attention. Sailing past Benares, John Gilling was reminded of the chapbook fiction of his youth, and a great deal of writing like his made explicit reference to chapbook literature, sometimes directly presenting itself as part of the genre, as did the title page to William Hall's *Diary* of 1848:

> The Diary of Sergeant William Hall, of Penzance, Cornwall, Late of Her Majesty's Forty First Regiment, Containing the Incidents Connected With Two Years' Campaign in the Scinde and Afghanistan During the Late War, to which is added the Sermon Preached to the Troops on the Sunday after the Battle, By the Rev. J. N. Allen B.A., Assistant Chaplain to the Scinde Field Force. Also, the Particulars of Numerous Shooting Excursions in India after Game of All Descriptions Including the Lion and Other Wild Beasts of the Jungle.[32]

T. Gowing's *A Soldier's Experience* of 1884 *was* a piece of chapbook literature of the almanac type, containing a copy of the will of Peter the Great, a list of battles fought by British regiments and anecdotes of famous soldiers.[33]

In the folk-fairy tale of chapbook fiction, hundreds of Jacks are sent out into the world, to kill giants or behead dragons. In a nineteenth-century development of this old tale, the soldier-hero abstracts himself from the reality of comradeship and the communality of campaigning, and presents himself as the lone and intrepid traveller and fighter, as William Hall did. It is important to note that in published accounts of nineteenth-century soldiering written by working men, it is rare for the communality of war to be presented, as John Pearman presents it.

The folk-fairy tale has served certain functions within western culture that it is appropriate to discuss at this juncture. There is a substantial body of literature concerned with the use that young children make of the fairy tale, in circumnavigating the exigencies and crises of development. Within this psychological and psychoanalytic framework, the fairy tale is seen to act as a vehicle for children exploring feelings of hatred and aggression and love and desire towards their parents. By using these tales, children may be assured that there is a solution to the conflicts they experience; and by using (thinking and dreaming about, playing at, drawing and writing about) the figures of the stepmother, the giant, the frog who is not a prince, they will come to understand and gain some kind of control over their painful and ambivalent feelings of hatred and attachment towards real mothers and real fathers.[34]

Within this psychoanalytic framework, Bruno Bettelheim has shown us too that fairy tales can suggest to young children that the weak and powerless (children, Jack the Giant Killer, Tom Thumb) may defy the great and powerful, and not be annihilated.[35] From a different perspective, Walter Benjamin has discussed the way in which the folk-fairy tale can be used as a structure of possibility against the dead weight of mythology, and the message of dour inevitability that the myths offer.[36] We do, in fact know from both psychological and historical sources that the folk-fairy tale has been used by and been useful to, a great many people growing up and surviving in this culture, over the last 400 years.[37]

So the working-class soldier's presentation of his tale, in a manner that echoes the adventuring of Tom Thumb, Jack the Giant Killer and Thomas Hickathrift, may suggest something of the same usage, may suggest that these stories, of lone and individual journeying and conflict, are written in this way for a particular purpose. What we should be alerted to above all, in pursuing this line of thought, is that the structure of the folk-fairy tale allows the expression of feelings about the self. It allows these feelings to be expressed in a highly conventionalised and formulaic way to be sure; but the soldier-hero, like Jack, can move through the emotions of fear, anger, desperation, loneliness and extreme aggression. What makes the world in which he journeys and battles is beyond his ken: he is a stranger in a mysterious universe, where things just happen; he is powerless and a tool of circumstance, like a child.

As a picaresque traveller, this kind of soldier-hero makes a circular journey, from his place of origin and back again, this time with a position in that social order made clear to him, his relationship with it established. So the lone soldier-hero of nineteenth-century military working-class biography wrote within a secular tradition, that of pilgrimage in a known and material world. Isabel Rivers has contrasted this tradition with that found in Methodist narrative, where the central figure journeys from this world to the next, the only fixed point for him being 'eternal and other worldly'.[38]

But it is not only a journey to another world, or to a celestial city that shows the hero-narrator to be a stranger and alone. Soldiers' tales are secular tales, and they can be read in the light of available models and available traditions. But some tension attaches to the use of the tradition outlined, and to the wrenching of individuality away from communality, which I have suggested is a feature of the nineteenth-century soldier's written story. I suggest that this tension is to do with an unacknowledged recognition made by these men, that what they were doing on these long journeys and during those years of war, was something *not to do with them.*

John Bunyan's *The Holy War* (1682) might be taken as the very pattern for nineteenth-century military autobiography, with its classic account of going for a soldier, that is echoed by so many men, including John Pearman:

> as they were crossing over the Country, they happened to light upon three young fellows that had a mind to go for Souliers[39]

> I was far from being settled although we made – good wages and not worked hard But I felt I should like to travel and see other Countries. . .so I made up my mind to be a Soldier and enlisted at once. ['Memoir', p. 190]

In *The Holy War*, the argument and the action belong to the Four Captains of Righteousness: they fight for something they understand and more or less believe in. There is no way of knowing if men like William Hall read *The Holy War*, though I am convinced that John Pearman must have, at some time in his life.[40] In the writing of men like these, there is a recognition that the war they fought was *not* like that, was not the same kind of war that the Captains of Righteousness fought. This recognition, of alienation from the purpose of war, is to be seen most clearly by considering what John Pearman achieved within the form of nineteenth-century military autobiography, that other published working-class writers, like William Hall, did not achieve.

By the time Pearman came to write, he knew that the wars against the Sikhs were not his wars: that they were wars of capital, of the landed interest, of the rich and powerful, of official Christianity. Knowing this, he was able to present his time in India as a time of conviviality and comradeship, an experience that was not bound by the expectations and ideology of his leaders, a time in which there was space to live and to tell his own story.[41] The denial of communality, the self-presentation of lone heroism, of self as Jack the Giant Killer, that is a feature of other working-class writing about military life in the same period, was perhaps an oblique recognition on the part of the writers, of something these men knew, but could not acknowledge as John Pearman did: that the ideological setting to their adventures made them strangers in the world.

In the pre-Crimean period, not only was military life remote from general social experience, but the army was itself cut off physically from the host society. Most soldiers served overseas, acting often as the agents of colonial foreign policy in a series of minor campaigns that has been called 'Queen Victoria's little wars'. In this series of small colonial wars, the policing function of a colonial army often merged with offensive action, and served as a way of labelling offensive action defensive.

The independent state of the Punjab was seen as presenting a severe threat to British India when its army crossed the Sutlej River in December 1845 – not into British territory, as was implied by British army command at the time, but into its own, that bordered the river on its southern bank. This territorial advance by the Sikh Raj finds its place in another history, in which the eighteenth century saw the eventual control of the Punjab by the Sikhs, and in which a resolution to survive as a people possessing a distinct identity had developed among them. Sikh power increased in the north-western territories as that of the Moghuls declined, and by 1765, the Sikhs were able to organise themselves into twelve military groups (*misls*), that governed most of the Punjab. A period of territorial expansion followed. Lahore was captured, and became the seat of Sikh government in 1799. The death of Ranjit Singh in 1839, conflict over inheritance of the throne and the growing ambitions of the *khalsa* (the military brotherhood of initiated Sikhs), all played a part in a move across the Sutlej in 1845.[42]

Of equal motivating force was Britain's evident territorial ambitions, and the move of men and artillery to the north-western frontier in the spring and summer of 1844. By the autumn of 1845, the invasion force (for it was clearly seen as such in Lahore), the largest ever assembled by the British in India, had arrived at the Punjabi frontier.

Several factions had emerged in the Punjab after the death of Ranjit Singh: his seven sons with their different claims to the throne; the Dogras of Jammu province; and a Sikh aristocracy. The Dogras were Hindu, and the Sikh grouping were members of the *khalsa*, so conflict often had a communal aspect. 'Ranjit Singh's youngest son, Dulip Singh was pronounced Maharajah in 1843, at the age of seven, with Hira Singh Dogra as chief minister. Dissent and weakness in the Sikh state had been watched with great interest by British India since 1839.

Briefly, after the crossing of the Sutlej in December 1845, the battles of Mudki, Ferozeshah and Aliwal were followed by the rout of the Sikh army at Sobraon in February 1846. The Sikhs were driven back across the Sutlej, and the British army advanced to Lahore, where a treaty was made in March with the Sikh *darbar* (the ministry that was to govern on behalf of the young Maharajah). Under this treaty, certain territories were ceded to the British. Peace did not last. The Second Sikh War saw the siege and Battle of Multan, and the Battles of Chilianwala and Gujrat. After this last defeat for the Sikhs in February 1849, the British annexed the Punjab in April 1849.[43]

All of these 'little wars', of which the Sikh Wars can be taken as an example, had in common a characteristic that has been called 'the emergence of a small-war mentality'. Across the emergent British Empire, the British army faced a wide variety of opponents, fighting in conditions and using techniques of combat that were not to be found in the textbooks of conventional warfare by which officers had been trained. Gwyn Harries-Jenkins has argued that this diversity of fighting conditions led to a rejection of military theory by the British officer class, as being irrelevant to the circumstances they found themselves in. In its turn, this rejection of theory impeded the development of military professionalism.[44]

When in his 'Memoir' John Pearman describes the kind of warfare that he was obliged to take part in, it was frequently to reveal the use of outmoded tactics,[45] and it is quite clear at many points that the officers who commanded him did not have a body of experience to guide them through the wars in the Punjab, and indeed, there was no collation of small-war experience until Sir Charles Callwell published *Small Wars: Their Principles and Practice* in 1896.[46] There was another factor, both military and social, that held officer attitudes towards these wars together: in military memoirs and military fiction of the period, great emphasis was placed on *battles*. Reading the mid-Victorian press, the public would learn little of the process of a campaign apart from the victories an army might gain. This emphasis on battles, by military hierarchy and in the public imagination, reinforced the belief of many officers that the study of military theory was an irrelevance. What this meant in John Pearman's case is that he was commanded by officers who had no general theory of climate and terrain, no theory of communications and supply to work by.

Pearman's 'Memoir' has been used, in fact, as evidence for the use of dangerous and outmoded tactics and control of the army by decrepit 'Peninsular men' during the Sikh Wars. For instance, in his account of the Battle of Chilianwala Pearman describes a stage disastrous for the British, when the Sikh cavalry broke into the line of the 24th Foot and did great damage, carrying off four guns. ['Memoir', p. 104] The Marquess of Anglesey uses Pearman's very brief account (of an incident that he did not directly witness) to outline the peculiarly inappropriate advance ordered by Brigadier Pope on this occasion, with no skirmishers sent out in front, and no men left in reserve:

> The blame for this debacle rests with those responsible for appointing Pope to his command. He was so ill and enfeebled that he had to be lifted into the saddle. He had never commanded more than a squadron in the field before. . . When he formed his nine squadrons in a single long line, leaving not a squadron in support, all confidence in him must have finally ebbed away. A more foolish formation, especially in a jungle with numerous obstructions, can hardly be imagined.[47]

There are in fact many accounts of such incompetence, poor leadership and tactical error to be found in both modern and nineteenth-century descriptions of the Sikh Wars, and they serve to reinforce a traditional history of the British army, in which it is seen sunk in tradition and apathy until the Crimean scandal throws a reforming light upon it.

Yet in fact, the Sikh Wars did see the development of new military tactics, particularly in the use of the artillery. The Peninsular War doctrine, enshrined in the warfare manuals of the first half of the nineteenth century, practically forbade the engagement of an enemy's artillery: fire was to be directed at the enemy infantry, as it was the infantry that was understood to be an army's essential fighting force. The wars in the Punjab saw a breaking away from this doctrine. Major-General Hughes, in his introduction to N. W. Bancroft's writing, shows how new tactics, involving large amounts of artillery fire, were refined during the sequence of battles between 1843 and 1849. Large quantities of artillery were moved ahead of the infantry and cavalry to engage, and to attempt to neutralise, the enemy battery. Meanwhile, infantry and cavalry moved together in a line until the artillery enabled the infantry to pass through the gun lines and make an assault. Horse artillery were used in a new way too, being directed to join cavalry units on the flanks, whilst field artillery supported the infantry brigades.[48] So evidence of military incompetence notwithstanding, in his descriptions of the Battles of Badowal, Aliwal, Sobraon, Ramnagar, Chilianwala and Gujrat, John Pearman is also describing the emergence of a new set of military tactics.

In the situation of small colonial warfare that John Pearman experienced, the personality of officers mattered a great deal, and was important for holding together an administrative structure, through 'the bonds of deference'.[49] John Pearman's testimony is important, because he shows that the deference so casually assumed by nineteenth-century officers and by twentieth-century historians might be a complicated, resentful and bloody-minded affair; and so it is worth pursuing the insights that Pearman offers into the relationship between officers and men a little further. He enjoyed the reversal of class relations that the battlefield might offer; ['Memoir', p. 191] and later, the 'Memoir' shows him trying to understand his own contradictory attitude towards order and discipline that the officer class partly represented. He was in no doubt about the occasions where mismanagement and poor leadership had cost the life of his peers, and in the writing of the final passages of his 'Memoir', the tyranny of the army and of officers over men took its place in his condemnation of all social tyranny. And yet, remembering the Battle of Gujrat he recalled affectionately the behaviour of Colonel White:

> Jest at that moment a 9 Pound shot struck the ground at the Colonels horses heels but Coln White did not – move or Look round his Brave old Face never moved with his White hair round it he only said stiddy men stidy make much of your horses men. I think there was not a man or a officer who knew Colonel White that didnot Love him such a happy Face and so kind to all ['Memoir', p. 121]

Are we to read here the bonds of deference? In one of his most interesting passages, Richard Holmes writes about the vocabulary of love and responsibility with which men have been led into battle throughout history: soldiers are called 'lads', 'boys', 'mes enfants'.[50] In a situation of extreme tension and fear, exposed and vulnerable, reduced to the position of a child, words addressed as if to a child take on the structures of comfort. But Pearman's remembered moment of affection for Colonel White was also an item in the drama of class relations: there was a contradiction in feeling affection in the situation Pearman found himself in, a situation where he was dispensable, a human being of lesser worth than his colonel, a mere item in the calculation of battle. This was a very military moment; but it is also an example of a psychological moment of class societies, recorded in different and convoluted ways in the nineteenth century, where people looked briefly across the wastes of difference and division and understood momentarily the possibility of other ways of feeling, other kinds of relationship.[51]

The impact of his own kindness, reflected back to him by a

common soldier, moved the young officer Daniel Sandford to tears in February 1849 after the Battle of Gujrat:

> as they lay on the ground with their mangled limbs they seemed grateful for any kindness and brightened up so when any of their officers came near them, that it made ones heart swell.[52]

These were psychologically useful moments for middle- and upper-class men (and for women of these classes, in other circumstances), allowing them to feel the dimensions of their own charity, and to use the misfortunes of the lower orders as a glass in which to read their own goodness.

Not all of the lower orders were grateful for the mere and paternal attention paid to them by their superiors: there is a quite horrible story told about the visit of Sir Henry Hardinge to the field hospital of the Bengal Horse Artillery after Ferozeshah in December 1845, and the outrageously clumsy comfort he brought to severely wounded men ('as if he must say something', observes George Bruce, who quotes this incident). To one young man who had been wounded by grapeshot passing through both cheeks, Sir Harry said:

> 'Well, my lad, I see you have two beauty spots on your face to take home to your sweetheart.' The lad abruptly said: 'I have no sweetheart!' 'That's quare. . . I thought soldiers and sailors had sweethearts wherever they went. But never mind my boy, if you haven't you will have, and that's some consolation. You won't be the less thought of for having a *little less cheek* than usual'.[53]

To feel affection in these circumstances (which N. W. Bancroft, who tells this story, insists some of his comrades felt) is an evasion of the real bonds that held these men together, and shows at the same time the need for love and affection in desperate circumstances.

'For the key to what makes men fight – not enlist, not cope, but fight – we must look hard at military groups, and the bonds that link men within them.'[54] The question of comradeship in armies and in battle has been explored perceptively and in great detail by several twentieth-century commentators, and John Pearman's evidence from his Indian years adds evidence to these accounts. For over 30 years he carried with him the names of the men he had fought with, ['Memoir', p. 266] and describes the care they took of each other in the firing line. The same Bancroft who recorded the nasty story above said that 'a soldier was nobody in those days, unless he had a comrade, no matter where he was, or what he was doing'.[55]

Comradeship was specifically organised for in the nineteenth-century army,[56] and it was this set of relationships that gives soldiers' accounts the curiously domestic tone that Pearman presents: his is the story of men who cooked and washed together and sat sewing in the barracks, as well as fighting together as friends. The conditions of battle usually provided for physical closeness. The square formation of traditional warface was still used in the colonial campaigning of the 1840s, often as a means of discipline, but also as a formation that offered great benefit in terms of psychological security. Men on horseback though, could not bunch together as closely as infantry in square formations could, and John Pearman fought most of his battles on horseback.[57]

When soldiers' tales are interpreted by historians, we are often invited to see their action in battle as the valour of simple men. The section of Richard Holmes' *Firing Line* that goes by this title is one of his most moving; but the delineation of courage and endurance is bought at the price of men's complexity, and of understanding their contradictory attitude towards the situation that they find themselves in.[58] The document that is introduced here, then, is valuable for the very difficulty of the feelings that it expresses. As readers, we can trace John Pearman's reaction to soldiering, to battle, and to the taking of human life, through the shifts of his text – though in the first half of the 'Memoir' he does not *present* them to us as complexities. But over the wider topic of soldiering in India, of being an agent of imperialism, a servant of John Company, Pearman was made conscious of his own attitude:

> And at the time I am speaking off India was to the White man a free Country we Could go where we liked no Trespass out there and John Company behaved well to us shared some of the Plunder with us Soldiers I mean in prize money not so the Queens Government and then John Company didnot make us work found us plenty of servants plenty of Grog and good living. . .Well with all the faults of a Military life there is more to live for then the poor man who in England is a free paid Slave ['Memoir', pp. 191–92]

He enjoyed the perks and the booty, though the particularity of his enjoyment lay in the pleasures of getting by, the physical and intellectual manipulation of circumstances, the stratagems employed to get a piece of meat, a horse to ride, a few hours' sleep on the muddy ground after a battle. He was conscious of an intensity of living then, a short space of time, certain to be limited either by death or things getting better, in which he could be both practical and intelligent.

But more than this, India gave Pearman immense freedom to inquire, to watch and listen, and to talk to a wide range of people. He was 'very fond of romeing about the Country and Converseing with the natives – a people I Always found very kind. . . some of our men used the Poor native very bad.' ['Memoir', p. 67][59] Analyses of late nineteenth-century imperialism have condemned the working-class recruit to jingoism, and our historical assumption is that official attitudes were held to by the common soldier. Whether or not this is the case for the later part of the century, John Pearman's manuscript is an important check on our translating these attitudes back over 50 years. A cavalry officer making the same journey as Pearman had recorded that

> No sooner had our anchor dropped, than the river suddenly swarmed with boats full of the wildest-looking savages, in a perfect state of nature, saving a dirty clout bound about their waists[60]

and John Pindar, a miner from Fife, who enlisted in June 1853 and saw service during the Mutiny, thought that he was contending with a 'stealthy, treacherous enemy of pure savages, to whom the laws of common humanity were unknown'.[61] Yet Pearman, landing at Calcutta, 'very much admired the Carrage of the Black men as they walked on the river bank or stood to look at us', ['Memoir', p. 6] and he admired the Sikhs as soldiers without having tc mention, as did Privates Baldwin and Ryder, that they had been trained by European officers.[62]

John Pearman learned a great deal by talking and listening:

> I once Said to an Indian Black man why do you trust and put such faith in the water of the Ganges. He replied I act as I was taught. You do the same. I could ask you why do you put such faith in Jesus you would say I was taught to do so) Now both are but theiry ['Memoir', p. 195]

Thirty years later he remembered conversations such as these, found in them his own roots for the anti-imperialism that secularism was publicising in the early 1880s;[63] and perhaps rewrote them:

> A True Musselman not a Mehomitian a Fire worshiper put me right on this Subject, Were I an Englishman he said I would worship the gun Sword & Bayonet only. See what it had brought your country. All her possessions. all her liberties all

her money, all her commerce all her advantages. . .Your
soldiers and sailors with their united arms was the argument
that prevailed with us. ['Memoir', p. 197]

In contrasting 'a true Musselman. . .a Fire worshiper' and 'a
Mehomitian', John Pearman was probably trying to distinguish
between Islam and Zoroastrianism, without the vocabulary to do
it. He was likely to have encountered Zoroastrianism in the Indian
army at this date, and men from the western states had recently
joined the army of the Punjab, bringing with them servants and
other camp followers from the Gujerati territories, a group that
probably included some Zoroastrians.[64]

Life as a policeman allowed John Pearman to cast the same
searching eye upon the religious differences and the religious
hypocrisies of rural Buckinghamshire; ['Memoir', pp. 167–9] but it
was sad, tame stuff compared with the elegance of the argument
against imperialist Christianity that he could report from the
Punjab of the 1840s, and the careful distinction that he was able to
make between 'a true Musselman' and a 'Mehomitian'. It was
India, and the contradictions of a soldier's life that first gave
Pearman the opportunity to worry at a problem, to make those
leaps in understanding which are given by the placing together of
two perspectives. His problem, as both a soldier and a policeman,
was that the intellectual contradictions that he dealt with were
grounded in his own experience, so what he *did* in his life, and
what he enjoyed doing, were often the groundwork for his
approach to wider and troubling moral questions. For instance,
about Chilianwala, the penultimate battle of the Sikh Wars (13
January 1849) and one that was disastrous for the British, with a
very high casualty rate,[65] he wrote:

> The Battle Lasted until Dark at night when both armys
> Stayed on the ground and the killed and wounded Lay were
> they Fell. . .the place was coverd with dead and dying that
> night I prayed to god that I mite never see that sight again In
> the night it came on to rain. . . Well as I said night Closed the
> sad sight and the rain Come down as if to Cleans us from our
> past Sin. for I verily believe man was not made by God to Kill
> his fellow man ['Memoir', pp. 107–8]

This elegiac summary concluded an account of a battle in which
Pearman was intensely involved as a soldier, and many years later
as a writer, and about which he conveys the same vivid and
controlled excitement that he does of other battles. It was in the
tension between what public service took from him, and the parts
of himself that had to remain hidden, that helped him abstract

meaning from the circumstances in which he had been so deeply involved. It was in this way that John Pearman came to know himself.

He moves then, in his 'Memoir' between a past that held its own meaning at the time that certain events took place, and the recasting of those meanings by the propulsion of new experience. Because it is almost certain that he wrote the manuscript in 1881–2, and because it is possible to trace a fair proportion of his sources in the contemporary newspapers and other publications, then the tendency on the historian's part is to attribute Pearman's analysis to the ideas he got hold of in his sixties. I think though that we should pay proper attention to his assertion that he had been thinking about these matters for 40 years ['Memoir', p. 169] and to consider what scattered evidence the manuscript holds for the development of men's ideas in the dynamic of dialogue, in the heat of barrack-room afternoons, or pressed together 'as Close. . . as the Fingers on our hands' ['Memoir', pp. 2–3] aboard the ships that carried men to fight for principles that only an extremely simple historical analysis will claim that they necessarily held as their own.

James Coley, Chaplain to the East India Company, joined the camp at Umbala in December 1845 and stayed on the field for the whole of the next year, seeing action at Mudki. Nobody wanted him, neither officers nor men – 'I grieve to find that there is very little demand for my services' – and he took to hospital visiting.[66] In the camp at Ferozepur he visited the hospital of Her Majesty's 80th Foot, and had a long conversation with a private soldier, which obviously shook him to the core. It is worth reproducing for the insights it offers into the possible state of mind, the belief system and cosmology of some of the men who made up the Army of the Punjab:

This evening at the hospital. . .a hardened wretch of the name of Ore told me, that he was a stranger to my principles and did not want me to converse with him. He said he had been brought up in unbelief and felt no uneasiness of mind at the prospect of dying an unbeliever. On my reminding him that he had a soul. . .he said that men need not be under any alarm with respect to futurity if he did his duty towards his fellow creatures. . . If he was corrupt, God had made him so. It was *unreasonable* to suppose that God would punish him for being what he made him. He did not believe in an evil spirit. He had read the Bible but did not believe it was the word of God. He had understood that the writings of the Apostles were forgeries, composed after their death. He spoke of the

Christian religion as an argument against its truth. He could
not believe that any men were ever so superior to each other, as
to be inspired by God. He could not exactly disprove the truth
of the Bible, but still he could not see why he should regard it
as false: on the contrary he approved the morality it
inculcates. . . He gave me credit for good motives and
intentions in talking with him, but would rather keep to his
own principles. . . Such cases, I know alas! too well, are not
uncommon among soldiers. . . I felt as if I were talking with
the Devil himself face to face.[67]

This is the language of debate, as reported by Coley: in his
transcription he reveals a man used to argument, to the rhetoric of
the appeal to reason. We may see here a particular expression of
that vast substructure of irreligion that Jim Obelkevitch's work
has shown,[68] and see Private Ore's argument as part of a more
general one, that belonged to a particular class and background.
What service as a soldier did was bring men together under the
banner of an overt political purpose, give a particular political and
narrative shape to a working life, and give men extensive
opportunities to talk. It is likely that John Pearman encountered the
ideas he dealt with in his 'Memoir' at many points in his working
life, and that his 13 years in the army were an important source of
them.

4
'A Low Order of Men'[1]

In January 1857 the first compulsory police act came into force.[2]
Buckinghamshire magistrates, sitting in quarter sessions, were
obliged, like the 13 other administrative counties which had not
formed constabularies under earlier, permissive legislation, to
establish a paid professional police force for the first time. John
Pearman, travelling to Aylesbury in March 1857, not only found
his way into a new administrative hierarchy, but was himself
representative of a much wider dislocation of place and circumstance than followed on the end of the Crimean War. In this year
of formation, Buckinghamshire Constabulary took on 153 men
(more than it was to recruit in the next five years put together)
and 19 of these men had just been discharged from the Crimean
regiments.

The County and Borough Police Act of 1856, and its legislative timing, was a response to a set of fears, of 'a footloose army' returning home. 'I fear the setting free of so many men who have been made familiar with blood and crime in their military life', said a magistrate at Epiphany Quarter Sessions in Aylesbury that January, and thus drew on a powerful memory that had been evoked in Parliament and the national press throughout 1856: 'Peace brought disastrous consequences in 1816. . .it was incumbent with another peace at hand. . .to legislate for the prevention of crime.'[3] This footloose army was joined in respectable imaginations by 'the whitewashed criminal thrown back upon his own haunts', for transportation began to be phased out in 1853, and the ticket-of-leave system established.[4] The preamble to the County and Borough Police Act mentioned the suppression of vagrancy as its primary justification, and it was in these terms, and with this rhetoric, that it was sold to the House of Commons. What is more, during the Crimean War the practice of stationing small detachments of troops in various parts of the country was discontinued.[5] John Pearman for one, thought himself a particular victim of this reduction in the size of the reserve army. ['Memoir', p. 153]

The footloose army of the respectable imagination – the army of the unemployed, the vagrant, the criminal, the discharged soldier – included in its ranks men like John Pearman, who became policemen in order to tide themselves over a bad patch. In the mid-Victorian years, all provincial police forces served this function locally, in provincial contexts: they were a way in which men could get themselves through a period of recession or unemployment, they were a way of finding something to go to when travelling from one part of the country to another, or from countryside to city.[6] Moreover, local police forces offered men the chance to manipulate their choices, in a way that the army, the other escape route from public or personal disaster, did not. The War Office and Parliament regulated military intake by altering age and height qualifications, and by limiting recruiting numbers from year to year, so there was never a free flow from the ranks of the unemployed to the ranks of the contemporary army.[7] Once in the army, it was difficult to get out as well (it cost John Pearman £5 to leave in 1857), which was not the case with joining a police force. Nearly 48,000 men joined English county forces alone between 1839 and 1874; about 12,000 of them were dismissed, but 24,000 of them resigned.[8] Only a quarter of the men who joined the Buckinghamshire police along with John Pearman in 1857 stayed for more than five years, and the majority – 47 per cent of his fellow recruits – left before the year was out.[9]

It was generally understood by police hierarchies throughout England that most recruits would leave within six months of joining. Social history, and histories of regulation and government, have scarcely yet begun to get to grips with the idea of a society policed by men like George Farey, born in Monks Risborough, Bucks., back home at the age of 22 after a failed enterprise in New York, in the force for 18 months before resigning; or with Harold Cheetham, brickmaker of Stockport, trade unionist and one time president of his union, in the local force for a few months in the 1860s until things got better[10] – or with the idea of John Pearman, policing Eton, living within the shadow of Windsor Castle, grimly patrolling the country lanes in his cart, brooding resentfully on the fact that

> In England 66 persons own two millions of acres of Land; 100 persons own four millions of acres 710 persons own one quarter of the whole soil of england and Wales. . .is not this a cruel monopoly of the Land given by god to us all. . .
> ['Memoir', pp. 163–4]

Back in 1857, John Pearman had used the newly formed Buckinghamshire Constabulary in much the same way as his fellow recruits had. He was unusual only in that he stayed – for nearly 25 years – and in that he was a success.

The majority of John Pearman's fellow recruits in 1857 were either natives of Buckinghamshire or of a neighbouring county. But comparison between the birthplace and last residence of men who did not fall into this category shows them moving from their birthplace closer to the south midlands, nearer to London, before making the next move, to Aylesbury and the police recruiting sergeant. The garrison towns of the south-east discharged their men onto the labour market in this geographical region (John Pearman was discharged at Harlow in February 1857),[11] and a month or so looking round, perhaps in London, was common. Charles Rose for instance, a Chesham-born watchmaker, came home after a year in the Crimea, worked at his trade for a couple of months, and then joined the new county police a few weeks after Pearman did.[12] But John Pearman was not coming home; and his turning to the police force was only indirectly to do with the Crimean War.

He had not served in Turkey. He had spent the war years training recruits, first in Lancashire and then at Sandhurst, where his skill with horses got him a stand-in post as Riding Master. His story (and his surviving family's story) was that he was promised a staff appointment which failed to materialise: it was given to a protégé of the Duke of Cambridge instead. John Pearman's grandchildren were told that

> the old man was so infuriated that he waylaid the Duke and grossly insulted him telling him he was no gentleman. . . as a result he was threatened with a court martial. . . but (his commanding officer) stood by his friend and managed things so that my grandfather was able to buy himself out.

It is highly unlikely that such an incident ever took place, as Pearman would certainly have been court-martialled if it had occurred; but it does make an extremely good story.[13] Undramatically, in his 'Memoir', Pearman recorded that 'I made up my mind to Leave if they would Let me which they did after a great deal of Trouble by my paying to them £5 after all my hard service'. ['Memoir', p. 153] He joined the police as a third-class constable, at the very bottom of the heap.

Soldiers were never popular with mid nineteenth-century chief constables, for levels of literacy among them were low, and it was held that they saw drinking as a necessary part of institutional life. But some particular disgrace must have attached itself to Pearman's name, for the experience and attributes that he brought to his new job gave other men who possessed them appointment at a higher level than his. He was a mature man (37 years old on signing on), unmarried, could read and write well, came with a reference from his commanding officer and was skilled with horses.[14] In this year of formation, what seemed to guarantee appointment as a first-class constable was previous police experience. But the Charles Rose mentioned above had none, was an undesirable ex-soldier, but was appointed to the second class. But whatever doubts may have been felt about John Pearman, he made good in a way that was rare among nineteenth-century police recruits. He was never fined, he was never de-ranked; and he made his unimpeded way up the police hierarchy.

In Buckinghamshire (and other counties) a hierarchy had been created and fixed in 1857. Officers were appointed as officers, and no working-class recruit could hope to climb higher than the position of inspector. Superintendents were born, not made, drawn from the middling sort of land agent, clerk, bailiff; and to get as far as being an inspector was rare enough. I looked in detail at the police careers of about 1,000 men for *Policing the Victorian Community*, and only four of them rose from being a constable to being an inspector. One of the four was John Pearman.[15]

It was Pearman's ease with all manner of people, his ability to talk and tell a tale, blend into the background when necessary, assume an identity, keep himself well-hidden, that brought him promotion. On several occasions between 1857 and 1864 (when he first became an inspector) he was sent out in disguise on detective work, and he records one of these periods in great detail in his 'Memoir'. ['Memoir', pp. 153–8] This kind of work was available for a few well-trusted county officers, for only in urban areas, and then not usually until the late 1870s, were permanent detective forces common. John Pearman seems not to have seen in detective duty what Alexander Clark, a detective officer of Aberdeen, writing in the early 1870s described as 'the thrill of the chase', the drama of the hunter and the hunted.[16] Some urban policing situations, like Clark's in Aberdeen, allowed pursuit and capture in the intricate map of court and alley, and in the quarry of the common lodging house. But detection in the rural areas consisted far more of a watchful passivity, a system of control operated by talking and listening, the machinery set in motion by information received. It is important to understand how very little freedom of individual action county policemen in this period actually had, whether they were on detective duty or not.[17] In the account of June 1859, in which Pearman 'dressed ragged' and it took him three weeks to find a clue, he could only act after reporting to his inspector. As he noted, it was lucky that a court of petty sessions was sitting, for without a magistrate to sign a warrant, he could have proceeded no further. ['Memoir', p. 156] Until the 1880s, the magistrate remained the administrative pivot of daily police operations in the rural areas.[18]

At the end of his police career, John Pearman acknowledged that in doing police work not only his skills and his attributes, but in some way his own self, had been drawn on. During his Indian years, as we have seen, he had been 'very fond of romeing about the Country and Converseing with the natives', ['Memoir', p. 67] and what the ratepayers of Buckinghamshire bought, when they paid for his labour, was something of his interest in other people and their ideas, his capacity to both play a part and to listen to other people's stories. But because it was only the use of the skill that was wanted, not the ability to forge social analysis out of experience, and out of all the stories he had read and listened to, then John Pearman had to say that 'I Cannot say much for the Policemans life he must be a special man & Look after other mens faults and shut his Eyes to all is virtues'. ['Memoir', p. 192]

The idea of liminality is popular among historians at the moment. A term taken from anthropology, that describes those figures in particular cultures who hover on the threshold of two worlds, and by whose position two ensuing sets of knowledge may be mediated, it is used to great effect by Dominick LaCapra for instance, in his critique of Carlo Ginzburg's *The Cheese and the*

Worms.[19] Ginzburg's work, his account of the heretical sixteenth-century miller Menocchio and the invented cosmology that emerged through questioning of him by the inquisition, is in any case of direct relevance to the writing of John Pearman; for in Pearman's 'Memoir', the same questions of the relationship of experience to knowledge, and of popular and oral culture to the world of books and 'elite' ideas are raised, as Ginzburg raises them through the figure of Menocchio.

Ginzburg defines Menocchio as a representative of popular culture, and argues that the miller did all his reading and all his thinking through the grid of this peasant culture, that the written word was secondary to orality, and that his invented cosmology was, in Ginzburg's words, attributable to

> a substratum of peasant beliefs, perhaps centuries old, that were never wholly wiped out. By breaking the crust of religious unity, the Reformation indirectly caused these old beliefs to emerge. . .[20]

But LaCapra's notion of Menocchio as 'situated on the threshold between popular and dominant culture' gives us instead the picture of a man with a deep interest in books and a passion for inquiry and controversy, a man who quite clearly used new ideas from what he had read and heard about, and who out of them actively constructed a theory that explained the world for him in a more or less satisfactory way. LaCapra also points to the particular position of millers in sixteenth-century European society: mills were situated on the outskirts of settlements; millers had commerce with economic worlds wider than the village, and with urban centres, and so on.[21]

So, though liminality as an idea is fashionable, it has a certain mileage to it. In *Policing the Victorian Community*, I described the way in which, by enforcing a particular kind of work discipline, nineteenth-century police authorities put constables into a position that could be described as liminal: working-class recruits were cut off from the communities of their birth and stationed at a geographical distance from them; they were dressed in a uniform, and expected to live by the rules of sobriety and self-discipline; and possessed of these attributes were sent out to watch a society from which they had but recently been removed.[22] In parliamentary commissions of inquiry and in chief constables' reports of the 1860s and 1870s I kept coming across a particular image: constables on night-duty are ordered to watch the beer-houses; they are to watch through the window, or the open door, and even then, to keep their distances from that light and conviviality inside. They are not to speak to the drinkers, not to step over the threshold or through the door that distances and makes theatrical what was until yesterday a familiar life.[23] Recently, discussing the role of the detective in novels and other writing of the mid-Victorian years, Anthea Trodd has shown the extreme tension and ambivalence that attaches to these fictional figures, for they, as working-class men, stepped over the threshold from the sordid and low public world into the sanctity of the middle-class home.[24] Of course, what is particularly interesting about the actual class and cultural ambivalence of the nineteenth-century police constable's position is that it was enforced, and that his masters had hopes of it: hopes that by taking working-class men and making policemen out of them, much larger groups of working people might be schooled in the social virtues.[25]

Being in an awkward position between two ways of life, two belief-systems – being in this kind of liminal situation – also has its effect on those who occupy that position. There are technically brilliant and persuasive readings of psychoanalytic case-study for instance, that invite us to see the maid, or the governess, in the nineteenth-century bourgeois household as she who is literally on the doorstep, she who breaks the enclosed circle of the ideal Victorian family, and who by her knowledge and her position is the very epitome of that 'something betwixt and between'.[26] I would not want to pursue this line of argument here, but would suggest that what figures like these have thrust upon them, and what shapes them as subjects is *information*. Servants have access to family secrets; policemen learn about the property basis for police distribution. Policemen (like Italian sixteenth-century millers, indeed) live on the edges of communities, both topographically and emotionally, and they too are in a particularly good position for obtaining reading material, hearing arguments, thinking through what has been presented to them in this way.

The trouble for John Pearman, as I think his writing shows, is that there was no story to tell about being a policeman. There are hundreds of versions of the soldier's tale; but for the policeman, only a bit-part in Punch and Judy, where he replaces the Crocodile towards the 1880s, and a bit later some pathos from Gilbert and Sullivan.[27] I have found no autobiography of a nineteenth-century constable.[28] If liminal, policemen are also comic figures, with big feet and funny hats, domestic shadows of the soldier, who may be despised, but who is glamorous too. Indeed, the debate of the 1850s that preceded the first compulsory police act drew constantly on the image of different kinds of army. Militias, and the yeomen and volunteer forces, might be the domestic reflection of the real thing, that acted out its drama in scarlet coat and in another country; but they still provided ways of understanding what a police force was, and what it was not, in the 1850s and 1860s.

Throughout his account of life as a policeman (which occupies less than a dozen of the Memoir's pages) John Pearman maintained a detachment from the work he did, displayed a written reluctance to become involved in the question of policing, or to comment on it as a moral or political activity. This is by way of striking contrast with his account of soldiering, which he understood to be a politically highly-charged activity, both from his readings in the anti-imperialist literature of the late 1870s, and from his own experience of the sub-continent. His analytical passion was therefore reserved for soldiering.

His detachment from a job that he did for a quarter of a century probably derived from several sources. It has already been suggested that it was dull compared with soldiering; but much more important than this was the fact that the policing of mid nineteenth-century communities demanded from police personnel a passive watchfulness as a means of social surveillance. This was not simply demanded from recruits; it was a taught skill, that might become a personal attribute of policemen themselves.[29] In some cases, and not just Pearman's, what watching did was to make plain to those who took part in this system of surveillance what was the class and economic basis of that machinery of control. John Pearman got the figures of land ownership in the 'Memoir' [pp. 163–4] from his reading;[30] but as a police officer he would anyway have known precisely the number of acres surveyed by policemen in Buckinghamshire, would have known that the distribution of constables and their patrol routes was largely dictated by the rateable value of property in each police division; would have known indeed that police divisions were themselves matched to the area of jurisdiction belonging to the traditional rulers of rural England – the country magistrates.[31] What the activity of policing could do then, for a number of men who worked at the job over a long period of time, was to throw a searchlight on the local workings of a system of control and management. It revealed yet more of what some men already knew about the way the world worked.

Soldiering, on the other hand, represented a distinct operation of state and government, usually in a situation removed from the familiar social one. There were anyway at the time of Pearman's writing, radical critiques of the army and British imperialism for him to draw on, and to make personal analysis easier to construct.[32] There were no such contemporary critiques of policing, and Pearman had to draw obliquely on a different kind of source to explain himself to himself as a policeman.

His reluctance to write about policing also had something to do with the way in which he saw a system of civil law as being intimately bound up with the law of the churchmen – this 'priesthood' – ['Memoir', passim] and the moral imperatives that were used by them to promulgate it. He identified this twin-headed enemy in much the same way as the freethought press did (he was almost certainly reading the *National Reformer* and the *Freethinker* when he wrote the 'Memoir') and it was much easier to see the connection between the two when discussing British imperial activity abroad.

There is a point in the 'Memoir' where he presents the job of policing in terms of straightforward contradiction:

> if you want to see Freedom you must leave England and look out some were else. . . But still I like Law and have always tried as a Soldier and a Policeman to maintain it and to keep up Disciplin. but when we think of God. and then our Rulers we look for the reasons why it is so maintained ['Memoir', p. 245]

To label those only as ambivalence would be to ignore the subtlety of John Pearman's understanding. He wrote more about law than he did about policing because he knew that the police were an aspect of a system of law, that – in the words of a modern sociologist of police – they 'function (by) maintaining order as defined by the group which supports them. . . they are appointed with the task of maintaining the order which those who sustain them define as proper'.[33] He saw the reason why the law was 'so maintained', why there was 'one Law for the poor and another for the Rich,' ['Memoir', p. 240] and he upheld the rule of law in his writing, in spite of his clear understanding of how it was used in his experience, to exclude some people from the commonweal, remove from them their right to the earth. Policing was coercive within this analysis, in that it administered this particular set of laws; and at the same time, it did not exist separately from that system of law. We could say then, that policing was beneath John Pearman's attention; or that he *was* paying it attention, but as part of the general system he was in the process of condemning. Certainly, a police force could not be understood as an army could, as a possible army of righteousness, fighting an external enemy. A police force could not either be, or in Pearman's ironic analysis of the British army's role in India, fail to be, an army of God.

Some of John Pearman's silence on the question of being a policeman must also have derived from his consistent assertion that in spite of promotion and good luck, he was infinitely connected with the world he was sent out to police, with the

whole of 'the poor Brotherhood'. ['Memoir', p. 194] He knew
that the poor might

> Break the Law or what is called sin. . . (but) The cause are not
> been the same with the rich as lay at the Door of the Poor and
> yet they sin but very little Compared with the Rich They may
> break the Law many ways and often but that is the Law made
> by man for his own ends not the Law of God. The Rich break
> the Laws they have made for their own ends and the Lawyer
> will Drag them out of their own Dirt for the Golden Calf) or
> money ['Memoir', p. 188]

His connection with the poor brotherhood that he policed was, in
fact, even closer than this, for on several occasions in India he had
been a thief. ['Memoir', pp. 25, 29, 39, 88, 129] However, he did
not explore this precise connection in his writing.

'It is not a happy life', he said after 25 years a policeman, whilst
admitting at the same time that 'I done very well in the Police
Force'. ['Memoir', p. 192] He did, and as a reward for other
pieces of detective work successfully accomplished, and his
exemplarily blank discipline sheet, he was rewarded with the
highest position that the hierarchy could offer to the working man
become a policeman: 'I was promoted to 1st Class Inspector in
January 1864 and sent to take Charge of the men employed at
Eton College and the Street.' ['Memoir', p. 158]

The place carried its own meaning: Eton the very school of
privilege, Windsor Castle greyly looming close by, centre of
kingcraft, the seat of 'the Godess Victoria. . . Defender of the
faith and Head of our Land for which she receives 85.000£ pr year
beside other Large windfalls'. ['Memoir', p. 232] If India
provided John Pearman with fuel for his republicanism, then the
evidence of his 'Memoir' is that his time at Eton forged past and
current experience into a coherent and radical analysis of the
society he policed, and that when he came to write that analysis
down in 1881–2, he drew on a set of skills that police work had
demanded of him, every day, for 25 years.

5
The Practice of Writing

All levels of police work in the mid-Victorian years demanded a reasonable proficiency in reading and writing, but particularly in writing. Country forces especially were spread thin, and the writing of reports and entries in occurrence books were effective means of supervising constables at outlying stations. 'This book', ran the notice pasted into the journals that were issued to all members of the Northamptonshire Constabulary, 'is to be kept in the form of a daily journal by the Inspector, Sergeant or Constable. . .in charge of divisions or stations. He will record in a neat and legible manner his proceedings during each day of the 24 hours.'[1]

After 1856, all local authorities asked their policemen for this kind of record keeping: police journals were open, public and official accounts of a system of supervision and control, usually examined weekly or fortnightly by superior officers. A recently published police diary, which was kept by a New York patrolman between 1850 and 1851, represents a different kind of writing, prompted by William Bell's own need for an *aide mémoire*: 'forced to remember the names and addresses of scores of suspected thieves and fences, he conscientiously started a ledger of the shops and dealers he had visited'.[2] The writing that English policemen of the same period took part in was actually prescribed, and John Pearman worked for a quarter of a century at a job that demanded the daily exercise of writing skills.

In some borough forces, journal keeping meant the joint filling-in of one ledger by several policemen.[3] But in the rural areas, police diary writing was a lonely, individual affair, making the day's deeds available for individual and prolonged scrutiny. It has been claimed that 'writing. . .by objectifying words. . .encourages private thought; the diary or the confession enables the individual to objectify his own experience'.[4] In looking at the writing experience of mid-Victorian county policemen, we need to consider the claim that any kind of autobiographical composition, in conditions of isolation, will usually have this psychological effect, will give this 'personal awareness of. . .individualisation'.[5] Within this psychological framework, it does not matter who the audience is, nor what suppression of personality may be demanded by the diary's official purpose. What matters is that an individual takes part in a process that makes the aural visible, and that places on the page in linear form a series of events that has happened to that individual.

It is likely that the hardcover notebook in which John Pearman wrote his 'Memoir' originally had an official police purpose (though it is smaller and thicker than other constables' journals I have read). He originally started writing in it at the back, probably on the penultimate two pages, where he made notes on a series of court cases in which he gave evidence in the period 1869–76.[6] (It is possible of course, that he copied out the contents of pages 267–8 at a later date.) He then gave an account of his military career on page 270, and moved back to page 269 to list the items of a family history. He concluded this page with his retirement from the police in October 1881. On the page before the court-case notes is a list of his fellow recruits to the 3rd Light Dragoons in 1843. These jottings at the end are an epitome of the story he moved on to tell in the front of the notebook: a brief autobiography, an army career, a list of comrades, a series of trials that reveal the failures of the rich and powerful.

Police notebooks and journals do not seem to have been at all consistently dealt with after they were filled up: had they been collected in, we should expect to find many more of them than the random volumes that turn up in constabulary archives. It was obviously quite common for policemen to keep hold of them: sometime in 1883 for instance, the eleven-year-old daughter of Warwickshire constable William Cooper got hold of his discarded journal and wrote:

> Mother is cutting up bits to put in our mattress. Father is sitting in his armchair rappity tapping with his nails Nellie is busy altering Mrs Bloxhams dress. . .and I am writing this but of course you can see this by my scrawly writing but I can write better than this when I do try this is only a bit of scribble to pass away the time I am yours truly Emily Louisa Cooper. P.S. I forgot to tell you where I reside, but I give it underneath. Police Station Tysoe[7]

Much has been written recently about the wide and sweeping changes brought about by the creation and use of writing systems within human societies. Walter Ong, for instance, outlines the effect of writing on individual consciousness with a list that includes the notion of individual motivation, the idea of character and the idea of human action as propelled from within.[8] But in introducing their study of the cognitive effects of an invented writing system on the Vai of modern Nigeria, Sylvia Scribner and Michael Cole comment on this method of proceeding:

It is striking that the scholars who offer these claims for specific changes in psychological processes present no direct evidence that individuals in literate societies do in fact, process information about the world differently from those in societies without literacy. They simply make assumptions about changed modes of thinking in the individual as the mediating mechanism for the linguistic and cultural changes which are the object of inquiry.[9]

'This is an entirely appropriate procedure for anthropologists, sociologists and classicists', they comment, but not for psychologists; and they go on to argue against the supposed universality of literacy's effects.

Neither does this seem an appropriate way for historians to proceed. But in fact, a text like that of John Pearman, or the official diary-writing of other nineteenth-century policemen, can allow a quite specific illustration of what is being argued against as generality by Scribner and Cole. Walter Ong, for instance, has suggested that one effect of acquiring written language is a way of seeing the world in which time is not so much a framework to, but rather a constituent of, human action.[10] The concern of police hierarchies with the management of time, the strict meeting at conference points, the detailed placing of the day's events in chronological order and the written recording of them, could all be seen as small and localised historical examples of the effect of writing that Ong has argued for. In demanding journal-keeping of their workers, police managers were concerned with the disciplining of personnel and with the ordering and management of particular communities; and the last was designed to be managed through the first.

It could then be argued that policemen were made to internalise the framework of industrial time in a more clear-cut way than were many groups of workers in the nineteenth century, and that the discipline of writing played a central role in this process.[11] Yet in fact, it is more likely that the framework of natural time, and the precise reckonings of the agricultural day and year, were one of the attributes that police authorities bought when they positively set out to recruit men from rural backgrounds.[12] In this case, then, writing could be said to have confirmed an existing psychological framework, rather than providing for it. Extant written texts from the past, roughly similar in style, and produced for clearly defined purposes like the diaries that nineteenth-century county policemen had to keep, can then allow us to test these claims for the universality or the specificity of writing's effect. Scribner and Cole suggest that there are no grounds for making 'sweeping generalisations about literacy and cognitive change', and that in order to support the thesis that literacy makes a difference to mental processes 'psychological analysis has to be joined with cultural analysis'.[13] This means that we need to know writing was used in particular contexts, and what its users understood they were doing by writing. A piece of writing like John Pearman's allows us to pursue these questions. We can let the words yield up some of the linguistic theories that the writer was working with, gain insight into the processes of thought that placed the words on the page in a particular way. At the same time, we can consider the content of John Pearman's writing, the actual ideas and beliefs that he was dealing with, their origins and transmutations. In this way, it will be suggested that the psychological process that we see at work in the composition of the 'Memoir' is itself historical evidence of the workings of a culture, and of the uses an individual made of it.

In order to wed psychological analysis to cultural analysis, writing has to be seen as language acquisition, that is, it has to be seen as part of a process taking place within the span of an individual life. People do not become literate all at once: John Pearman's text itself shows that the learning of written language can extend through half a century. In his particular case, the process was mediated by the fact that he was a working-class man who could write, and write well, but who had received little schooling. He wrote an informal English in a society that, by 1880, was so clearly laying the foundations of formality, was establishing so clearly the canons of correctness, that an editor 80 years on felt obliged to take a lawnmower to his prose. What is more, John Pearman was writing in a literate society where written English was not constituted in simple opposition to oral language,[14] or where speech functioned as the possession of the disinherited with formal written English the province of their rulers.[15] Rather, he wrote his 'Memoir' in a society where there was a complicated and constant interchange between the written and the spoken, where ideas read about became absorbed into the ideas people already had cognisance of, and where oral traditions helped interpret the written word.

The approach taken in this section of the introduction deals with real psychological processes undergone in real historical circumstances, and it has to be said at this point that the argument deals in different terms and at a different level from what is outlined by Gareth Stedman Jones in *Languages of Class*. In his important piece on 'Rethinking Chartism', Stedman Jones has argued that social experience is organised by language, or rather, by specific political languages that allow individuals to articulate sets of experiences in particular ways.[16] In the case of the Chartists, so this argument goes, it was not simply lived experience that propelled large numbers of people, in the 1830s and 1840s, into understanding that their social situation resulted from political injustice. Rather, it was the structure of understanding that radicalism provided, and the articulation of that radicalism in forms of language, that allowed people to attribute economic and social evils to a political source. This language – precisely, metaphors and other figures, rhetorical structures and chains of argument and reasoning – was met with in Chartist speeches, in journalism and other literature of the movement, and it directed people's understanding in certain ways.[17]

As far as the content of radical thought is concerned, this argument is of some importance in John Pearman's case, for it is clear that the written and spoken structures of radicalism had organised his political understanding, at some point in his life. Particularly, the radical understanding of foreign trade as an evil seems to have been both used and elaborated by John Pearman in his analysis of imperialism, and the connection he made between imperial expansion and questions of ownership and profit in Britain.[18] This point will be returned to in the next section, when Pearman's political reading and political writing are dealt with at some length. What is important here, over the question of consciousness and written language, is to point out, as others have done, that Stedman Jones' analysis rests almost entirely on newspaper articles and newspaper reports of speeches: on that historical elision that has already been noted: of simply assuming that written language is a direct and transparent representation of what it was that was said.[19] What is more, a particular understanding of language is conveyed here by Stedman Jones, but not really made explicit. For in 'Rethinking Chartism' language reception (listening to language, reading it), and the production of language are not really seen as psychological processes. The great crowds of Chartists figured in Stedman Jones' argument clearly were psychological beings, took hold of particular forms of language, appropriated them, used them; came to reorder what they knew through that language; came to think in different ways. However, as we are dealing with that most impermanent of all historical evidence, spoken language, we have no direct access to that process, and Stedman Jones can only present his anonymous crowds of Chartists as the subjects of language, as highly effective rhetorical figures in his own historical narrative.

But written language – treated as written language, and not just as speech-written-down – allows something different. In John

Pearman's case, we are dealing with a user of a writing system, and through what he wrote we can gain access to his active use and reordering of many languages (including the language of radicalism). The historian's attention to written language allows some access to those long-lost processes, allows the presentation of its users as both psychological and historical beings.

Commenting on nineteenth-century working-class writing, John Burnett notes that 'after letter writing, autobiography was. . .the most common form of personal literary expression'; and he singles out the spiritual autobiography as the form most familiar and available as a model to nineteenth-century working-class writers. Both *Destiny Obscure* and David Vincent's *Bread, Knowledge and Freedom* present overwhelming evidence about the use of the autobiographical form by nineteenth-century working-class writers,[20] and the writers themselves, whose work Burnett and Vincent reproduce and comment on, suggest reasons for the absence of diaries and journals from the corpus.

An autobiography is the survey of a life from a momentarily fixed viewpoint, an attempt to make sense of the past and to marshal events and the experience of relationships into a coherent narrative sequence.[21] Often, the autobiography was undertaken at the end of a working life, in conditions of greater leisure than had been experienced within it. Burnett mentions lack of time and opportunity working against the practice of journal-keeping.[22] To this list can be added lack of space, and peace and quiet in many households. What is more, journal-keeping demands a constant outlay of money – money spent on a luxury that was the first to be abandoned in times of trade or domestic crisis. The gaps in John O'Neal's journal (*A Lancashire Weaver's Journal, 1856–1864, 1872–1875*) are directly related to the times when he was very short of cash.[23]

The working-class autobiographer was, according to David Vincent, committed to a double task of 'analysing (his) own past and that of the working-class community. . .only by understanding himself could the working-class man understand the world in which he lived'.[24] The impulse to understand himself is what I think we must finally see as John Pearman's motive for composition, in it read the magnificence of the attempt; and its final failure. Its success as a piece of self-presentation can be found, for instance, in the places where, with startling clarity, Pearman conveys his experience across the years, the moment of landing in India for example, where 'it was a sort of Strange sight to us', and 'every thing was new allthough strange to us'. ['Memoir', pp. 5, 6] At other moments a feeling, a sight, a sound is conveyed by the similes of spoken dialect: the men lying on the ship on the outward passage 'as Close togeather as the Fingers On our hands', the foreyard snapping 'like a Carrot', the way the women 'did scrawl out' when Private Potter ran after them with a human skull, the troops spreading out 'like a Lady Fan'; the wounds of the dead washed by rain, 'as White as Veal'. ['Memoir', pp. 2, 3, 14, 33, 109] We can start to read its failures in the narrative disjuncture that has already been mentioned,[25] and in what that disjuncture actually represents of John Pearman's understanding of himself; and his failure to achieve that understanding.

The 'Memoir' does not, in fact, fit altogether smoothly into the autobiographical pattern that Burnett and Vincent have outlined. For a start, the second half is only occasionally written as a life story. Rather than writing narrative here, Pearman produced a piece of writing that operates as a kind of dialogue of ideas, into which he inserts autobiographical items at different points. A typical shift of topic in this way is to be found on pages 188–9 of the 'Memoir', where reflection on the way in which the rich can evade the consequences of breaking the law leads to a reflection on the life of the poor: 'we cannot find much to live for ours is a life of heavy toil to get a bare living and to amas money and Whealth for the great men of the day.' Generalised reflection then leads Pearman to his own story: 'But I must be very thankful I have never been out of employment or without a Shilling since I first took to Keep myself at the Age of 13 years & 9 months.'

Second, and as the example above indicates, Pearman did not set out in a deliberate fashion to survey his past from a fixed vantage point. The possible use of letters home, the Sikh Wars, and more tendentiously (for we do not know what he read during the course of his life) the model of the military autobiography, all did dictate the use of narrative and an overtly autobiographical approach in the first half of the volume. But in the second part, where his position as policeman and indeed the job of policing (except for the adventure story of detective work in disguise) could not be discussed in the dramatic and clear-cut way that soldiering could, he abandoned autobiographical structure. It is indeed, quite common for the simple past-tense narrative structure of autobiography to collapse when the writer moves close to the moment (or the time) of composition. But John Pearman stopped the linear presentation of events 25 years before 1881–2, when the soldier's tale came to an end. He dealt with the ensuing (and very long) period of his life by setting up, working through, and arguing against a certain number of ideas. He wrote then in response to contemporary events and contemporary reading, and in this way, writing the 'Memoir' may have functioned as diary-keeping in the 18 or so months of its composition.

Walter Ong has pointed out that the personal diary was 'a very late literary invention, in effect unknown until the seventeenth century'. In outlining the ways in which writing can be said to change people's way of seeing the world, Ong presents diary-keeping as a heightened expression of a psychology shaped by written language, with its nervous movement between self-as-writer and self-as-audience, and its devices for the 'internalisation of consciousness'.[26] Did writing the last part of the 'Memoir' serve John Pearman in this way? We have to assume that here, Pearman worked through ideas that he had talked to others about, that they were part of a common stock of debating points, with no one single source, and that he configured an audience in order to work through them. He was obviously reading widely when he wrote the 'Memoir' and some of his reading is reproduced in his writing. Stylistically, the 'Memoir' is a trying-on of many different voices; and we will at least be able to consider Ong's claim in the light of some quite specific evidence.

Finally, in matching the 'Memoir' against claims made for nineteenth-century working-class autobiography, there is no evidence that Pearman expected that what he wrote would ever be read by anyone else. He did not announce that the 'Memoir' was written as a guide for his children, or for a wider audience, both of which were common didactic purposes in the construction of nineteenth-century working-class autobiography.[27] He used the privacy of its pages to record an unhappy marriage, the sadness of a relationship that was 'I suppose much the same as other peoples'. ['Memoir', p. 208] Two pages of his essay 'Is Marrage a Failour' are cut away. Whether he or someone else did the cutting, their excision could be read as the clearest internal evidence offered by the text, that he did not expect it to be read.

Having made this point, it is important to acknowledge that the imagining of an audience is a necessary psychological condition for writing: simply, it is not possible to write without knowing that writing can be read, and without postulating an imaginary reader of some sort. Indeed, on many occasions, Pearman actually addresses an audience, and at one point refers to 'another part of this Book', ['Memoir', p. 243] (though he may have meant 'notebook', or 'volume' here). And the volume *was* read: whoever spoke to the reporter at his funeral in 1908 gave a version of his life that was closely tied, by content and style, to the first half of the 'Memoir'.

What John Pearman came to understand of himself through the act of writing is unclear. The 'Memoir' is a collection of jagged observations, difficult shifts of topic, incomplete self-portraits. He did not smooth himself into the rounded character who makes a journey through life, but rather presented the unfinished items of a psychology. The 'Memoir' is an account of thinking as much as it is of living.

John Pearman was a literate man, though the errors he made in writing may serve to disguise this fact for those who are unfamiliar with the processes involved in acquiring and using written language. Many adult learners of the system are hampered by their lack of familiarity with formal English, but this was not the case with John Pearman, who had a long acquaintance with it from his work; from the legal language that, as a police officer, he encountered on a regular basis, particularly in court; and from his reading. This knowledge of formal English shows up in his spelling, where he shows a mastery of the lexis of the law which is not evinced in words that demonstrate the same phonetic principle of written English, but which are not legal terminology. This knowledge of formal English, which was certainly much wider than that of most working-class people of the time, was used by him as an organising principle of his own writing; but within that framework, as has already been suggested, he encountered the difficulties that written English presents to *all* its learners.

If we look at the errors that John Pearman made in writing, we can begin to assess what linguistic theories he was working with when he made them. A brief consideration of low-order written errors – in spelling, in tense agreement, in sentence cohesion – will then lay the foundation for considering larger questions of structure in writing, questions of the rhetorical organisation of passages of text, and cohesion within them. This brief consideration should serve to demonstrate ways the linguistic evidence offered by informal texts can be used as a device of historical interpretation.

It is a commonplace within developmental linguistics that the mistakes people make in speaking are revelatory, that is, they give access to the ongoing construction and use of the linguistic theory that the user is working with. Thus someone learning English, either as a child or as an adult acquiring a second language, may discover the -*ed* rule for some English verbs, and overgeneralise the rule, adding -*ed* to verbs that are not regular in this way, producing such errors as *sitted* for *sat*, or *runned* for *ran*. These mistakes allow a possible reasoning process to be reconstructed. Written errors allow many of the same deductions to be made, and writing, by fixing speech and making it permanent, allows analysis to be made across the years.

Earlier in this introduction, an argument was made for a connection between the ability to write, and an individual's reading capacity.[28] But in fact, both capacities have their origins in speech, in that writing depends first and foremost on the understanding that sound can be symbolised, and reading on the understanding that those symbols can be brought back into speech – can be read. John Pearman's writing allows us, to some extent, to make a historical reconstruction of the spoken language he used and transformed in the 'Memoir'. The simplest way of starting this reconstruction is to look at the way he spelled words.

John Pearman spelled from speech. All users of written English do this, or rather, all those who learn to write have to make the necessary connections between what is spoken, and what is written down. Later, writers move beyond this simple, one-to-one connection between articulation and written symbol, to a connection that allows questions of meaning and lexis to influence how words are put on the page.[29] Yet articulation always remains a major source of information for all writers who have to think how to spell words, however advanced they may be. Examples of Pearman's use of articulation in spelling are *an* (and), *as* (has), *is* (his), *sildom* (seldom), *ingaged* (engaged), *distroy* (destroy). Modern Surrey and Buckinghamshire dialect speakers pronounce these words in the way Pearman spelled them;[30] and the last three errors show with a particular clarity one of the inherent difficulties of an alphabetic writing system: the similarity in vowel sounds, and in the appearance of the graphemes that represent them.[31]

The samples above are spellings made from the most basic and simple analysis of written English that a writer can make, of syllables based on the arrangement of consonant–vowel–consonant. On an equal number of occasions, John Pearman mis-spelled words from a learned phonetics. A phonetic analysis of English, that is, an analysis and representation of the language according to the vocal sounds it is composed of, can be learned from many sources. Since about 1890 a majority of children in English schools have been taught to read and write by methods that emphasise a consistent relationship between speech sounds and certain clusters of letters. But as has already been noted, John Pearman cannot have been taught to read in this way.[32]

It is possible to discover the phonetic principles of a language from experience – from personal reading – and that is probably how John Pearman came to make the connections he did. The majority of his spelling errors involved the substitution of perfectly possible, but formally incorrect, letter clusters to represent certain vowel sounds: *althow* (although), *clew* (clue), *dought* (doubt), *idear* (idea), *sweap* (sweep). Connected to this spelling strategy, where he remembered a correct sounding, but conventionally inappropriate phoneme, was his tendency to misremember certain letter sequences that are used to represent certain speech sounds. What he ended up doing in a small number of cases was to use an inappropriate phoneme that could not possibly represent the sound he meant it to represent: *afread* (afraid), *beginging* (beginning). On a few occasions, he reversed letter sequences as in *agian*, and *greive* (grieve). These last two categories of error show that as a practised writer he was relying as much on visual memory as on spelling from speech.

Written English presents all its users with the problems of homophones, words that sound the same, but that have different meanings. John Pearman had problems with *where* (were), *piece* (peace), and *their* (there). Words like these are predictable only by context, and they result in slips of the pen that are made by literate and experienced writers all the time. Proof-reading usually eliminates them; but as we have seen John Pearman seems to have largely stopped correcting his own work in the second half of the volume.[33]

A small but significant category of error in the 'Memoir' does seem to be due to a general lack of proof-reading. *Calulation* (calculation), *posseion* (possession), *squbble* (squabble), are not phonetic errors, but errors of omission and visual recall that writers can correct if they want to. This kind of scanning would also have eradicated the few errors that were caused by line-break: *im*/mitation (imitation) and *som*/thing (something). In general, John Pearman found words like 'calculation' easy to spell – latinate words made up of regular syllables. He spelled words like 'assistance', 'attention' and 'apprehended' correctly, not *because* they were latinate, but because they are the vocabulary of the police notebook and evidence-giving, words he had a lot of practice in spelling.

The largest category of error he made involved either not knowing, not remembering, or over-generalising from, a rule of written English, for instance the rule that the function of the final -*e* in words like 'come' is absorbed by the added ending -*ing*, and that the final consonant in words like 'equip' is doubled when an -*ed* ending is added. But he had in general discovered this rule for latinate words, as is clear from his use of such a rule in appropriate contexts: *marvell* for 'marvel' and *ungratful* for 'ungrateful'.

There is one final category of error made by John Pearman in spelling words, that cannot simply be put down to faulty visual recall, nor to the misremembering of spelling rules. These are errors that arise from lack of tense-agreement. As Mina Shaughnessy, discussing the productions of modern emergent writers, has observed, 'verbs probably create more difficulties for writers. . .than any other part of the grammatical system. This is not surprising when one considers the many ways in which verbs can go wrong in formal English.'[34] Some of the errors that Pearman made in the agreement of tenses probably arose from the dialect he spoke – writing *do* for 'does' and *drove* for 'driven', for example. The tense system of English is notoriously irregular, but even the regularities can cause difficulties, especially for a writer whose spelling strategy relies heavily on articulation, because the inflections of the regular verbs (*-ed*, *-d*, *-t*) tend to get lost in speech.

This last set of errors, of tense-agreement, connects with a set of difficulties that can take us quite close to the specificity of a working-class man becoming a writer in mid–Victorian England. Errors that arise from failing to make tenses agree are matters of cohesion, of making agreement between parts of a sentence. They are allied to large questions of cohesion, to the problems facing a writer who is working at the development of ideas through long pieces of text, like John Pearman was. In fact, Pearman's use of punctuation in the 'Memoir' can lead us to a consideration of these larger issues of written language. We have as yet no history of punctuation, though we badly need one; for there are good grounds for seeing this apparently functional and low-level aspect of a writing system as the means by which its users signal complicated relationships of self and language – as I hope the following discussion will suggest.

All writers have to negotiate the space between spoken language and written language, for whilst writing has its origins in speech, and whilst the first steps in writing acquisition are dependent on learners knowing that speech can be written down, written language is 'a separate linguistic structure, differing from oral speech in both structure and mode of functioning'. This distinction, made by L. S. Vygotsky, holds good even though we may come to talk like books, and the ordering of our speech may come to be modelled on what we have read.[35] It is by punctuation that the writer is made aware of the distinction and tension between speech and writing, most commonly by being forced to separate his or her narrative from the spoken words inserted there – by the use of quotation marks. But at other levels too, by marking text to show the intonation and stress of spoken language, by dividing the words and phrases up in certain ways, the writer is forced continually to contemplate how written language is like oral language, and how it is not.

Rules for punctuating written English were in the process of being established in the second half of the nineteenth century.

George Holyoake, teaching 'practical grammar' via the printed word in the 1860s and 1870s, told his audience that

> It was at least a century after the discovery of the art of printing that our present marks of punctuation were introduced. About that time a perpendicular stroke, like a parenthesis without its curves, was used to designate the pause of a comma. The notes of exclamation and interrogation were not used till the early part of the last century.[36]

Holyoake himself urged restraint on emergent writers, thinking that the only essential marks of punctuation were the comma, the dash and the point of exclamation. Schooling and fashion will always affect an individual's choice of marks, no matter what the contemporary rules for usage might be (indeed, what I have often interpreted as John Pearman's invented system of brackets may be his use of the possibly very old oblique stroke, that Holyoake mentioned). But no matter what John Pearman's experience of punctuation was, he wrote for the main part within the grammatical framework of the sentence, though he did not always signal this grammatical unit by the use of capitals and periods. As is the case with most emergent writers of any age, the line had an organisational meaning for him that it does not actually possess grammatically: he tended to capitalise words at the beginning of new lines, and frequently filled up the empty space at the end of a line of script with a dash or a period.

Within this general observation of sentence boundaries, he often used individual marks inappropriately, or omitted them altogether:

> Now the Best Love we have for each other is to Love him for our own advantage For Instance when we find a part of the world that would be of use and a Profit to us. We at once Covit the same. but then it is peopled – with a dark skinned race Gods people but what of that ['Memoir', p. 165]

> Looking at Cain and able or the First Jealousy cain murdered his brother able this as the appearance of the Savage age and nothing is spoken as of any kind of Manufactury of Tools or Buildings Therefore had they not have fell as we are told in the Book of Genesis God intended that they should remain in a State of Nature ['Memoir', pp. 183–4]

By comparing the extracts above, which do not observe Pearman's line endings, with the relevant passages in the 'Memoir', the reader will observe the materiality of the writing process that he took part in: writing for John Pearman was something that fitted into a real space, that was framed and bound by line length and page size. Yet, in spite of this belief in the physical framework of the task he used the sentence form, which is an organisational principle of written language, not of speech. His observation of it shows that as a writer, he had moved far beyond the point of believing that writing is just speech written down. But

> the mature writer is recognised not so much by the quality of
> his individual sentences as by his ability to relate sentences in
> such a way as to create a flow of sentences, a pattern of
> thought. . . an idea in this sense, is not a 'point' so much as a
> branching tree of elaboration and demonstration.[37]

When John Pearman attempted to control his argument 'in passages of thought', he was not always able to maintain cohesion through a tree of elaboration. This can be seen happening in the latter of the two passages above, where the difficulty seems to be connected with the problem of transcribing spoken words – or rather, what *would* or could be said in speech, on paper. In dialogue, he would not have needed the connective 'therefore', which dictates the subjunctive 'had they not have fell' (which in its turn goes wrong), he might have said something like 'if they didn't fall', or 'if they hadn't fallen'. The writer works alone, without the support of an interlocutor.

Yet on most occasions, John Pearman moved beyond the difficulties that lie in the relationship between speech and writing, and achieved a manipulation of meaning in written words: attained a kind of rhetoric *of writing*. In order to see how he achieved this, it is necessary to briefly look at some of the places where he used the stress and structure of spoken language, and some of the places where he failed to achieve cohesion in the written form. It is also important to look at the *topics* that brought him his success in this aspect of the writing system he was using.

Lack of tense-agreement has already been mentioned under the heading of spelling, but it connects as well to the broader questions that have now been raised:

> My firm belief is man was sent into the world to be happy &
> joyful as all other animated nature are it is the artificial Law
> that cause so much misery ['Memoir', pp. 162–3]

'Nature are' and 'artificial Law that cause' are mistakes that probably would not be made in speech (though it is just possible that the second is a dialect form). Writing presents *images* of meaning that are not available for scrutiny in the moment-by-moment interaction with an interlocutor, and at this point of composition, Pearman probably saw the items of nature –

animals, birds, flowers. This imagery may have caused him to use
the plural form of the verb. An error like this is a direct and
simple result of the psychological mechanism involved in writing.

Far more interesting for current purposes are the places where
John Pearman lost control of the written form because of the
content of what he was writing. Towards the end of the passage
describing the 'first jealousy' quoted above, he grows angry with
the crude hypocrisies of imperialism:

> but the Christian race ignor the will of God and say they must
> be made Christians God Cannot be right to keep them in a
> State of nature But here is the rub if they were Left as they are
> we should not be able to take possession of their Land and then
> *Tax* them to have a piece of it again and in a few years we can
> send them a Bishop and make them pay for him also. Oh John
> Bull you are a great rouge ['Memoir', pp. 184–5]

The argument is furious at the end, and the summary the writer
achieves is drawn from the form of the soliloquy, something that
hovers between speech and writing. Perhaps his brief quotation
from the most famous of all soliloquies in English reminded him
of this device.

His most obvious difficulties as a writer came when he was
trying to construct an argument like this, half-figuring a
disputant, hovering between speech and writing. Dialogue on the
other hand, which he wrote without the same difficulties, is
controlled directly (and punctuated) by the pauses and stresses of
spoken language transcribed.

At some points, it seems that John Pearman deliberately used
the devices of speech in order to construct a written argument.
There are many points in the text where he imagines an audience,
brings them clearly forward, and uses them as a device for linking
points and moving an argument forward:

> man as Prostituted that Law and made artificial Laws to suit his
> own purpose and Aggrandizement which as nothing to do with
> God, *Look at the pride of the Church* the Bishops must have his
> Coach. . . ['Memoir', pp. 159–60]

> he wished to be the reformer of his day. *but if we look* at the
> middle ages Galilee was burnt ['Memoir', p. 162]

> O John Bull you are a great rouge Thou shalt not covit, nor
> desire *Now let us look* at our many views of religion. . .
> ['Memoir', p. 166]

they love not their own kind *Another word in the Christian Dogmus I could never understand* that is the word Omnipotent ['Memoir', p. 170]

I must say I done very well in the Police Force. *But as I said before* it is not a happy life. *But what am I thinking off* how much of happiness is the lot of the poor ['Memoir', p. 192]

The italicised passages show the momentary return to the rhetoric of spoken argument, in order to construct a written one.

Very early in the 'Memoir' John Pearman strove for literary effect, often by the use of irony: 'But Little did we think', 'Makepiece But wrongly named'. ['Memoir', pp. 6, 8] He noted of one fellow soldier that 'I shall again have to speak of him'. ['Memoir', p. 70] But these are different devices from the ones that can be observed at the end of the 'Memoir', where the shifts of topic become those of writing rather than those of speech:

I have always found them to have peace of mind and no doubt that is the much talked of Heaven. But we must build up a hope of some kind ['Memoir', p. 235]

'But we' is a learned device of written rhetoric.

As a writer, John Pearman had come rapidly to understand and use rhetorical questions. For example, describing the illogical behaviour of Christians at funerals, he asked

Why did they weep. Men weep at the grave when they are to have the Fortune of the desease or a part in a short time Why do they weep surely it is astounding to see such weeping when by his acknowledged Dogmus he is told to rejoice and be of Great Gladness ['Memoir', pp. 168–9]

Repetition shows Pearman's conscious acknowledgment of its usefulness. In a passage like this, the imagined interlocutor or audience hovers in the background; sometimes, the writer brings them forward, the crowd of ghosts from campfires in the Punjab, exhausted soldiers' desultory talk on hot barrack-room after-noons, the beer-house gathering of rural Buckinghamshire, and addresses them directly:

True we have some hours of rest from labour. But should you have a Family that is taken up for them – But should you be so unfortnate as to be out of work you and the Family have much to suffer ['Memoir', p. 189]

The audience is also present in places where, by using this kind of rhetoric, he can treat the ghosts as the subject of his argument:

But did any man know a Bishop on the Benches at the house to
Vote for any Cause that was to benefit the poor man I have
looked for it from them for the last 40 years but have failed to
see them Love their neighbour as theirselves ['Memoir', p. 169]

But there were arguments that were much more difficult to
control by using the devices of speech in this way. Here, using the
linking devices of spoken narrative, he has to leave his
qualification to the end, where it serves only to diminish the force
of his argument:

True the poor man is robed of his birth right by the acts passed
in Parlement and the acts of our Great landed property men
and then again the poor is much robed by the High profits
Charged by his Fellow man for gold is god, and man will do
anything to get it at least most of them ['Memoir', p. 171]

However, in general throughout the course of writing the
'Memoir' John Pearman learned about expanding an argument in
writing, not by tagging qualification onto the end, but by using
opposition as amplification:

But then the Deplomicy of the Parliment is to Keep 3 fifths of
the Population poor and to keep them Content with being poor
and if Distress is to severe why make a subscription for them
but they must be kept poor or they would not work to keep
the other two fifths in Comfort ['Memoir', p. 206]

Here, the devices of spoken language are controlled to construct a
written argument; but earlier in the text, as for example on pages
165–6, it was the tension between the form, which was
constructed as narrative, and the content, which was argument,
that got the writer into difficulties. He rescues himself though
towards the end of the passage in question, by addressing the
subjects of his narrative directly: 'The next step is you must pay
for the Loss you have put us to. . .' ['Memoir', p. 166] It is not
possible to do this in speech. It is at a point like this (and there are
many of them) that John Pearman started to structure his
argument as written discourse.

Sometimes the transitions between writing-as-speech-
transcribed, and writing as discourse, are less clearly marked than
they are in the passage just discussed. For instance, in the long
argument about the hypocrisy displayed by Christians at funerals
on pages 167–8, it is only possible to say that the transition occurs
somewhere about the phrase 'and you see the Husband weep', at
the bottom of page 167. As he wrote this passage, perhaps John

Pearman became aware of one of the neatest and most satisfying devices of written language, that is, the use of repetition through the expansion of a basic formula ('you see the Husband weep. . .'). It is noticeable that when he is using this technique, his punctuation becomes less erratic than it often is. Here, he was in total control of the written form, as he was in other places during the writing of the 'Memoir'. In the following extract too, memory and distance promote ease and confidence. He remembers an aspect of being a soldier in India that is briefly uninterrupted by his anger at current imperial events. This is a passage based on the structure of spoken language, yet liberated from it. He is in perfect control:

> at the time I am speaking off India was to the White man a free
> Country we Could go where we liked no Trespass out there
> and John Company behaved well to us shared some of the
> Plunder with us Soldiers I mean in prize money not so the
> Queens Government and then John Company didnot make us
> work found us plenty of servants plenty of Grog and good
> living if they were Thieves and stole the Country I must say
> that gave some of it to the Blood hounds who hunted down
> the rightful owners ['Memoir', pp. 191–2]

A simple marker of this control is the fact that this piece can be punctuated in a perfectly conventional fashion. And though it is structured by the cadences of speech, its writer elaborates *within* the sentence form, in a way that he would not be able to do whilst talking.

John Pearman's punctuation is, then, a reliable guide to his progress as a writer, and is most revelatory as evidence when we can see him using it to negotiate between the systems of spoken and written English. For instance, in the passages on pages 196–8 of the 'Memoir' (also quoted on pp. 49–50 here), where he used the argument of 'an Indian black man' to present his own, his punctuation is formally correct. Using dialogue in writing does seem to draw the writer's attention to the differences between speech and written language and, by bringing the distinction between the two into consciousness, makes the system easier to control.[38] We can learn something too, from his imperfectly learned, and perhaps invented system of marks. He had not been taught about commas, and he often employed a period when a comma is needed.[39] Here, for instance, discussing his 'nature', he wanted by some means to signal a pause, the place where he stopped to consider before he went on to make a deliberate evaluation of his own personality:

my Nature was not to take pleasure. But to watch the way and
doings of Mankind and to learn if possible what he as to live
for ['Memoir', pp. 189–90]

He used this partly-invented system to show the passage of
time: describing the cooking of a bullock's head after the Battle of
Badowal on pages 27–8 of the 'Memoir', he indicates the time it
took to cook by using two full stops. Here time (the time in
which the meat is cooking) stands still. The rapid sequence of
events that follows is not punctuated, and the swift passing of
time is thus conveyed. Later on the same page, he used full-stops
to indicate movement and rhythm, a deliberate human breaking
up of time: 'on the way again at 4 miles an hour . quick . march'.

Here, the invented system works perfectly well. In other places
it is quite clear that he would have been helped as a writer by a
better formal knowledge of punctuation. Punctuation marks help
enormously in the reviewing of one's own written text. On pages
176–7 of the 'Memoir' where he deals with a complicated
argument about the history of the tithing and Christian misuse of
a Jewish system, he probably would not have lost control of the
argument if he had been able to see, moment by moment, where
he had got to.

Yet it is the moments of self-consciousness, quite reliably
signalled by imperfect punctuation, that offer the most useful
interpretative devices for the 'Memoir'. The moments where there
is textual evidence of his realising and understanding something
about writing, are moments of psychological revelation across the
years. There are several examples of this conscious and sudden
understanding of writing and writing-as-speech-transcribed.
Pearman used the 'Memoir' to make notes for himself as a writer,
often putting into brackets a kind of shorthand *aide mémoire*:

It is as easy for a Camel to pass through the Eye of a Neadle as
a rich man to enter the Kingdom of God and Why because they
enjoy not the Earth (Cast Cast) distroy their happyness
['Memoir', pp. 169–70]

He had learned about the caste system in India, and often used the
idea to comment on divisions in other societies. In the next
quotation, he uses brackets to make his own equation of a
Christian god with a heathen idol:

the Lawyer will Drag them out of their own Dirt for the
Golden Calf) or money – (God) ['Memoir', p. 188]

His developing understanding of writing as a system in its own
right is also shown where he uses quotation as ironic commentary.

Here he discusses the way in which the great names of history were actually men who committed crimes:

> Marlborough his 1000s and so did Wellington. . . they are all Famous in history for Great men. But say Kill one man) are for what there is the rub) say Plunder or what ever it may be he must be Hangd he is a little Murderer. . . ['Memoir', p. 179]

Late on in the 'Memoir' he uses an elaborated irony, not taken directly from speech as those examples on page 78 of this introduction, but making a point by its use that might well be lost on a physically present audience:

> the men at the Helm of this Great ship [say] we must not Let them rise they wont work for us then we must not let them Starve but make a Gathering in Bad times so as to keep them Contented what more can they want ['Memoir', p. 233]

Although, as has already been noted, John Pearman uses the similes of dialect throughout the 'Memoir', it was only towards the end of its composition that he used idiomatic language as a figurative device:

> But the *Great* and *Rich* donot Care much wether this is sin or not they take it as it comes and the devil get the Last as the old woman say when she and the world was at logerheads ['Memoir', p. 224]

For a writer to present a contrast not only between the formality of writing and the idioms of speech, but also a contrast between the subjects of the passage, the 'Great and the Rich', and the commentary of the poor, is a demonstration of what advances in written rhetoric John Pearman had made through the straight-forward process of writing his 'Memoir'. This kind of literary learning can obviously be achieved without overt instruction.

A few pages earlier than this he had used for the first time another device of written language that draws on the contrast between the spoken and the written. His account, between pages 215 and 221, of his great family crisis of late 1867, is dealt with in detail in the next section of this introduction; but it is important to note here that it rests on the indirect reporting of speech, and that the successful use of indirect speech is a mark of the writer in control of the medium, and conversely, is one of the greatest stumbling blocks to achieving mastery of the written form. A useful way of teaching it is to ask learners to write dialogue and note its difference from indirectly reported speech.[40] John Pearman provided himself with this particularly appropriate kind of practice.

We need to consider briefly what it was that prompted this first and only use of indirect speech in the 'Memoir'. The Master of Eton has told him to get out of town, for his children have scarlet fever and the students are about to return from holiday. As a writer, John Pearman inserted the order from the Master that propelled the narrative, into the narrative itself. ['Memoir', p. 216] By reporting it indirectly, he emphasised its enormity, its inevitability, its status as the very feature of the story being told. A few lines later, when he recounts a meeting with the doctor of the village he was making his way towards with his family, an interchange in which class antagonism and class contempt are quite naked, Pearman uses direct speech. ['Memoir', pp. 220–1] The doctor here has a status in the drama, a part to play; but he was not the author of the drama itself, as was the Master of Eton, Dr Balston.

What has been described is not a device that was *deliberately* used by John Pearman, but his understanding of the meaning of the event he recounts was recorded in one way rather than another, and his choice of presentation is textual evidence of his feelings about the matter. However, there are other places in the 'Memoir' where he was quite clear about both being a writer, and what constructing an argument in writing is like. An example of this is to be found on page 183, in the passage beginning 'I write with full cognisance that all men are brothers'. At other points he refers back to what he has already written. Controlling text and argument in this way demonstrates consciousness of being a writer, and enjoyment of what he obviously thought was a particularly striking and well-formulated point: 'No no as I have said before the faith hope and Charity of the Christian is the Cannon. sword & Bayonette' ['Memoir', p. 225] There is a much more elaborate example of this awareness of being a writer in his essay 'Socialism v Atheism'. ['Memoir', pp. 199–207] These nine pages are constructed around a series of Biblical precepts which illustrate Pearman's definition of socialism – 'By Socialism I mean a Just and comparative equal – Division of Capital. Property and Labour. and the right of the people to the land' – and which stand as an ironic exposure of the hypocrisy of Christianity. But he was not entirely familiar with the essay form, perhaps using here the journalistic model of articles in the freethought press. He did not draw his argument to a conclusion, but moved abruptly into a long autobiographical piece and a discussion of his marriage. The way in which general social and political arguments both confirmed, and at the same time refused entry to his own experience, is a constant feature of these pages.

The political arguments he manipulated stopped short of

allowing him to deal with what he knew of himself as a social and emotional being, and the shifts between argument and experience, are usually as abrupt as the one just indicated. But there is one place in the 'Memoir' where he achieves a perfect match between them:

> look at the difference of the Start in life our Queen had a noble start compare that with the Gutter Children of the earth and look at their start they surly have nothing to thank God for. Now by a Close Calculation of the birth rate it would take about 65 generations from the time of the Christian era to the present time to produce our Queen. . . Now it would take the same number of generations. . .to produce me and when I look back for only the past two generations of my Family what an amount of temptations we have to endure to avoid and to look at if what our parsons Calls sin to git a chance to live while our Queen and the Lords & Dukes fare of the best, the poor Children of this – Carrupt earth can get for them. . . ['Memoir', pp. 239–40]

He is in perfect control of the argument here. The place where he enters his own calculation – 'me' – is perfectly timed. It is at this point that he enters both this particular narrative, and the difficult history he is dealing with. He makes his theoretical mark upon the world, analysis and feeling working towards a delineation of himself within historical time.

Writing, then, played a psychological role in the political journey that John Pearman made in his lifetime, particularly in the hurried journey of 1881–2, and the 'Memoir' is a document that shows the difficulties that lie in the attempt to put lived experience together with a learned form of analysis. Some of Pearman's failures are those of anyone who makes the attempt by using written language. Writing is linear, it places one event after another, whilst living is experienced in a different way.[41] The *argument* with which he filled up his pages, his consistent abandonment of the linear narrative of autobiography, was probably an attempt to capture the inchoate, the intense living and thinking that the words were meant to represent.

The constraints of this linear autobiography were ones that John Pearman explicitly recognised; but much more of the 'Memoir's' dislocation can be attributed to the resistances that political theory offered to the forms of feeling – anger, longing, irony, contradiction – that he wanted to embody. The *matter* of Pearman's struggle, which centred on his understanding of modern freethought and radicalism, and their connections with older analyses of society, is the topic of the next section of this introduction. The feature of the 'Memoir' as a whole is its writer's transformation of an old event by new experience, as the experience of reading about British imperial exploits in the newspapers of 1881-2 transforms the meaning of the events that he first described in a letter of 1849. In eight pages the letter of 1849 which Pearman copied out into his notebook summarised six months of campaigning which the 'Memoir' expanded into a much longer account. The way in which he used the letter as a set of working notes can be seen in the following extracts, where in the later account he attributes to the soldiers he is describing a motive that embodies the cynicism about colonial enterprises that he had learned from the current condemnations of the secularist press:

after a deal of delay we reached Lahore on the 30th October and Formed an Army of About 7000 strong & 3 Troops of Guns . 18 . in all The Enemy under the command of Rajah Shere Sing was then laying at a Town Called. Wuzzerabad on the Bank of the river Chenab about 70 miles North of the City of Lahore. On the 2nd of November we crossed the river Ravee north side of the City of Lahore under the Command of Genl Curton ['Memoir', pp. 252-3]

We continued our march Untill we came to Moodkee here we halted 3 day for the Infantry and some foot artillery our camp now came up to 7000 men. We then march to Ferozepoor where we joined more of the army and we had to Cross the river Sutlej and took our route to Lahore – which we reach in the First week in November and now we was 20 Thousand Strong all arms. We then Crossed the river Ravee and made for Jallunder and then Direct to river Chenab to the Town of Rannuggar on the Chinab. In the morning we all marched about 8 AM and now to find the Enemy and as the Boys would say to get Batta or Prize money. Rajah Shere Singh was with his army at the Town of Wuzzerabad about 60 Thousand men and we made for that place which is on the Bank of the river Chenab about 70 miles north

> of the City of Lahore. our
> army at this time was under
> the Command of Lieut
> General Curton
> ['Memoir', pp. 76–7]

Two pages later, in the second account, the one of 1881–2, John Pearman describes the general inspection of the army by Sir Hugh Gough on 20 November, before the Battle of Ramnagar, who 'spoke a Lot of Stuff to us of Laurals to gain for our Country and honor to the regiment But not a word about the Pension you would get if you got Cut about'. ['Memoir', p. 79]

The rest of the 'Memoir' shows that this attitude was not the result of a simple cynicism. He was capable, as we have seen, of presenting the difficult tension between being one of the 'bloodhounds' who hunted down a country's rightful owners, and the fact of those bloodhounds being working men, who deserved a rightful share of the booty. ['Memoir', pp. 191–2] Presenting the two passages above, and the shifts that the writer of them had made across 40 years, shows the difficulty of incorporating analysis in narrative, and of adding new ideas to old accounts. By the time John Pearman had reached the middle pages of the notebook, he had generally worked out a method of resolving these difficulties (though he never did resolve them completely).

Throughout the whole of the 'Memoir', it was India that offered a scene for the transformation of old accounts by the propulsion of new ideas. Edward Royle has pointed out how attractive the East in general, and India in particular, was to freethinkers and secularists because it offered 'an instance of another religious culture different from and (it was believed) superior to that of the arrogant Christian west'.[42] The only point of comparison we have between John Pearman's contemporary use of events and their transmutation by memory and theory is in the use of the 1849 letter, and its reconstruction of 1881–2. Dialogue was a marked feature of the reconstruction, both in the example above, and in general. Discussing the religion of the 'True musselman' ['Memoir', p. 197], Pearman makes a modern condemnation of Christianity by having it come as a direct quotation from 'an Indian Black man'. This comes close to a deliberate device for linking past experience and present under-standing, and these passages of quotation are certainly among the most correctly rendered (in the formal sense) in the whole of the notebook. This is the means by which John Pearman found to make his past active in his present.

We can say then, that the written text of one working-class man of the mid-nineteenth century shows some of the cognitive and intellectual effects that can be brought about by the acquisition and use of a writing system. The text itself offers evidence of an individual moving through a set of ideas, reviewing them: changing his mind. The historian cannot say that these changes would not have taken place had John Pearman not used written language in this systematic way; but it can be pointed out how inseparable were these processes from John Pearman's experience as a worker, in which writing was practised on a daily basis for 25 years, and more importantly, how inseparable they were from the cultural context in which he wrote, and the class position that he occupied in that culture. This is the topic that will be dealt with in the next section of this introduction.

6

The Propulsion of Experience

In 1867 a crisis occurred in John Pearman's life. He had by this time been stationed at Eton for four years, and life was reasonably comfortable, though the children (five of them by 1867) had been ill off and on all through the previous year. In August 1867, the oldest boy caught scarlet fever, and the events that followed on this were the dramatic enactment of the ideas that John Pearman later came to articulate in his 'Memoir'. In the longest autobiographical piece in the second half of the notebook, he told the story, which involved being told to leave town by the Master of Eton for fear of his family infecting the students, having great difficulty in finding both a place to take the children and transport to get them there, and a dramatic and bitter exchange on the road to Winkfield with the doctor of that place, who tried to prevent them from reaching the inn where Pearman had found a refuge for them all. ['Memoir', pp. 215–21]

Fifteen years later, at the time of writing, it is clear that John Pearman was a reader of newspapers and other forms of political commentary; we can assume that this was also the case in 1867, and note that in May of that year the Conservative government tried to prevent a Reform League meeting in London, and shut the people out of Hyde Park.[1] A further and connected incident occurred in August;[2] and whilst John Pearman did not write about

a contemporary political setting to his own August of 1867, given
the length and anger of his narrative, and the arguments within
the 'Memoir' that draw on the event itself, it is possible to see
August–September of 1867 as his moment of radical revelation,
the time when the precise meaning of the grey castle across the
river was made plain, and when privilege and possession spoke in
a clear voice, and showed him exactly where he stood.[3] By the
time he came to write the 'Memoir', John Pearman was a
republican, with no doubts at all about his feelings towards the
'Godess Victoria', and a world in which 'the Lords & Dukes fare
of the best'. ['Memoir', pp. 232, 240] This section of the
introduction will consider Pearman's efforts in the period 1881–2
to find a contemporary political analysis that would give form to
his experience.

He certainly found vocabulary and arguments in modern
secularism, but he had genuine difficulty with many of the ideas
he took from it. For instance, he could not cast off the Christian
notion of sin, though he very much wanted to, because it had a
social and emotional resonance for him that secularist argument
could not deflate. The struggle between theism and atheism was
part of the structure of nineteenth-century freethought,[4] but John
Pearman did not engage with this argument at all, consistently
utilising the theoretical egalitarianism of Christianity as a vehicle
of radical protest. Yet throughout all the uncertainty and
difficulties that we can see him having with the central tenets of
freethought, and through all the dogged reasoning that makes up
the 'Memoir', his condemnation of kingcraft was clear and
unwavering. John Pearman was a republican, and he knew it.
Indeed, if his style and tone of voice was adopted from anywhere,
the *Republican* seems to offer the possibility of having been a
model for him, more than does the *National Reformer* (though the
latter was much more widely distributed). There was a revival of
republicanism in 1881–2, and the royal event of 1882, the
marriage of Prince Leopold, was condemned by the *Republican* in
both a cartoon and in the form of a petition against further grants
to the royal family until it made its financial affairs public.[5]

About a mile away from Pearman's police cottage at Eton lived
another member of the uniformed working class, Hubert
Simmons, the eponymous 'Ernest Struggles' of his autobiography
of 1880, station-master for the Great Western at Windsor. He,
too, had moved to the area in 1867. It is difficult to imagine a
personal narrative more different in purpose and tone from John
Pearman's. Hubert Simmons told his life story as staccato music-
hall comedy, using stock characters, type-cast names, twirling
moustaches and funny hats. He wrote a comedy of the working

class made acceptable, the plot of his second volume pivoting on
the comings and goings of royalty at Windsor station. The
apotheosis of sycophancy is reached when, out for a walk in
Windsor Great Park, 'Ernest Struggles' beholds

> the most beautiful picture that imagination can paint, but it was
> no imagination, it was life itself. There encircled in the woods
> in an open space was the Queen of England, the Princess
> Beatrice and two little princesses gathering primroses.[6]

Meanwhile, just over the river, Inspector Pearman brooded on
'the Godess Victoria', and the start she had had in life compared
with 'the Gutter Children of the earth'. ['Memoir', p. 239]
   In fact, Hubert Simmons did get truculent towards the end of
his autobiography. His resentment at the treatment meted out to
him by the railway company led to his resignation (he missed the
royal bustle then, of the wedding year). His gesture of defiance
was to tell his readers to send for further copies of his book by
post rather than paying for carriage by rail, thereby saving
themselves 3d, and reducing the profits of the Great Western. But
the form he chose for the telling of his story could not really
support his anger: pantomime does not allow for the expression of
class consciousness, nor class antagonism. This was not the case
with John Pearman.

It was as a working man, and within that central definition, as a
working man who had been both a soldier and a policeman, that
John Pearman wrote his 'Memoir'. Within this framework of self-
definition, many of the concerns he represented seem to have been
mediated by contemporary secularism and freethought. 'Freethought gains the elite of the working class', claimed the
Freethinker in 1888,[7] and had G. W. Foote known about John
Pearman, he might have claimed him as his own too (though
Pearman, a historical and emotional member of the 'poor
brotherhood', would probably have argued the point). There was
a rapid growth in membership of the National Secular Society in
the years 1881–2,[8] and Pearman's mention of Bradlaugh, the only
contemporary political figure he names, confirms Edward Royle's
argument, that popular understanding of secularist struggle was
mediated through this 'popular hero – the champion of the masses
against the classes, of right against might and of the people against
their corrupt and oligarchic masters'.[9] Bradlaugh probably had a
further personal appeal as a political iconoclast for John Pearman:
he had been a soldier and had briefly written about the effect on
the individual of being one.[10] There was probably no branch of
the National Secular Society closer to Eton than Reading,[11] but

circulation of the *National Reformer* (and other freethought newspapers) expanded rapidly in the years 1880–2, and Pearman, now retired, was in a better position to get hold of and to spend time reading them.[12]

It is a mistake though, to restrict the search for influences on John Pearman to the publications of the National Secular Society, or Charles Bradlaugh, or indeed to the years 1881–2. We should remember rather the possibility of multifarious influences and connections, F. J. Gould's account for instance, of scepticism and secularism in Great Missenden in the 1870s, where he was schoolteacher and knew of 'at least one book-case that held freethought volumes'.[13] But even a diffuse and variously transmitted secularism in the 1870s could not be the sole source for Pearman's political understanding. He spent 25 years policing a farming area, and his knowledge of the tithe system was detailed and sophisticated. He added his own particular knowledge to a more general condemnation of land ownership to be found in the freethought press; but he probably got his history of tithing from John Bedford Leno's *Anti-Tithe Journal* of 1881.[14] Leno himself worked in the printing office at Eton College in the mid-1840s, and thought that the most important thing that he had done in this period 'was starting in the royal town of Windsor a branch of the Chartist organisation'.[15] There was anyway a tradition of dissent in the town, stretching back to the Commonwealth, when Windsor was strongly Puritan and anti-Royalist.[16] If emphasis is laid overmuch on the sources of the *National Reformer*, the *Freethinker* and the *Republican* in the following pages, it is because there is evidence that Pearman wrote the 'Memoir' in 1881–2, and it is clear that he was reading these journals in that period. When he moved to Albany Road in Windsor in the autumn of 1881 when he retired from the police, he faced the site where the Labour Hall would be built in the 1920s.[17] If he had not been reading the radical press before this date, it would have been easy to get hold of it afterwards. The weighting of the following argument towards these sources then, is only the way it is because we are on more certain historical ground here than over speculation about print-room chat at Eton, or the endurance of Commonwealth traditions in nineteenth-century Windsor.

It is appropriate at this point to consider the particularity of a member of the uniformed working class having access to the radical tradition, both its local and national manifestations, and to its modern transmutations, as it has been suggested that John Pearman did. For instance, it is possible that Pearman's condemnation of British imperialism could have one of its sources in Shelley's 'Queen Mab', that most widely read of nineteenth-century radical poems.[18] Pearman's vocabulary suggests that it could have been one source for his own analysis of war as 'the statesman's game, the priest's delight/ The lawyer's jest, the hired assassin's trade'.[19]

But though John Pearman might, through such a usage, come to see his own past as 'legal butchery', enacted 'beneath the burning sun/ Where kings first leagued against the rights of men/ And priests first traded with the name of God',[20] we should acknowledge the tension that this stock-in-trade antimilitarism of the radical tradition might place him in. When Richard Carlile asserted that 'nothing exists in animated nature of so horrible a character' as a soldier,[21] we should note the personal and experiential difficulty that John Pearman might be placed in reading these words: for Shelley and Carlile were commenting on the contents of a man's life, which had not been lived dishonourably.

The history of ideas and the psychology of learning both show us the uselessness of simple notions of transmission, and we need to explore John Pearman's political understanding from the premise that its sources were multifarious. In discussing the philosophical underpinnings of nineteenth-century secularism, Edward Royle has pointed to the idea of philosophical necessity, which allowed freethinkers to combine the idea of regularity in nature with 'an exultation of the powers of reason'. At the same time, and following this philosophical trajectory, the freethinker was provided with 'a secular system of ethics to match the secularised concept of natural law'.[22] Yet John Pearman's writing takes us to that vague and undocumented place where published theories meet other convictions, other sets of ideas. When he wrote that 'God made animated nature all ruled by a certain Law of its own', ['Memoir', p. 159; see also pp. 162, 163, 167] his evident use of a modern secularist vocabulary elsewhere in the text should not make us think that he was working within the framework of a secularised concept of natural law. He seems rather to be suggesting that the law of nature, or natural law, is a higher law – a pre-existing law, which mankind has abused and corrupted. ['Memoir', pp. 159–60] The idea of a true equality or righteousness existing in the beginning of things was widely used by different radical constituencies in the nineteenth century, and that is partly what Pearman is doing here.[23]

Were we to base our understanding of Pearman's discussion on its ideational content alone, then it would be possible to say that 'God' and 'nature' get elided in his text, and to place this elision within a deistic tradition. But to do this was surely not Pearman's

intention, for in terms of disputation and argument, he *needed* God
– as an argument – in order to make certain points.[24] And at the
same time, God was more than an idea and an argument, for
towards the end of the 'Memoir' Pearman expresses certain
doubts about his existence as an entity. (This point is discussed
below.)

Along with all these possible traditions, sources and trajectories
(which must include the historian's trajectory, which makes
connections that are not apparent to the historical actors he or she
is dealing with) we should note as well that the vocabulary of
natural law and natural justice was very widely used within the
land reform movement of the 1870s and 1880s.[25] So in reading
John Pearman's 'Memoir' we need to be aware that a man might
use the vocabulary, the rhetoric and indeed, the arguments of
freethought and its philosophical underpinnings, but at the same
time be conducting his own debate in religious and deistic terms.
Our understanding of Pearman's usage must give space then, for
individual imagination and individual cosmology; and neither
should we forget possible literary sources for striking phrases,
borrowed, used, their sources forgotten, or never known.[26]

Finally, just as we do not know exactly what it was that
brought Private Ore to that hospital bed in the Punjab where he
used rationality to debate the existence of God with the Reverend
Coley,[27] we have to remain agnostic on the precise meaning of
Pearman's 'certain Law'. Private Ore said that he had been
brought up an unbeliever; to understand what it was that took
John Pearman to the point where he could doubt the existence of
God then that substratum of unbelief that Ore revealed needs
considering;[28] but so does the terrain that Pearman's own thought
and writing led him into.

Slipped into the 'Memoir' was a folded sheet of paper in which
John Pearman gave instructions for his funeral. (p. 249) 'To Be
Buried' can be interpreted as a request for a secularist funeral.
John Pearman's assertion is that death 'is the end of all men for in
my travels over the Globe I find this is the end of all. . .' He was
saying that out of his own experience he had discovered that 'we
live only by and with the liveing'.

Whilst the freethought press was not the basis for John
Pearman's political analysis, newspapers like the *National Reformer*
were the possible source of much of his political vocabulary.
'Priestcraft', the idea of the Christian 'dogmas' perverted to serve
political ends, the notion of 'idolatry' and of religious practice as a
'fetish' were useful encapsulations of ideas that he was already
working on.[29] Perhaps too, some of the concerns about personal
and sexual relationships that secularism made a matter of public

discourse helped Pearman to analyse the failure of his own marriage. The *National Reformer* published a long article on 'The Future of Marriage' in October 1882, and his sense of dissatisfaction with the relationship in which he had spent 25 years was possibly prompted by reading like this.

He made explicit reference to issues of freethought on pages 202–3 of the 'Memoir', writing that

> there is not a religion on the whole earth that Gives fact of this future state all is a Theory. Now the whole of the Clergy and our learned men know this and the same was as good as said in the house of Commons when Mr Bradlaugh refused to take the oath

It is likely as well, that the figures he gives for the Queen's income were taken from Bradlaugh's *Impeachment of the House of Brunswick* (or perhaps from George Standring's recasting of Bradlaugh's figures in an issue of the *Republican* of November 1881).[30] It is almost certain that he was reading the *Freethinker* and the *National Reformer* in August, September and October 1882, for his condemnation of the established church's involvement in the Egyptian crisis after the defeat of Arabi Pasha at Tel-el-Kebir,[31] his sarcastic repetition of the prayer for British troops delivered up by 'our Great medicine man (who) has once more sent his Instructions to the God of Battles', ['Memoir', p. 172] uses the same imagery as these two newspapers. The *Freethinker* in fact, ran a lead story in October 1882 under the headline 'The God of Battles' (which is discussed below), though Pearman does not *directly* quote from it. What is more, both the Egyptian campaign, and the earlier Boer (or First South African) War were connected with the Irish reform crisis of these years, in the same way that Pearman made this connection.

However, making connections like these was not dependent on being a reader of the radical press. The exiled maharaja Dulip Singh (who had been 11 when his and Pearman's experiences had coincided once before, in India in 1849) was provoked by the Egyptian crisis into reflecting on exactly what he had lost to British imperialism in the 1840s. In a series of letters to *The Times* in August and September 1882, he claimed back his fortune from the British: 'my case at that time was exactly similar to what the Khedive's is at the moment. . .'.[32]

Things would be easier if John Pearman *had* copied passages from newspapers and books, for then it would be possible to say with certainty that his concern with property, ownership and the possession of land made him read Henry George's *Progress and Poverty*. There was an English edition of the book by early 1881, and George visited the UK for the first time in October of that year. In the summer of 1882 a sixpenny edition of his book came out, and George was much in the news (particularly in the papers that Pearman was likely to be reading) for he was arrested in Ireland in August.[33] All that it is possible to say though, is that it is highly likely that Pearman did read *Progress and Poverty*, and used some of its arguments, especially those to do with the aculturalisation of different parts of the globe.[34] Places where the style of Pearman's argument seems to mesh with that of George are indicated in the Notes to the transcript of the 'Memoir'; but for a man whose understanding of land ownership was tied up with an emergent class analysis of possession and exploitation, George may have made ultimately unsatisfactory reading.

The kind of use that we can clearly see John Pearman making of contemporary political analysis is exampled below. The first extract is from the *Freethinker* article of October 1882 just mentioned; the second is likely to be Pearman's transmutation of what he read here:

THE GOD OF BATTLES
Last Sunday, in response to the Archbishop's invitation the churches and chapels echoed with thanksgiving to God for our 'victory' in Egypt. . . Sir Garnet Wolseley was appointed Commander-in-Chief of the expedition because of his tried ability. He was supplied with the best staff officers and the very pick of the British and Indian armies. . . Yet after all this, the clericals have the impudence to say that God almighty gave wisdom to our officers and courage to our men. . . Our military success in Egypt was a dead certainty from the first. As soon as it was found out that none of the European powers would interfere. . .out comes the Archbishop of Canterbury with his prayer for victory. . . then the Archbishop of York rushes out shouting 'Glory to God! He's done it all. Hallelujah!'. . . Is God the God of other nations as well as the British; and does he hear their prayer as well as ours? If so, how does he decide between opposing armies?. . . The God of Battles is a relic of fetishism. Nations of old prayed to their god because he *was* theirs and no one's else. . . But our God of Battles never shows up in such fine form. He is nothing but a ghost behind a curtain, a poor puppet in the hands of knaves for fleecing fools. . .

The Archbishop's war cry Our Great medicine man has once more sent his Instructions to the God of Battles, our army in Egypt. He begins, – O Almighty Lord God – King of all Kings and governor of all things that sittest on the Throne judging right; Now if the archbishop believe this god who governs all things. . . Why does he presume to instruct him. The he says, We Commend to Thy fatherly goodness our men etc. But as if doubtful of this fatherly goodness he teaches god his duty to the British section of his Family Forgetting that his fatherly goodness might have an equal interest in our Egyptian brothers for if god be father the Soudanese and Aribs are our breth ['Memoir', p. 172]

What probably happened here is that John Pearman used the rhetoric of the *Freethinker* to comment on an earlier prayer of August 1882, which he could have read the text of in *The Times*, a local newspaper, or which, as an inspector of police and expected to attend the established church during his working life and perhaps keeping up the habit in his retirement, he could actually have heard delivered from the pulpit.[35]

The two passages placed together show that John Pearman was not a passive recipient of secular ideas – of any ideas – but rather that they gave him the vocabulary and the rhetoric to express what he already knew, from other sources, other arguments. What is more, it may be that Pearman's use of these contemporary forms gives access to the popular and unwritten understandings on which the literary and intellectual manifestations of secularism were based, but which, at the same time, it could not fully mobilise.[36] One function of the 'Memoir' then for us, may be the account it offers of a not entirely successful two-way traffic.

What John Pearman was a specialist on was imperialism, and what he looked for in the press in the early 1880s were sources of information on the First Boer (First South African) War, and the current crisis in Egypt. The encroachment of the Boers into Zululand in the late 1870s had led to the nation's partition by a settlement of 1879. At the Pretoria Convention of 1881, the boundaries of the Zulu nation had been left vague. It was argued that this vagueness – presented as flexibility at the time – afforded protection to the Zulus; but it was really an argument about Britain's limited liability in Africa.[37] The way was left open for Afrikaner encroachment into Zululand: by the middle of 1882 the Boers had established two kingdoms in Africa, and Britain had done nothing to protect the Zulu territories.[38] The secularist press gave an account of these events that John Pearman was able to use, by putting the Zulu Wars together, as he did, with British support of a corrupt regime in Egypt: 'Are the Egyptian, the Arab, the Zulu, the Afghan, the possessors of hearts and souls in which the voice of God never speaks–'[39]

For John Pearman though, understanding imperialism meant more than merely utilising definitions found in the press. He had been personally involved in its history: imperialism had made him what he was, had provided the tension between involvement and detachment that he knew was the mark of his own personality.[40] What came to the fore for him in 1881–2 was his own experience of British imperial exploit in India. 'India, next to Ireland, was the country most frequently used to exemplify the results of British imperial policy', remarks Edward Royle in *Radicals, Secularists and Republicans*,[41] and both were used by John Pearman. Ireland, in his view, was most particularly bound up with the question of land ownership and land taxation:

> Looking at the treatment of Ireland conquered by the sword
> 700 years back and kept in Bondage all those years. I think they
> are in want of a Moses very much for if we read right we can
> see that they are more Taxed than the Israelites was by the
> Pharoah ['Memoir', p. 187]

The Irish Land Bill was passing through Parliament in 1881, and the *National Reformer* reported on its passage in detail.[42]

John Pearman saw ownership lying at the base of imperial venture, and the analytic connection he made between the two enabled him to see British policy in Ireland in the same light as the policy he had helped implement in India:

> as a Half Bread Welshman I must hate the English as the Irish
> Hate them and I have long time wished that some thing would
> turn up with england & America so that England mite get a
> sound beating by them the Irish would then be able to get back
> their own Country again ['Memoir', p. 234]

England's first arenas of imperial venture had witnessed the methods that he was familiar with from his time in India: 'the Scot and Welsh are much the same The Gun sword & Bayinet is the unity of the whole.' ['Memoir', p. 234] Here he echoes arguments that he had used much earlier on, about the conjunction of greed and Christianity in the conquest of the sub-continent. But the analysis he made of Ireland's position lacked the specific condemnation by religious argument that he was able to use when writing about India. He knew a lot more about colonial exploit in India than he did about the Irish situation; knew more about India than did Annie Besant for example, writing on India and Afghanistan in the *National Reformer* of 1878–9.[43] His careful distinction between types of religious belief and practice in the north-western territories may have been a proud and personal display of knowledge more detailed than that presented in the secularist press. What is more, his dislike of Roman Catholicism would have prevented his uncovering of such subtle distinction as far as Ireland was concerned.

His identification with the subjects of British imperialism was at once personal and intellectual. His mother was Welsh;[44] he knew how the Irish felt; the 'Indian Blackman' and he were victims of the same system; and then, in 1882, 'the Zulas can tel in what the Christian as done for them.' ['Memoir', p. 198][45] He saw himself the same as these people, for he understood the system that lay at the foundation of all their exploitation, and his own. This kind of analysis, in which feeling illuminated experience and theory, meant that he avoided the racism that has been pointed to in the journal of William Bell.[46] What is more, because his understanding of different religious forms was a sophisticated one, he avoided much of the cheap racism of the popular freethought press, where condemnation of religious practice might be bought at the price of telling stories about converted and gullible darkies falling from trees because Christianity had convinced them they could fly – not Pearman's style at all. Yet it must be emphasised that, as in the mainstream of secularism, Pearman was extremely prejudiced against Roman Catholicism.[47]

Pearman's interest in religious cultures was connected to another concern of secularist thought, that of anthropology and the study of distant and 'primitive' peoples.[48] He used his knowledge of the 'new anthropology' to further his own argument against both the dogma of God's omnipotence, and against imperialism, joining the two together on pages 183–4 of the 'Memoir', and asking 'was Adam & Eve when made in a Savage state or was they in that State called Barbarian or was they made in a State of Civillization. . .'. He goes on to argue that if there were such a thing as a state of nature and God wanted that state altered, then it would happen at once 'without the aid of men sent to Preach religion to them', their real motives in so doing being to 'take possession of their Land and then *Tax* them to have a piece of it again'. His central argument was not about a denial of God, but was an exposure of the social uses that certain doctrines – 'the dogmus' – had been put.

Discussing the psychology of freethought (or at least of its leadership) Edward Royle writes of men from whose eyes the scales had once fallen, determined to reveal the truth to others in a similar way.[49] There is the same grim, dogged pursuit of the ridiculous, the hypocritical, the style of one who only displays what stands to reason, in John Pearman's writing; but it does seem that he was after something very different from the average provincial secularist, and there is danger in confusing this method, some of which was borrowed, with his intention. However, on some occasions the adopted style of inquiry and argument that Pearman used *is* a reliable guide to intention. For instance, his essay 'Socialism v Atheism' is very similar in tone to a typical article in the *National Reformer* of early 1882, which refused to do 'any injustice. . .to the memory of Jesus of Nazareth'.[50]

But Pearman was not concerned with the central arguments or the techniques of freethought. He was not interested in denying the existence of God, nor in exposing the falsely shored-up authority of the scriptures.[51] What he wanted to do was to understand and expose a social and political *use* of Christian theology which justified the exploitation of large numbers of people by a set of men who had no legitimate base for doing so. He pursued this point using the vehicles of 'omnipotence' and 'sin'; and he was quite aware that these twin pillars of orthodox Christianity presented him with an intellectual challenge that matched the subtlety and convolution of their use:

> Another word in the Christian Dogmus I could never understand that is the word Omnipotent ['Memoir', p. 170]

> I have offtimes laid and tried to reason in my own mind Beleiving in God to be Omnipotante ['Memoir', p. 195]

> the temptation of Break the Law or what is called sin is very great with the poor I Cannot but think if there is such a thing as Sin ['Memoir', p. 188]

> Well what is the meaning of the word of sin. . . I cannot understand the word sin ['Memoir', p. 206]

> I write with full cognisance that all men are brothers in the Flesh and if some are criminals by the artifice Law made by man they will be coequal in the eye of God or if not so our Criminal Class must have been borned to sin by the omnipotence of Gods will oh what is sin)) (*The Question*) ['Memoir', p. 183]

Sometimes, by the use of ironic illustration, as in his satiric account of forcible conversion to Christianity ['Memoir', pp. 165–6, 242–3] John Pearman could outline satisfactorily the intellectual problem of omnipotence. In the last quotation above, he connects the notion of omniscience with original sin, and starts to frame the question in a new way.

In these twin concerns, Pearman represented a mainstream of nineteenth-century puzzlement and anguish. Robert Cooper's much published *Lecture on Original Sin* of 1839[52] set out the arguments that were being rehearsed in the popular freethought press 40 years later: that the theory of omnipotence was irrational and cruel; that an omnipotent god could not, in the light of reason, allow certain things to happen – and yet did. This was Private Ore's problem too: 'If he was corrupt, God had made him so. It was *unreasonable* to suppose that God would punish him for being what he made him.'[53]

This central cruelty to the spirit and the intellect could have its Biblical supports entirely undermined, and this was the most important technique of mid nineteenth-century secularism. But though John Pearman knew his Bible, he was not consistently interested in using his knowledge to perform this act of deflation. He shared a wider psychological anguish at the idea of omnipotence, and gave clearest expression to it at the end of the 'Memoir', when dealing with the subjects of imperialism he wrote:

> Then were is God with his Justice he dont Chrush this dambed peice of Iniquity for if there is a God it must greive the Spirit of God ['Memoir', p. 226]

and a little later

> Oh when I think of God and *Justice* I think Why do he not do away with all King Craft what rot somthing like Justices ['Memoir', p. 249]

His analysis was, in the end, resolutely social. When he used the technique of textual deflation it was to demonstrate that the idea of the law of God had always been used as a *political* argument, always used to social and coercive ends. He looks at the laws of Egypt and Rome and concludes that

> there was but a small difference in the then Laws. Civil. Military or religious the Great object was then to keep the poor to work for the great in power. . . the same is our Laws now in a Lawlised Nation wherever it be three fifths of the whole people must be poor and very poor to work to keep the State ['Memoir', p. 226]

Within secularist thought, it mattered whether or not there was a god; but to John Pearman, that was not the main issue. For him, the idea of God was an *argument*, the cruelty or beneficence of which could be used to explore the material world.[54]

What did matter to John Pearman, what he wanted to find out, and what his 'Memoir' was partly written to discover, was whether sin was an action against God, or the idea of God, or whether it was an action against natural justice; and then, having made that distinction and that decision, whether immorality was a

sin. His most sustained argument on these points is to be found
on pages 206–7 of the 'Memoir': God asks of men only justice; but
justice is defined by men, and in a divided society it is perverted
and manipulated to 'keep 3 fifths of the Population poor and to
keep them content with being poor'. It is with this formula that
Pearman reaches a conclusion. That we can see the achievement of
the analysis should not serve to disguise the real struggle that
went into its making:

> Well what is the meaning of the word of sin. As it anything to
> do with Justice I cannot understand the word sin. I know when
> we offend against the law of man that is not sin) Sin must be
> somthing against God. . .

The individual struggle of many nineteenth-century working
people must have been to free themselves from the bondage of an
official ideology that presented them with the authoritarian
hopelessness that John Pearman took issue with on these pages of
his 'Memoir'.

An article in the *National Reformer* of April 1882 concluded its
analysis of 'Christianity' by pointing out that its doctrines taught
people that 'the source of goodness lies *outside* of humanity'.[55]
This argument connects directly with Pearman's experience: he
knew it was men who set up the edifice of law that defined some
people as good and some as bad. In his own struggle, it is clear
that he used both the tenets and the rhetoric of the freethought
press to argue his case with himself. But essentially, his concerns
cut a swathe through the processes of secularism, for they
belonged to a political tradition that popular freethought drew on
– 'a common stock of populist ideas, anti-clerical and anti-
aristocratic' – but the roots of which the movement did not fully
understand.[56]

John Pearman used the ancient rhetoric of natural law, opposing
it to 'artifice Law', or 'the Laws of the Parliament made by man',
arguing that 'the poor man is robed of his birth right by the acts
passed in Parlement'. ['Memoir', pp. 183, 206, 171] Within this
framework, Christianity sometimes became for him a vehicle for
radical protest, an image of fairness, otherwise called Justice, that
stood as a consistent reference point for what ought to be:

> My firm belief is man was sent into the world to be happy &
> joyful as all other animated nature are it is the artificial Law
> that cause so much misery in the world and not the law of
> God. . . Jesus the Nazerien. . .said in his Eleventh Command-
> ment Love yea one & another as I loved you. Now the

Best Love we have for each other is to Love him for our own
advantage. ['Memoir', pp. 162–5]

In places like this, John Pearman's writing would seem to
illustrate a historical continuity of thought and feeling, to be
linked to a radical tradition that it is always tempting to trace
directly back to the seventeenth century.[57] Given that this is a real
historical and political temptation, it is important to note that the
Land and Labour League used the idea of the Norman Yoke, the
Saxon Commonweal and the authority of the scriptures in
support of land reform in the 1870s.[58] So these ideas and forms
of analysis were re-emphasised and given articulation in the
decade before John Pearman started to write. The source of his
ideas here is probably no older than that; and indeed, he would
not have had to be a political radical to highlight the political
figures he names in the 'Memoir'. He mentions Charles
Bradlaugh and Oliver Cromwell, using Cromwell to articulate
certain ideas about democracy. ['Memoir', pp. 194, 197][59] The
other political figure he employs is Jesus the Nazarene, out of
whose teachings he constructed a definition of socialism that was
probably learned from his reading of the early 1880s, but which
also had its deeper roots in his assertion of the rights of 'the poor
children of the carrupt earth':

> Jesus was a Socialist he preach it from first to Last and such is
> pure Christianity. . . By Socialism I mean a Just and
> comparative equal – Division of Capital. Property and Labour.
> and the right of the people to the Land. Read their Masters
> words Jesus said Sell whatever thou hast and give unto the
> poor ['Memoir', pp. 199–200]

The term 'socialist' was being used in the secularist press in the
late 1870s. In 1877 the *Secular Chronicle* was urging its adoption,
and the *Secular Review* discussed socialism and land nationalisation
in 1878. These papers, and the *Republican* (which defined socialism
in 1880 as 'the groans of down trodden people yearning for a
share of liberty and justice which belong by natural right to all
humanity') were much more open to the idea of socialism than
was the *National Reformer*; but Pearman could also have learned of it
as a set of ideas from this source, in the winter of 1882–3, where it
was debated in hostile tones.[60] But in fact, John Pearman knew what
he meant by socialism in a way that suggests he constructed a definition that was drawn from wider sources than the secularist press.

It is in fact possible to argue that John Pearman made an original
intellectual contribution to the radical tradition he inherited,

however long or short we consider that tradition's roots to be, and no matter how we mark out its philosophical trajectory. He took a tradition, and reformulated it to include his own experience of imperialism, for he had literally *seen* the appropriation of the earth by kingly power, had indeed been one of its 'hired bravos', in India, in the 1840s:

> we find a part of the world that would be of use and a Profit to us. We at once Covit the same. but then it is peopled with a dark skinned race. . . what of that. . . So we wish to make Christians. *I.E. Covit* their country it will bring a good return for the outlay. . . Well may Dan. *De.* foe) in his work put man Friday neck under Crusoe. Foot we see this every day and yet these very Christian men make a very Great Cry about the Slave. oh were is Gods Justice ['Memoir', pp. 165, 241]

> The life of this dark Kingly power, which you have made an Act of Parliament and Oath to cast out, if you search it to the bottom you shall see that it lies within the iron chest of cursed Covetousness, who gives the earth to some part of mankind, and denies it to another part of mankind; and that part that hath the earth, hath no right from the Law of creation to take to himself and shut out others; but he took it away violently, by Theft, Murder and Conquest.[61]

The conjunction on the page of these two pieces of writing, the first from Pearman's 'Memoir', the second from Gerrard Winstanley, offers a suggestion beyond which it is impossible to go. On the face of things, there is no way that John Pearman could have set eyes on anything written by Winstanley before 1899, and John Morrisson Davidson's *Four Precursors of Henry George*.[62] Winstanley was rediscovered through the work and publications of the English Land Restoration League and the Land Nationalisation League; but what John Pearman could have taken from their presentation of Winstanley's work was only available after he had completed the 'Memoir'.

Certainly, in the setting up of the Land Reform League in 1880, all the *ideas* about ownership and possession that Pearman deals with in the 'Memoir' were debated, and made accessible through newspaper reporting.[63] But what is striking about the two passages quoted above, is the similarity in style and vocabulary, particularly Pearman's use of 'covetousness' (which echoes throughout the 'Memoir'). Indeed, the freethought press that reported on the progress of the Land Reform League did *not* offer John Pearman a model for the intellectual leap that was his own, of seeing in the appropriation of an empire by Britain, particularly

in the annexation of the Punjab in the 1840s, a modern version of
an old story, whereby those who have possession of the earth take
more of it away from others, and shut them out from its
enjoyment.

The suggestion must remain literary and rhetorical. And yet:
John Pearman spent most of his life in the area from which the
majority of the Parliamentary Army had been recruited during the
Civil War; Windsor had always been a rebel town under the
shadow of a royal castle; ideas can live longer than centuries: they
were talking about Winstanley in the Welsh valleys in the 1790s,
and quoting the Levellers in the 1820s.[64]

John Pearman's writing is a reminder of the arrogance that lies
in assuming that people 'get' their ideas from somewhere, that
social and political analysis is always taken from above, from
published sources. The 'Memoir' can stand as a description of
how people respond to other people's ideas, in written form. But
those ideas could not be responded to at all if they did not speak
to what the listener or reader already knew, knew not out of some
innate knowledge or experience, but from all that one encounters
during a lifetime:

> All one has is. . .texts or documents. . . in ones own time one
> gathers far more than most people realise from just these
> versions of an endless documentation. . .[65]

All the books, all the ideas, all the arguments encountered
reflect and echo each other through what historians have come to
call a lived experience: the measure of a life lived out in historical
time. The point of assessing that process in John Pearman's case is
to make the simple but important point that the ways of reflections,
the assimilation and reordering are the province of a man with
little schooling and an imperfect command of formal English, as
much as they are of those of us who can name the endless
procession of texts and who can reflect (because we have been
taught to do so) on the interaction between what is known and
what gets said. To say this is not to claim that the processes of
education are unimportant. George Holyoake, the infidel and co-
operator, believed that the right to grammar was akin to the right
of self-defence laid down in Magna Carta;[66] and John Pearman
clearly would have been helped in his quest by a more complete
mastery of a language system, and a topography of a system of
ideas. Where the material he was working on resisted his
meaning, it was often because he did not yet know what that
meaning was: here, the technical ability to make the ideas and
words work for him would clearly have been of great help. It is
quite obvious that he could have been taught to do all of these

things, very easily. At the same time, there is a magnificence in the intellectual leap that he made with his limited repertoire of analytic devices (which were of course, most potent ones, in spite of it all).

John Pearman's political analysis was bound up, indissolubly, with his need to understand himself as part of a social world. He used everything he had access to by way of analysis. The 'Memoir' is witness to his search, which is a more general and enduring one, for a politics that will allow entry to forms of feeling and thought not officially delineated; that will recognise people's need to express what they know about themselves, and the world that has made them.

7
Public and Private

John Pearman wrote a life story that was framed and bound by public events. He described his passage from railway servant, to soldier, to policeman as a 'Public Service of 40 years in uniform', ['Memoir', p. 159] and the format of the military memoir that he partially used as a model in the first half of the notebook dictated this narrative allegiance to the public drama of wars, and battles, and the appropriation of great tracts of land under hot and distant suns. But within the conventional framework of nineteenth-century military and working-class autobiography, we should notice the oddness and particularity of the radical soldier's tale.

The most commonly used device for expressing difficulty and ambivalence in nineteenth-century working-class autobiography was through the depiction of childhood.[1] Indeed, this was an autobiographical device that cut across classes until the later part of the century: to write of a particular childhood and its vicissitudes is to write of that part of the self that cannot be absorbed into the central story, and through which feelings of being unwanted, unloved, unfinished as a human being, can be expressed without disturbing the rounded edges of the adult character who is being created in written words.[2] But John Pearman did not use this device: his story begins with his enlistment at the age of 24; and his life begins as a worker ten years before that when 'I first took to Keep myself at the Age of 13 years & 9 months'. ['Memoir', pp. 1, 189]

The method John Pearman chose for expressing his doubts and uncertainties about himself was through a discussion of his marriage, and a presentation of its failures. It is at this place that he feels what he is most clearly: 'I have always been a very Careful man. . .'; and it was the place where he felt unloved:

> she as a very bad fault that is Ingratitude. she was always ungratful thinking man had nothing else to think of but her and then it didnot matter what you gave her in the way of money she never was thankful. . . Perhaps had I been a man otherwise I mite have been better thought of ['Memoir', p. 209]

He must have been the most extraordinarily difficult man to live with. He did not allow Elizabeth Pearman to manage the house-keeping – 'I would always be Master of the home and I spent the money as I found my wife was not up to the mark in laying out money to the best advantage.' ['Memoir', pp. 208–9] They obviously quarrelled over the upbringing of the children; it seems that he must have constantly reminded her how lucky she was not to have to go out to work (as a county policeman's wife she was not allowed to); he had a very bad temper. He calls the 'blist of married life' his ability to give the children a treat, not the emotional or sexual relationship with his wife: 'I know my wife never had much affection for me.' ['Memoir', p. 212]

His complaints, his dour and uncharming efforts to be fair to her, his damning of Elizabeth Pearman with faint praise, show that he wanted something from the relationship, something that he did not get (scarcely perhaps, knew what that thing might be), the wanting and the dissatisfaction expressed most clearly in the story of the song-birds:

> I was always very fond of Birds and when I was first at house keeping I got some but my Wife found much fault with them so as to get to hot words so I gave them up at once and here was one of my home comforts gone ['Memoir', p. 213]

In recent years, the caged bird has been so firmly established as a female metaphor that at first it may seem faintly absurd to follow John Pearman here into the terrain of his own feelings about him-self and the kind of man he was. But, in fact, it is easy enough to take this image and trace its course throughout several accounts of nineteenth-century manhood, see it as an emblem of a particular kind of restriction and containment.[3]

We could start to follow John Pearman here by considering his attitude to family discipline (the laying out of the housekeeping money, his condemnation of 'Children loved beyond reason', his evident pleasure in organising his family on their yearly outing to Sandhurst). It is this pleasure in order and discipline (which elsewhere in this introduction has been explored as a love of law) that leads us to the central contradiction of John Pearman as a man; indeed, it is the contradiction that he as a writer leads us towards, but that he was not able fully to understand.

His pleasure in the ordering of a family was part of a wider enjoyment: the early part of the 'Memoir' is full of references to the seductive beauty of military order. John Keegan and Richard Holmes have both recently given us historical examples of the delight felt at witnessing great armies in battle array.[4] Soldiers frequently recorded this delight in their autobiographies: J. W. Baldwin of the 9th Foot wrote of the 'superlative grand parade' at the camp after Sobraon, which 'almost turned me giddy with delight';[5] and even the Reverend Coley joining the camp at Umballah felt 'a sort of enthusiasm in beholding. . .the marching of an army'.[6] Some years after this, Robert Blatchford recalled talking to veterans of Alma, one of whom said that ' "It was a very pretty sight to see. Our lines and the French lines marching up like a picture".'[7]

Just before the Battle of Aliwal, John Pearman watched the artillery and infantry 'Spreading out like a Lady Fan':

> it was a Beautyful Plain for miles The Sun Bright & Clear.
> There was the Enemy in our Front 3 or 4 miles Long and
> Looked Splendid. and as our Army came into Line as Steady as
> a feild Day. I sat on my horse and Looked at the two armies. it
> was a Lovely sight ['Memoir', p. 33]

He thought the two regiments on parade at Umballah 'a pretty Sight when in Line', ['Memoir', p. 66] and again, before the Battle of Ramnugger saw the 14th Light Dragoons 'come on in Pretty stile so Steady and Strate'. ['Memoir', p. 85]

'Pretty' can mean 'fine' or 'beautiful'. It is also a word one chooses when one wants to express the littleness, the appropriability of something, something one could perhaps, by merely looking take and hold: the tiny brush strokes that make the soldiers' figures on the black and white medallion decorating a Worcester teacup. John Pearman's pleasure in this order, and in its beauty, and the way he made it imaginatively his own, is seen most clearly here, in the littleness that 'pretty' expresses.

But he could not make the word or the world his own, nor possess it; for he was one of those toy soldiers, whose brains might soon shatter and fly with the sound of 'a Banbox full of Feathers' to be scraped from another soldier's face: John Pearman was in the picture. That he could not resolve the tension between his understanding of the world and his experience of it, between wanting to be loved and being the kind of man he was, between his love of discipline and the corrupt system that upheld it, between the glory of soldiering and the slaughter of men – were all to do with the nature of what he was describing here, in the pages that follow: with the material and political constraints that are the subject of his 'Memoir'.

In successive editions of his *Practical Grammar*, George Holyoake had tried to explain what the importance of a perfectly managed writing system might be to its possessors, and what that writing system actually was. He used the analogy of Nature, and described a 'grammar of nature', a 'general system of the world', telling his readers that the natural world was arranged and ordered like a system of written language:

> The most ignorant persons know something of the sky, the earth, and natural objects – they know that objects are great and small and vary in kind – they have seen rivers swell and flow – they know that fishes swim, birds fly and men walk. The knowledge of the agreement and arrangement of the words. . .which express what we thus s~e, hear and understand is grammar.[8]

But people must come, as John Pearman did, to describe all of what they see: what men have done to the world as well as the fishes that swim and the birds that fly. The very act of writing about this world reveals its disharmony, the disjuncture between what is seen and what the observer knows of his or her position within it. Caged birds do sing; but it is an imperfect song: no final harmony. The bars are shadowed on the mind, are made a way of seeing – that both permits and prevents.

Part Two

Note on the Dating of John Pearman's 'Memoir'

I think that it is possible to date the manuscript with some certainty, and to say that it was written between October 1881 and the winter of 1882, and possibly also during the early part of 1883. There are two circumstantial supports for this dating. First, as I have described in the introduction, John Pearman retired from the Buckinghamshire Constabulary in October 1881 and then had time to read and write. Second, he makes no reference to any historical event that occurs after 1882. All the references are to incidents of 1881–2, or earlier.

On page 172 of his MS. he mentions 'our army in Egypt'. This is almost certainly the British army dispatched in 1882 to occupy Egypt after the defeat of Arabi Pasha at Tel-el-Kebir in September 1882. This army remained in occupation for a very long time, but the context indicates that John Pearman is describing a recent event. There is no mention of the Mahdist ambitions to free the Sudan, nor the Mahdist destruction of an Egyptian force under the command of a British officer in 1883. John Pearman does not mention the death of Gordon at Khartoum in 1885.

On page 180, he writes of 'the archbishops warcry'. The text of the prayer offered by the Archbishop of Canterbury for the safety of the troops in Egypt will be found in *The Times* of 7 August 1882. It was read in churches over the next few months.

The reference to the Zulus on page 198 of the 'Memoir' is probably a reference back to the defeat of the Zulu nation by the British in July 1879. Cetewayo, defeated King of the Zulus, visited Britain (and the Queen at Windsor) in July 1882, an occasion for the national press to laud 'the dusky warrior', and for John Pearman to reflect on what British imperial politics in South Africa had done for the King's subjects. The charter mentioned here is almost certainly a reference to the convention signed between the British and the Boers in 1881, after the British defeat at Majuba Hill, at the end of the South African (or First Boer) War of 1880–1.

The third reference on this page could possibly be to the Burma War of 1885. But it is much more likely (given the references above) that a train of association led John Pearman here to think back to the Third Burma War of 1853, which had always been presented in the radical press as resulting from a Christian arrogance and roughriding over native sensibilities and customs, as could be witnessed in the recent and current South African and Egyptian ventures.

On page 236, Pearman quotes a verse about the Guards leaving Windsor. The Army Lists show the 2nd Battalion of Grenadier Guards leaving for Egypt between August and September 1882.

On page 242 the reference to 'Stanleys game' clearly indicates his travels in Africa of the 1870s, not his Emin Pasha expedition of 1886–9. The radical press made it quite clear that Leopold of Belgium (in whose employ Stanley was) had designs on Africa.

The dates of possible newspaper and pamphlet sources of John Pearman's references and further reading will be found in the notes to the transcript of the 'Memoir'.

I am certain in my own mind that I have dated this MS. accurately, and indeed, the Pearman family have always believed that it was written at this time. What gives me pause for thought, in the watches of the historian's dark night, is the reference to 'Burmer' ('Memoir', p. 198), which does not quite fit the structure of reference outlined above. (But then, neither does Pearman's reference to Napoleonic betrayal of Polish aspirations in the period 1797–1815. See note to p. 179 of the 'Memoir'.)

Though it cannot be said with any certainty at what point after October 1881 Pearman started to write his soldier's story, I think that by the late summer of 1882 he had reached the Battle of Chilianwala in his account ['Memoir', pp. 101–9]. Memories of this battle explicitly linked his past experience and current political understanding, specifically on page 108 of the 'Memoir', where he appears to me to insert the language of analysis into narrative for the first time (though he has been *cynical* about British imperial motives before this). The soldier's story will soon be over, for he now only has Gujrat to describe. By the time he has written 50 more pages, analysis, or interpretation, will be his dominant mode.

Note on the Transcription
of John Pearman's 'Memoir'

The following transcription is a literal one, that is, it reproduces John Pearman's spelling, punctuation and grammatical construction with absolute fidelity. The transcript is laid out to show his line endings, because these, along with the other features just mentioned, allow the reader to follow his progress both as a writer and as a thinker in a way that is not possible in an edited transcription.* The reader will have noticed though, that in quoting from the transcript in my introduction, I have not adhered to Pearman's line endings in this way. This is for simple, practical purposes, to save space; and because here I want in general to draw attention to the content of his writing, rather than to the linguistic features of a passage.

John Pearman did correct his own work, though not consistently. What the reader has here is John Pearman's corrected version of his own prose. I have indicated major excisions made by him, in the notes to the transcript, but have not given the reader the original spelling of words that he corrected.

John Pearman wrote an extremely neat modified copperplate, that is very easy to read. The only problem I encountered with his handwriting was with the letter 'c'. In his graphology, the only letter that is not distinguished by feature between upper and lower case is 'c': only size allows the reader to determine whether or not a capital was intended. The reader will have to trust me to have made the right choice.

Where John Pearman records a date, I have also placed it at the head of a page of transcript. I have inserted battle names at the head of pages.

*I now really regret my edited transcription of the story 'The Tidy House', where I put the words on the page according to the conventions of reading teaching (in natural phrase units), rather than showing the children's line endings. Had I done this, then many readers would not have been able to think that I was attributing some kind of poetic intention to the children who wrote the story. (Carolyn Steedman, *The Tidy House*, Virago, 1982, pp. 28–9, 41–54.)

Memos of Late
Sergeant John Pearman of
H. Mgt 3rd or Kings own Light Dragoons

Enlisted at the Essex Serpent
Public house Charles St Westminster
London

On the 26th August 1843 and
was sent to the Depot at Maidstone
in Kent for Drill & Instruction
The regiment being in bengal in
the East Indies
Remained at the Depot at Maidstone
until the 4th June 1845 on which
Day 60 3rd Light Dragoons and 60
ninth Queen Lancers was Marchd to
Gravesend and embarked in the
ship (*Thetis*) Also 40 men for the
80 Foot and 4 men for the 39 Foot
there was also 13 women and 37 children
with us) and 4 young married women
of the 3d L. Drg was smuggled on Board
and taken out with us without Leave

⁓

June 1845

2   It was a very fine day and many
people accompanied us both Friends
and sweethearts, so time past merrily
on the road the Band of the Depot –
playing. Also the Band of the 16th Lancers
Depot from Maidstone. We arrived at
Gravesend about mid-Day . and was
soon embarked). The Bands playing
Fare the well Love now thou art going
over the wild and Trackless sea –
Smooth be the wave and swift wind
Blowing though tis to Bare the Far
from me) and when all was on
Board the good ship, The word was
given to whey Anchor and then the
Band played God save the Queen
We was now employed in geting
out our sea Kits and utensals for
Cooking and being told off into Mess
6 Each Mess . and then we got our –
Hammocks down and shown how to
tie them up and get into them we
where as Close togeather as the Fingers

Memos of Late
Sergeant John Pearman of
H.dll 3rd or Kings own Light Dragoons

Enlisted at the Essex Serpent
Public house Charles St. Westminster
London
On the 26 August 1843 and
was sent to the Depot at Maidstone
in Kent for Drill & Instructions
The Regiment being in Bengal in
the East Indies
Remained at the Depot at Maidstone
until the 4th June 1845 on which
Day 60. 3rd Light Dragoons and 60
ninth Queen Lancers was Marcht to
Gravesend and embarked in the
Ship Thetis) Also 40 men for the
80 Foot and 4 men for the 39 Foot
there was also 13 women and 17 Children
with us) and 4 young Married women
of the 3d L.D. was Smuggled on board
and taken out with us without Leave

It was a very fine day and many
people accompanied us both Friends
and sweethearts, so time past Merrily
on the Road the Band of the Depot —
playing. Also the Band of the 16th Lancer
Depot from Maidstone - We arrived at
Gravesend about Mid Day. and was
soon embarked). The Bands playing
Fare the well Love now thou art going
over the wild and Trackless sea —
Smooth be the wave and swift wind
Blowing though tis to Bare the Far-
from me) and when all was on
Board the good Ship, The word was
given to Way Anchor and then the
Band played God Save the Queen
We was now employed in getting
out our Sea Kits and Utensils for
Cooking and being told off into Mess
6 Each Mess. and then we got our —
Hammocks down and shown how to
tie them up and get into them we
where as Close togeather as the Fingers

June 1845

3   On our hands . on the morning of 5th
     June we was at Dover and some one
     Came on Board from Dover with orders
     we then made sail and all was –
     very pleasant the Wind Fresh and on
     the ships quarter) But in rounding
     the North Forland Light House our
     Fore yard snaped like a Carrot and
     we had to put into Deal for another
     after which we stood out to sea by
     the Isle of Wight . and by the needles
     on the 8th June Lost sight of Land and
     most of the men very sea sick *But*
     in a few days more) most of us was
     becoming *sailors* and got well
     had but Little to do on Board ship
     play Cards and sing in fine weather
     Parade twice a Day once for health
     Clean feet and Body and once for
     Muster. Food was very good and
     I got very Stout . a Comrade named
     Hamilton a Tailor Learnt me the use
     of the Neadle which I found after

5   We Laid the ships too – Waiting for
     the Pilot at Length a Small Ship came
     to us a short of Smack or Like one
     and about 8 or 9 Black men on it the
     First we had seen they had Red cap
     on their Head their Body Bare their Legs Bare only
     a small Cloth round the middle it
     was a sort of Strange sight to us
     they talked to the Captain and made
     many Gesticulation which was their usual
     way when talking. One came and he
     took Charge of our ship to Pilot
     us over the sand Heads and up
     the river Ganges . as far as Dimmond
     Harbour . Where a number of Ships
     was at anchor . Ships from all nation
     here we Change for a River Pilot –
     who took us up to Calcutta . the river
     Ganges is a Lovely river and many
     hansom Pagodas on its Bank . Garden
     reach is a Lovely place. In fact –
     after our Passage every thing

4 to be very useful to me we past the
Peake of Teneriffe . but it only looked
like a Cloud we was a Long way off
We saw no more Land until we was
in the Bay of Bengal about 116 Day
we were 120 Day on Ship all told
on our Passage we caught several –
Porposes and we ate some of the Flesh
I did not much care for it, we caught
also several sharks & inside of one
we found a steel tobacco Box a
pipe part of a Straw Hat and part
of a mans shoe.) we saw very few
ships on our outward passage we
had old Neptune Come on Board –
when under the (*Line*) with the –
usual fun those who would not
be shaved had to pay a fine which
was in *Grog*) The Ladies Excepted
we had two play when the Ship
Lay becalmed. I played in Both
in Macbeth I took Banco . on our
arrival at Tiger Isles and Sands Heads

October 1845

6 was new allthough strange to us it looked
very Lovely I very much admired
the Carrage of the Black men as they
walked on the river bank or stood
to Look at us . it took us two days
to get up the river. But about 5 o'clock
Afternoon 3rd October 1845 our ship cast
Anchor in Front of Fort William at
Calcutta the Garrison Major Came on
Board and said we where a Fine Lot
of young Lads as he wished to see
(But Little did we think that here
4 Months has past one third of our
60 Lads would be no more but such
was the Case. That night we Lay
in Front of Fort william I cannot
forget that night we was nearly
mad the heat between Decks and
the Mosquitos.) no man ever can
forget. The next morning at 5AM
we was put on a Steam Boat and
taken up to Chinsurah where we
was Landed on the Morning of

October 1845

7   the 4th October 1845 . after 120 days
on Board . our things was carried to
the Cantonments by the Black servants
and as soon as we got into our
rooms there was a very nice Break
fast for us Consisting of Beefstakes
soup and many other things which
we did good justice to.after being
so Long on salt Food. We had a —
Parade at 10 AM got White Clothing
served out . took our sea Clearance
money and Like Soldiers went off
at once to spend it, at night we
Could not sleep what with the heat
and the noise the Jackals made) there
was no sleep and plenty of Musquito
humming round your head in the
morning before it was light the Black
men came into the rooms which are
very Large open rooms only Iron and
wood rails for Walls . they set at the
Foot of your Bedstead and with a
Large Earthen vessel on their Head

❧

October 1845

9   Amount to 2 or 3 in 24 hours
those that died in the Day we Burried
at sun down and those that died
in the night we Burried at 5 A.M.
Like the rest we soon got use to it
take things altogeather we enjoyed
ourselves at Chinsurah on the morning
20th October our 59 men (one dead) and
Foot soldiers of the . 80 . 50 . . 62 regiments
all under Command of Major —
Mythyus was taken on board the Boat
Soomes and William Bentick . 210 in
all towed by steam Boats first to
Callcutta then down the ganges and
then into the Sunderbuns or the Floating
Islelands . this if all others is the —
worst place for Musquitoes they eat
you alive at night the Boats anchord
in mid river for fear of Wild Beast
there were plenty to hear at night
and a great number of Aligators
of all sizes from a yard Long to four
yards and as Large round as a small

October 1845

8 hold 2 or 3 Gallons. Calling out hot
Coffee Saib this was done so much
that my Comrad by name Makepiece
But wrongly named threw a Boot at
the poor fellow broke the vessel and
the hot Coffee run down his body but
didnot scald him.) of course he
had to pay for the Coffee . at this
place there was in my time no want
of Grog and the men were half tipsy
all day Canteen open all Day with
a Sentry to see no Licquor was taken
away but you could bye 16 Drams
or 3 pints one Dram for one rupee
or 2 shillings and this arrach or rum
was over Proof . 5th October Wm West
of ours was taken with Collerar –
and died in a few hours and one
of the 80 Foot his Wife and baby all
Died in 12 hours of Collerai There
was about 2000 Recruits and a
few Invalids in the Barracks
and the Deaths from all Causes

10 horse in body (but they only Lay in
the water or on the Bank I never
knew anyone touched by them
myself.) our officers shot at many
of them.) Poor Marten McGee was
taken with Collerai and died the
2nd Day we Burried him near a
Mosque on the Bank in a Gutteree
or Cotton quilt his Wife greived
very much they were both Irish
but nice people. She married again
one Thomas Fleming at the regiment
We was Packed in these open Flat
Bottomd Boats like Pigs in a pen
men women & children with not –
room to Walk and at night we
nearly Lay one on the other. the woman
and Children at one end of the
Boat the soldiers at the other a
Lasting Disgrace to England the
Blacks could Pity us.and in this
way we went up to Allahabad a

October–December 1845

11   Distance of nearly 600 miles and
      the Food we got was bad sometime
      salt rations the men grumbled in
      Fact nearly mutinied and then it
      was made better. We see many –
      Strange sights on the river ganges
      the dead Bodys floating down and
      Large Birds eating the Flesh as they
      went along. Some times our Boats
      got a ground and that caused
      much delay at Length we had no
      more wood or coal to get up steam
      and men were sent on shore to Press
      men to fill the Boats up we called
      at many place Dinnapore. Mongeah
      and Bannares and other places
      But the Country had become a very
      sameness and we cared but Little
      about anything most of our time
      was taken up playing cards.) Some
      times we was allowed for an hour
      on the Bank to streach our Legs and

October–December 1845

13   to our new Camp Ground about
      7 in the morning pitched Tents
      Got Breakfast had a Sleep and
      then went out to see the place and
      some days I went to shoot small
      Birds & other things all went on
      well until we arrived at Cawnpore
      where we had our Inspection for –
      Major General Sir Joseph Thackwell
      who Gave us Gt Praise for our Conduct
      and General appearance we remain
      at Cawnpore several day it was
      very hot and a Great deal of Sickness
      was in the Station we Lost 2 men
      Srg Robinson from Fever and his
      wife Collerai and Jack Hawkins
      was Left Back when we March and
      he died also with Bowel Complaint
      about the 4 Day after leaving Cawnport
      we came to an encampment where
      the 53 Foot which regiment march one
      day in advance of us they had a
      man Die and had burried him in

12 We made the most of it on our
arrivial at Allahabad we was
taken into Tents about a mile from
the Fort and remained several
Day and roamed about nothing
to do and got very happy forgot all
our illuseage on Board the Boats I
don't think Soldiers Bare Mallace.
I was in a tent with Sergt Major
Baker his wife 3 other women Mrs Freind
her husband . Mrs Barnes & Mrs Dalton
going to their husbands at the regit
But Barnes was killed before we got
there and she married Sergt Parker
a Tent in India holds 16 men four
in Each Corner the arms in the –
middle of the Tent. We commenced
our March. 3rd Light Dragoon in Front
and Changed alternate Days the 4th
Day from Allahabad we had 3 men
flogged *100 Each* Drunk on rear Guard
we marched before daylight and got

14 a Tope of Mango Trees but the Jackals
had taken the Trouble to get him up
and pick his Bones his Head was off
his Body and the Flesh eat off and
the Skull and Jaws was together and
Covered with Blood. the women had
Jest arrived in Camp and got out
of their Aekeres a man of our regt
named H.G. Potter took up the Head
and run after the women with
it and very much alarmed them
they did scrawl out Potter was stoped
3 day Grog for his pains. We had
a Parade at 5 Clock PM under the
Trees When sad to say the men fell down
on Parade as fast as they could be
Carried to the Hospital tent some
17 or 18 had to be taken in it was
a Jungle Fever that attack us. on the
road as they was Carried in the
Dullies or Stretcher with a cover over
the Blood run from their Mouth, and
Nose about 30 Sick was now being

October–December 1845

15   carried in Dullies by Black men
on the road Mrs Barnes every day
on their arrival in Camp got water
and washed the Blood and dust
from the Poor Fellows mouth and
got oranges for them we had to take our
turns to wait on them. Poor Joe Blake
Died first and we Burried him on
the side of the Road I was Lance Corporal
and read the Funeral service over
him. The morning we arrived at
Lucknow Poor Jack Coe and James West died
we Burried them in an officer Compound
outside Lucknow I was one of the party
to Burry them and was in the City
at the time the Trumpet sounded
and had to run for it to be in time
we now for the First time heard
the Troops on the Front Station was
taken a Campaine against the Sikhs
a war like race standing some of
them much over 6 feet high some
6 feet 6 inches. We now shaped

January 1846

17   And with such arms we was
taken into action 21st January
1846. After geting out arms we still
kept in the rear of the 53 regiment
and march for the Kurnaul Station
and on our arrival we found the
Station filled with women & children
of Different regiment and a few
old and sick Soldiers but no Doctor
our Doctor had to attend the sick
for the 3 days) we remaned we
Lef the women and Children of
the 53 and our Detachment here
and moved on to the Front with
out any encumbrance. The second
night at Kurnaul there was an
alarm that the Enemy was on us
we was turned out in Line and
Loaded with Ball Cartridge but
after remaining two hours we was
sent back to our Tents but to Lay
with our arms ready. All Pass
over right we now commenced the

16 our Course to Dehli to be served out
with arms and amunition but I
must say we had twelve stand of
old arms with us the old Brown Bess
with Flint Locks these was for our
Guard. When we arrived at the old
City of Dehle we Past through the
city and Pitched our Camp at the
Lahore Gate and remained nearly
a week Great delay when men was
wanted at the Front at Length we
was served out with arms and
Each man had 120 rounds of Ball
Cartridge . But Strange as it may
appear the old 12 Stand of arms
was retained by the men although
there was 100s of Thousands stand of
armes in the arsenal . the Gun I
had was deficient of a Cock to hold
the Flint Gun of Pt Goodwin no screws
to hold on the Lock the Gun of
Private Roberts had no ramrod
several others was like them

18 March in right earnest sometimes
twice a day and all our talk and
hope was shall we be there in time
to get the *Medle* . About the Fourth
Day from Kurnaul we had a second
March at 8 at night and about 10 P.M.
I was on the advance Guard with 6 men
we was about ¼ mile behind the
rear Guard of the 53. Suddenly that
regiment sounded form Square which
they did. The rear Guard about 20 men
remained out and Formed by them
selves we being recruits we did
not know what to do I fell my
6 men in under a Tree it was very
Dark our detachment form a Square
When some few of the Enemy's men
Cavalry rode round us and Left
us neither Party doing anything
we ended our march that night at
12 midnight Pitched our tents at once
in Front of a Mud Fort by name
Bus . se . an next morning after

January 1846

19   Breakfast we went out to Drill and
while at Drill an orderly rode in
and it sounded Dismiss and then
strike tents and in half hour we
was again on the march no one
seem to know where no road over
sand through Jungle anyway at
about 4 o'ck afternon we could see
a Large Camp and soon found out
it was our own army under the
Command of Sir Harry Smith one
of the 16th Lancer Came as our Guide
into the Camp at 5 o'ck. we got our
tents and put them up and
made some tea had a wash and
went down to 16 Lancers to see
who I knew But at 8 ock was
ordered to our own tents to here
General Orders read which were
that the whole Camp would get the
next day ration and march at
12 midnight in one colum and
[added later] The Rations was not got by our Detachment

✎

January 21, 1846. Engagement at Badowal

21   Major Mythyus in Command Gave
the order to Load But Several of
us Could not as our Guns was
no use we now got an order to
move to the Front . and at that
Moment a Ball Came and Knocked
Down Five a Corpl for the 80 regit.
his leg knocked off he said Comrades
take my purse I took his gun and
tost my own away we steped over
them and past on but had not
got Far when another Ball Struck
Harry Greenbank in the head and it
sounded Like a Banbox full of
Feathers Flying all over us he was
my Front rank man and his
Brains nearly Covered me I had
to scrape it off my Face and
out of my Eyes and Taf Roberts
my left hand man was nearly as
bad our Guns now commenced to fire
on the enemy we still continued
the march sometimes towards the

January 21, 1846. Engagement at Badowal

20 move onto the Cantonments of
Loodeanna . we got on the march at
1 o'ck AM it was very Dark & Cold
for India we march all the morning
with only one halt about ½ hour. and
about 10 AM 21st January 1846. I was
Looking to our Left . Front when I saw
something Glissen in the sun rays
I said Sergt Major Baker there is
the Enemy. he replied you be damb
he had been very Drunk Just before
we march & had been down to old
mates in the 16 Lancers. He had
hardly replied when . Bang . Bang .
and two Balls Wised over our heads
a third Ball went into a regiment
of Sepoy and knocked over 3 or 4
men the 53 was taken ground
to the Left when a Ball passed
through them striking the ground
in Front of us Close to me and
Bounded over our heads at this
time we was not Loaded But

✒

22 Enemy and at other times towards
Loodiana men Falling Every few minutes
no man of the 53 regit or our Detachment
ever can forget that day. Forced march
for some day previous and marching
that day from one AM until 5 in
the Evening over 30 miles and under
an Indian Sun with Brown Bess
120 round Ball cartridge and Coat at
our backs. Nothing to Drink on the
road some of the mens toungs were
protruding from their mouth at Last
the men could go no Farther the enemy
Cavalry Following Close on our rear
to cut up the Straglers. Sergt Major
Baker became beat and Lay Down he
said I cant go any further. I said
for god sake George think of your
wife and Children . he had two he look
at me and said I cant a Private
named Robson a fine young man
Lay Down with him we moved
on a Little when the Cavalry was

January 21, 1846. Engagement at Badowal

23   about to Charge us we was ordered
to form Square but was unable to
do so we made one corner but got
Confused Roberts said to me Jack be
steady we will have one each and we
both up with our Guns. I had not suffered
so much from thurst as some men
Roberts made water in his Cap and
Drank it. Just as we became so
Confused the 16 Lancers Came down
at a Trot in open Column of Troops
and Wheeled into Line between us
and the Enemy and Save us or none
of our Detachment would be here to
tell the tale they Troted towards
the Enemy Cavalry but they would
not stand for the Lancers they
retired The 53 was at this time
nearly all Fell down but begun
again to rally and so did we
but not until many of our 200 had
Fell Down and been killed Ted

⁓

January 21, 1846. Engagement at Badowal

25   Must have been killed. The enemy
took all our Baggage and the Stores
of all the Hospitals, killed all our
sick and the wounded on the field
and took about 20 Prisoners one
of them being Doctor Banyon of
the 62 foot who had Fell out from
our Detachment to see the wounded
men one of the Prisoners of our regt
named Cumber was taken prisoner
with another of ours on George Cooper
Cumber was striptd naked for
there sport and when naked and
being hunted about for sport
he managed to run from them
they Fired several times at him
he said but misted him he came
to Loodianna about 10 At Night
naked he found his way by
following the noise . on our march
that day my meat was about
Half Cooked and was the round
[added later] I got a piece of meat in the night

24   Mouse Henry Hazard and many more
      I forget their names as Last we
      got in right of Loodianna 3 or 4
      miles off when Sir Harry Smith Came
      to us and Looked at us with tears
      in his Eyes He said poor Boys Lay
      Down now and rest for a time Sir
      Harry shot the two Guides himself
      they was to have taken us wide
      of the Enemy to Loodianna but they
      took us into range of the
      Enemy Guns . Where we lay down
      there were a Large Shallow Pond and
      into this we all went to drink there
      was horses Camels Elephants men
      Bullocks all at once the water nearly
      Like treakle but down it went while
      this was going on many of the 16th
      Lancers were fetching in men of the
      53 and our Detachment on their
      horses in Front of them and by
      this means saved many men
      that had they not have done so

                    ✒

January 22, 1846
26   bone of the Shoulder with a peice
      of meat attached this had in my
      Haversack I sucked this and that
      what stoped my thurst but when
      I saw the others so bad I past it
      along the Ranks Each having a
      suck it was soon gone this was
      all we had that day next morning
      we called the roll there was 17 of
      my regit recruits missing 14 of which
      had been killed out of our Detachment
      of 200) 49 was missing 31 was found to
      be killed and 16 made prisoners
      by a man who had Charge of the
      Enemy Guns a Diserter from the
      East India Companys Troops in
      1836 he had rose to the rank of
      general of Artilary.★ Sir Harry –
      Smith came and Look at us on Parade
      on the 22 and told us there was
      no rations to be got Each man
      would get two rupees and do the

★ this Deserter Saved the 16 men Lives as Prisoners

January 22, 1846

27   Best we could with. I and two others
       went into the Town to try and bye
       something to eat. But we could not
       get anything the natives had got–
       nothing and all the men in camp wanted
       I got a Rams Head with the wool on
       this we took to camp and when we
       got Back we had a Pound of Elephants
       Cakes gave to Each man. I soon eat
       my Lot one of the men got an Earthern
       Pot as Large as a pail this we made
       use of we made a fire put water
       into it and put it on the Fire we
       then scorched the wool off the Head
       and washed it and put it into
       the Earthern pot to Cook . it had
       stewed about 2½ hours . When we
       heard a great Stire in Camp and
       we received orders to Strike Tents
       and march all was now on the
       Stir in quick time. A man named
       Williams tried to take out the Head

January 23, 1846

29   So we was well off . the next morning
       23d I began to look out for something
       to eat Drew my Bayonet and went
       about the Camp I got some coffee from
       a Sepoy and stole two peices of meat
       about the Size of an Egg each these
       I put on the Embers of an old Fire
       to cook and save my coffee. But –
       before they was done a young officer
       came to me and said where did you
       get them Pearman I replied with
       my Bayonet to be sure he sat down
       by the embers and looked at the meat
       roasting in the Embers. they were
       nearly done . When he snatch one
       peice I took the other and we
       Both Eat it I gave him a Little
       of my Coffee and then we went to
       Look for more to eat. I see
       many more doing the same. This
       young officer above named belongd
       to our regiment. he had to ruff it

28   When he broke the Pot and the Broth
run on the ground he got the thanks
of the Boys we then pull the Head
to peices and the Lucky man got a
peice it was so hot it burnt your
mouth but we got it down and workd
at the tents at the same time we had
become use to ruff it. It sounded
fall in so we Bundled the tent on
to the Elephant and run to Parade
ground fell in told off and was
on the way again at 4 miles an
hour . quick . march ½ We now heard
the Enemy had Changed their Camp
and we was going to take up their
ground which we did about dusk
the Enemy had gone 8 or 10 miles
on to Aliwal. And we was now
at *Bud . de wal* where the Battle was
Faught on the 21st some got tents
at night and some Lay on the open
ground we got 3 tents for our men

◥◣

30   the same as the rest he after all
was very cheerful and a good fellow
he became a Captain and exchanged in
to the Scot Grey as Paymaster when
they were in the Crimea his name
was *Colt* Many of the men killed
on the 21st was found and Burried
and some of the men was found
dead in the Village of *Bud di wal*
where they had been plundered and
no doubt killed as they were naked
we found some of the mens things
and the Hospital Stores of the 16
Lancers broke up and Distroyed
this made the men very angry
and it soon spread at Last –
some of the men of the *Artillary*
set fire to some of the Houses
which was soon on the ground
In fact we Distroyed the place
on the afternoon of the 23 a man
of ours named (Peter Locket) (a character) came

January 23–28, 1846

31   into Camp He had been Left on
      the Ground dead Drunk when we
      march at midnight on the 20th Jany
      from Jugron to Bud di wal and
      this was the first we had seen
      of him Major Mythyus Tried
      him by a Drum Head Court Marshel
      He was Sentenced to an 100 Lashes
      which he got that night and he
      was put into the 16th Lancer Hospital
      tent. There now came an order
      for our recruits Tents to be Broken
      up The Infantry to join some of
      the regiments and the remainer of
      ours Joined the 16th Lancers I went to C
      Troop and my Comrade was a Lance
      Corporal of that regiment we remaind
      until the morning of the 28 Jany
      doing regular Duty with the rest –
      those who could. But on the Evening
      of the 27 January who could ride well
      was to be taken to Coln Alexanders

∽

January 28, 1846. Battle of Aliwal

33   and Trotted along to the Front along side
      the 16th lancers who threw out skirmishers
      to the Front. We march in 3 contigious
      Columns Battle array. our Gun 2 in
      Front followed by two more and two
      behind them and then the spare horses
      rode by the Black Sizer or Horse Keepers
      About Half past 8 in the morning we
      Come in sight of the Enemy when we
      came to an Halt and the Infantry
      and Foot artilery began to get into a
      Line Spreading out Like a Lady Fan
      it was a Beautyful Plain for miles
      The Sun Bright & Clear. There was the
      Enemy in our Front 3 or 4 miles Long
      and Looked Splendid. and as our
      Army came into Line as Steady as
      a feild Day. I sat on my horse and
      Looked at the two armies. it was a
      Lovely sight. But soon to become
      Devils. It sounded advance and on we
      moved I could see the Skirmishers of

32   Troop Horse artillery to do Duty as they
had Lost many men and was short
of men . And on the morning of the
28th Jany between 5 & 6 Clock Adjutant
Smyth called Little Jacky Smyth
of the 16 Lancers took us through
the Camp in the Dark all Confusion
with the Camels and men and regiments
geting together at Last we found
Coln Alexander Bengal Troop of horse
artillry. When he Hollowed out to
Alexander.) He stammered in his
speach. Here he said take these
young Devels . for I am adjutant
quarter Master. General and every
thing else this morning . Good bye
Coln. and away he went Coln Alexander
said Can these Boys ride Sergt Darling
replied all of them. The Coln then
said to Sergt Douglas of the artillery
mount them and Lets get on the
road . we was soon on the horses Backs

34   the 16 Lancers was fireing their Carbine
and at 10 minutes to 10 A M the First
round shot about 9 Poundes passed
over our Heads it Sounded Skirmishers
in and Back they came at a Trot we
was now about 12 hundred yard from the
Enemy our Guns Got the order to Trot
and on we went covered by the 16th Lancers
to about 700 yard from the Enemy the
Coln shouted action Front unlimber and
Prepare for Action No 1 & 2 to the right
3 & 4 to the Front 5 & 6 to the Left we all
Dismounted and Held the Horses when
Bang went our Guns and about the 3
Shot I see was Makeing holes in the
ranks in front of us. We remaind
more than Half an hour in this way
when we Limbered up mounted our
horses and with the 16th Lancers and
3rd Native Cavelry took ground to the
Left more than a mile past the 53 Foot
to near an Nellar or deep water Course

January 28, 1846. Battle of Aliwal

35   at this time the Fireing was Terriffic
and Looking back the plain was
Covered with wounde and dead men
and horses and peices of Broken
Guns Jest at the time we was going
to Dismount a Shot struck my horse
and down he went with me I was not
hurt we was in a Cross Fire from –
the Enemys Gun and we had 7 horses
Down at once in my Gun No 5 out of
the 8 horses We had Lost several men and they
was geting short and so was horses
Private Steel of ours a Ball struck him
in the Head and Down he went our
man who road next the Gun had both
Legs cut off with a Ball through the
horse. We Limbered up again and
I. and Jack Reeves rode on ammunition
Boxes when a shot came struck the –
wheel Close to me smash it and the
spoke struck Reeves in the Thigh but
did not hurt him much it all mist

January 28, 1846. Battle of Aliwal

37   Fire again at the Broken ranks with
Grape and Canister shot which made
great havoc . at the time the 16 Lancers
Charged the 31st foot, Queens and the Gorkars
was Chargeing the Infantry and into the
Town of Aliwal and Drove the Enemy
in Front of them. There Army now
seemed to be in Full retreat towards
the river where there was a Shallow
Ford which took them to the Fortress
of Valore But before they could get
over the ford we had taken all their
Gun 67 and one that was nearly over
the river in the Ford our No 2 Gun –
fired a Shot at it knocked it off
the Limber into the water that made
68 Guns there was 5 Guns taken by us
and the one in the water made
6 the Trop) Very fine Guns inlaid with
Brass on Limber and wheel
the Gun Chased. 2 was sent to Calcutta
Musaiin 2 to Windsor Castle and one

36   me We had to put on a spare wheele
and on we Went again with Fresh
horses from the rear brought up by
the Black Sizers or hoselers. We now
Galloped Close to the Enemy About 300
yards and Bang Bang went our Guns
to a good tune and done something
to think about at this time I looked
to our Left and see the 16th Lancers
Comeing on at a Trot then Gallop I
took off my Cap and hollowed out
the first Charge of British Lancers
the Enemy formed Square But the
16th Lancers went right on it and broke
it and such Cuting and Stabing
I never saw before or since I run
and pick up a man named *Wise*
Shot in the Leg and put him on
our gun Carrage . I then run and
pick up Sergent *Steargen* Shot in
the neck and put him on the Gun
Carrage with *Wise*) and then we open
[added later] These two men belonged to the 16th Lancers

✒

38   was made a present to Prince Waldemarr
of Prussia who at the time was making
a Tour in India with his staff he found
Lord Gough army and was present in
one or two Battles this ended the Battle
of Aliwal We returned back to where
they had Camped and there found
all the articles that had been stolen
from the officers Bungalow at Loodianna
before they set them on fire . I took off
my Dirty thing and put on Clean ones
from a Camel Trunk belonging to the 56
Foot Also found a Dozen Bottles of Brandy
but Coln Alexander Made me Brake them
we picked up the wounded and then
got an old Sikh Tent and put it up
we got our food and Grog and had
a Sleep and Felt all right in the
Evening the Black Servant brought
me the Late Sergt Major Barkers Pony
when me and Harry Proud of the 16 Lancers
went into the Enemy old Camp to see
Sikh [he practises spelling this here]

January 28–February 9, 1846

39   what we Could make I rode the Pony
and Proud walked we had been at it
about Half an hour it was now got
very Dark we had Loaded the Pony
with Sikh Gutteree and other things
in the Front of me I held them down
on the Pony. I see a Sikh Soldier Crawling
towards Proud when I called out Look
Harry . who turned round and gave
him a blow on the Head and he Lay
very quiet after that we then went
Down to our old Sikh tent were some
of the 16th Lancers was and gave them some
of the things and some we parted with
for Grog. I tied the Pony up and
put the saddle under my Head and
Lay down on one of the Sikh Gutteree
a Luxury at those times I was soon
assleep and when I awoke in the
Morning the Pony was gone some
of the Bright Boys had been about –
before me and sold it and was

✦

January 28–February 9, 1846

41   27 Miles in Length about 43 Thousand
men the 9th Queens Lancers on the
Left. 3 Light Dragoons in the centre
and the 16th Lancers was at the right
the Distance between was filled up
with Infantry and Artillery and –
Cavelry Native and European the
Enemy Lay on the Banks of the
Sutlej river in the entrench Camp
with about 120 Guns and 70 Thousands
fighting men we arrived in Camp with
the 16 Lancers as we got our food with
that regit. but still rode the Horses
of Coln Alexanders Troop of Bengal
Horse atillery about 3 oCk afternoon
9th February 1846 and acting regimental
Sergt Major Johnson Came to take us
to our regiment and several men
came with him we took a parting
Glass with the 16 Lancers and artillery
men and march for our own regiment
about 13 miles more we got there about

40   Spending the money I gave the saddle
away about midday I was very nearly
Shot a Pt named Goodwin and me –
took a walk and were Looking at the
Field and the Dead. I had just cut
off the Hair and part of the scalp
of a Dead Sikhs to make a Black Plume
and was Looking at a very Large Dead
man near 7 feet High and Large with
it. When some one fired a shot from
the Town of Aliwal which struck
the ground about a Foot from me
so we made off to Camp again and
got our Dinner. We had a Standing –
Camp 3 or 4 Day and then we moved
again up the Country marching some
times right some times Left at Last
we got orders to join the main
army at Sabraon under the Command
of Sir Hugh Gough. The Camp was a
very Large Camp it Lay in almost a
Line in echellon of regiments and was

42   8 oClock at night was seen by Lieut Coln
White then in Command of the regiment
told off to our Troops and took to them
by the Sergt Major who told us off to horses
as far as the horses would go for the
regiment was short of horses so many
had been Lost in the previous Battles
of Moodkee . and . Ferozesah the men of
the regiment behave well to us they
had got all that Lay in there power to
make us Comfortable and we had a
very nice supper the officers sending
us things from their mess tent we
was Called and Christened from that
night the Draft of the Bayonet
Battery on account of our marching
with Guns and Bayonet with the 53
and being engaged with that weapon
at the Battle of Bud de.wal on the
21st of January and if any of the
Draft got into trouble for years after
our adjutant would say Colonel this is one
[added later] John Sullivan

February 9–10, 1846

43   of the Bayonet Battery the Colonel –
would then say are poor Boy and Let
them off saying dont you come here
again hor else I shall punish you
very severely mind. But many is the
time I have heard him say the
same word to the Draft the Coln
never forgot us At the Regiment as
we was in our tents talking to the
men about 12 midnight for having
so much to tell the men of England
and so many questions asked we
had not been to sleep although
so very tired. Sergt major Kelly
Came down the Troop and gave the
order that the men would mount in
the morning befor daylight and make
no noyse and the recruits who joined
on the 9th and got horses would go
with the regiment those without –
horses would remain on Guard
in Camp and take Charge of the

February 10, 1846. Battle of Sobraon

45   When our Batteries open Fire with the
Long 32 Pounders which took the Sikhs
somewhat by surprise as a such a fearful
Amount of Bugling and Tom Toming
and Druming instantly succeeded they
soon return the Fire from the numerous
Batteries in their entrenchments and
after a few shots to try the range their
Practice became really admirable one
of our men Dick Neve of C Troop had
his horse shot and was ordered to the Camp
the regiment was in Clos Column of Troops
We must have been at the time from 1000
to 1200 yards from the Enemy According
to the Position of our Batteries which
were all on the right or Left opposite
to there Left or right. But a very short
time had elapsed when there round
shot shells and shrapnels came as fast
as possible to our own Batteries and
amongst the Troops then drawn up –
pretty well out of range of the Long

February 10, 1846. Battle of Sobraon

44   things I had a horse and went with
the regiment we got on our horses and
march Down towards the Enemy Camp
about 5 oCk in the morning of the 10th Feby
1846 the Long 32 Pounders was already
Down and in Position and the rocket
Platform Fixed the Guns and rockets
Pointed to the Enemy Camp. We could
here our Army on the move in the
Dusk each regiment and Guns Geting
into there proper places as told off
the night before in the Divisions at
20 minutes after 6 oCk AM our Long
32 Guns sent us several shot into
the Enemy Camp and several rockets
The Enemy Camp at this time had
not made a move and didnot –
Know we was so Close down to them
our Guns ceased fire and we waited
until they got out of there tents and
to their Guns in these Intrenchments
for theirs was an entrench Camp

✳

46   bound. We had in the regiment an half
breed Greyhound and the Poor thing kept
runing after the spent Ball until the
Poor Bitch could run no more but she was
not hert. Still there shot came among
our Infantry Killing and wounding a
few. And such Cannonade and noise
as was now taking place no Thunder was
ever equal to it you could hardly here
your Comrade speak a Long side you
Excitement it was Truly. Our Batteries
was firing at a most rapid rate and
at an easy range into the very heart
of the entrenchments hitting the Bridge.
of Boats and even to the other side of
the river for most of our artillary and
field Batteries had advanced to an
Easy range and the fireing appeared like
Practice in Woolwich marshes . from 7
AM until about 12 noon this fireing
was maintained and receieved the
round shot bounding Playfully and

February 10, 1846. Battle of Sobraon

47   Spitefully over the plain, at about 10
AM All the Troops for the attack had
been collected in their brigades and
the Brigades was united in their several
divisions. The order was now given
to advance and General Gilbert Division
throwed out skirmishers to attract the
Enemy from the right and Left The
whole was now moveing slowly to the
Entrenchments so as to enter them by an
assault and as soon as General Dick
and Smith had gained an entrance. I see
Abercrombies sappers makeing a Lodgement
on the Works but not before the 50 foot
and 62 and 80th and 10th regiments of
H. Majesty had been once turned back
from the Batteries and again taken
up the Charge oh what a sight to set
on your horse to look at these Brave
fellow tried several times to get into
their Camp and at Last they did
but oh what a Loss of human life

February 10, 1846. Battle of Sobraon

49   the Front. The horse artillery of Dick division
Cantered to the Front some few hundred
yards and poured in a tremendous
discharge of Grape the infantry coming
up in Lines open a musketry fire
when within an easy distance and
Sir Harry Smiths the same. It now for
some miles round the Camp become
a musketry fire with the artillery
oh what a Thunder Genl Gilberts division
was now advancing from the centre
which was taken up by the other –
division and forward the Long line
of Infantry went 2 deep for several
miles in Length. The Enemy's shot
now came in amongst the men and
it seemed difficult to fill up the
Gaps made But on they go. But British
Troops are not to be detered But no
one could Exspect to Escape such a
fire as the Enemy was now pouring
in their Grape at point range

48   God only knows who will have to answer
for it. After the Infantry got some
Cover until the Sikhs had been driven
out from the entrenchments The 1st
European Bengal regiment did good
service and a regiment of Ghoorkhas
with them a Brave Mountain race
our regiment 3rd Light Dragoons being
in the centre we could see a Great
deal of the feild . But such a tearing
and rending of the atmosphere has
never been heard before in this Country
after we had gained a Lodgement the
fireing slackened a Little and ours did
likewise and now comes the time
of strife orders came for all the regiments★
to stand to arms Gnl Gilbert now threw
out his Light Infantry the whole about
100 yards to the Front to make the De –
monstration of attack while on the
right and Left the whole of Genl Dick
and Genl Smiths Divisions moved to

★ regiments had been dying down for a long time

✎

50   our Artillery Closed up to Quarter Distance
followed by the 3rd Lt Dragoons my regt
The advance of the Army was now
Changed from line to Echellon and
now the Troops Advanced it was about
11 oCk AM Genl Dick Division had reached
the Entrenchments and was fighting
Like Mad. A rush was made forward
by the 31st regit of European with
a Shout. The Ghoorkhas close with them
they are Dressed in Dark Green a very
Brave race from the Hills they kept
time and pace with our english –
regiments. The Sikhs was fighting
Bravely for their Guns and Camp
and our men ment to have them
and have them they did. But oh
to tell the Loss the 1st Bengal Europeans
had but 167 men on Parade next
morning the remanes of a Noble
regiments. The Sikhs now began to
retreat but gave us parting

February 10, 1846. Battle of Sobraon

51   Shots as they Left the parapets of the
Entrenchments. The Colours of two
English regiments were now planted
on the Batteries. The Enemy now
formed themselves in strong Close
Battalions to make good their retreat
to the Bridge of Boats across the
river sutlej behind their Camp
It was now our tern it was given
Forward 3rd Kings own Light Dragoons
A word the Colonel used when he
was in a good temper and on
we went by the Dead and Dying
and partly over the poor fellow
and up the parapet our horses
scrambled one of the Sikh artillary
men struck out at me with his sponge
staff but mist me. Hiting my horse
on the hind quarters which made
the horse bend down I cut a round
cut at him and felt my sword
strike him but could not say where

✍

February 10, 1846. Battle of Sobraon

53   Coming Back to the regiment when
we Caught it. The Enemy was now
rushing to the Ford as the Bridge was
Broken and on Fire and being choked
up with a Mass of Soldier Camels and
horses with some artillery and Carriages
some of the Boats got Loose and the
river being raped at the time the
whole Mass was turn into the river
and from what we where told . It –
was beleived that about 10.000 Souls
Perished in 10 minutes or a quarter
of an hour. Sir Harry Smithes Division
Came up the river bank and killed
thousands of the Enemy while they
endeuvered to Cross the river
We now Possessed the Entrenchments
and Camp takeing all their Guns
nearly 100 in All and the Dead
Sikh Bodies that Lay at their Guns
and at the parapets they certainly
where a brave Enemy. and I must

52   there was such a Smoke on I went
with the rest through the Camp at
their Battalion which we broke up
our regiment at this time was not
300 Strong Recruits all Told out of
700 that took the field on the 12th.
December 1845 and this was 10 Feby 1846
in this Charge we Lost 23 men 4 of
them out of my tent. But two of
them was there own Fault Jack –
Marshall who had been *drinking*
several days I was *told* he went out
After the Fighting was nearly over
to attack a Sikh on horse back and
his Comrade seeing he was Likely
to get the worse of it as we all could
see. Bill Driver a fine young man
6 feet high. Troted out to his assestance
and just as he got to Marshall who
was Jest Killed a shot came and
Struck poor Bill he threw up his
arms and down he Came his horse

✌

54   Say that their retreat from the Camp
to the river was as Steady as Could be
Although we Charged and the artillery
raked them where ever they was able
to say nothing of our Infantry with
shot and Bayonet. There was heaps
of dead besides what was Drownd
in the river. There was all their
regular or Aean Battalions. None
of our Army Cross to the other side
of the river we had done enough
The Battle of Sabraon the most –
severely Contested of anyone in the
Campaign was over and our Victory
Complete But had the 9th Lancer and
their Cavelry Brigade been on the other
side not a man of the 70 Thousand
would have been Left. When the
Duke of Wellington heard of this Battle
he was Commander in chaif of England at
the time. He said it was a second
Waterloo and ordered the Tower Guns

February 11, 1846

55   to fire a surloote which they did
at 12 midnight awakening Half London
he ordered a medle with the ribon –
Colours Waterloo reveresed which we
all got Also 12 months Batta din
for prise money £7–12s–6d I Cannot
recolect the Exact Loss on our side but
I think the number was 5000 Killed
and wounded . Most of the army
returned to Camp about 3 in the
afternoon as our Camp was Left
Standing. We soon got into our tents
the Bobagees brought us our Dinners
and it sounded Grog. So we made
a good meal had a Wash and
then Lay Down for a Sleep and in
a very few minutes all that was
not for any Duty was fast asleep
Forgetting all about the past. on
the morning of the 11th Febry a Party
was sent out to Bury the Dead I
remained in Camp but I heard

February 13–18, 1846

57   here we had a Standing Camp for
some days with Plenty of Duty on
Guard and as soon as you came off
Guard you had to reconitre the Country
that done you was told off for the
out Laying Picquet when you would
be half the Day and night on horse
Back on Verdit or Pattroling as soon
as you had come from this you was
for Laying Picquet not to take –
off anything only the Bit out of the
horses mouth and hang it on the
saddle which was on the horse on the
14th our Camp was visited by the
Maharajah Gholab Sign Dewan Deena
Gath. Fakir Nooroodan . Bhzee Ram
Sign and 10 or 12 others on very Large
Elephants with Splendid Traping –
nearly all Gold and their Dress was
splended. Some Little understanding
was come to us all the Prisoners taken
on the 21st Jany at Buddeewal was sent

February 12–13, 1846

56   the men say it was a Dreadful
sight. The Farriars was sent out to
shoot what horses remaned alive
with wounds on the Battle Feild for
Poor Brute they suffer much one
of our Horses had one of his hind
Hoof knocked off and the Poor Brute
kept Galloping about for a Long
time at Last one of the men Left
the Ranks and Shot him. On the
morning of the 12th We Commenced the
March at 5 AM and Got to *Khoonda*
Ghat about 3 oCk we crossed the Bridge
of Boats over the Sutlej river with
the artillery into the Paunjaub the
First regiment of our Gallant army
to enter the enemys Nation and we
march as far as 2 miles into it on
the morning of the 13th with all –
the army across we march to Kussoor
about 10 miles we found the Fortress
Evacuated so we took Possession

⟶

58   into our Camp and Each man was
given some rupees by order of the
Maharajah the men was Glad to get
Back again they did not say they had
been illused in anyway. on the 16th
Feby enroute for Lahore which City
we reach on the afternoon of the 17th
and Pitched our Army round the City
for several miles on the Plain of
Meen Meer. The Sikhs old Drill ground
on the 18t Febry we our regit 3rd Light Dragoon
was ordered on Guard off honor Dismounting
in the Great Dubar tent for the Signing
of the 13 articles of the Treaty. In the
tent was Sir Henry Hardinge Sir Hugh Gough
and the Staff officers and about 200
of us with Drawn swords the Sikh Chief
had also their Guard of Honour it was
a Grand sight the ceremony took 2½
hours and then Sir Henry Hardings
the Govenor General of India ordered
the durbar to be Broken up at the

February 22–April 7, 1846

59   Same time he took Possession of the
      Young Maharajah 12 years old named
      Dulun Singh for safity and to be sent
      to england. After this over our duty
      became much Lighter as our Campaign
      was over and Part of the army was
      marching Back to their Quarters. My regit
      Commenced the March back early 22nd
      march the Sun was now geting very
      hot and before we reached our Station
      the hot winds begun to blow. We
      arrived at Umballah on the 7 April
      1846 and took up the Barracks which
      at that time was not finished
      there had been about 700 women
      and Children in the Barracks for
      safety belonging to different regiment
      and a Great number of officers
      Ladies had taken up the officers
      quarters but these were being sent
      Back to their own regiments the
      53 foot was Also at Umballah the

～

April 1846–September 1848

61   a month after our return to quarters
      soon forgot the one dead some of them
      had had 3 or 4 husbands one that was
      Married made her Sixth Husband she
      married Sergt Gooderson of H Troop
      in May we got our Batta money –
      £7–12–6. Each and most of us had
      money we had made on the Campaign
      Lute) I sent £5 home to my freinds
      and it was near 12 months before they
      got it off Msrs Cox & Greenwood of Craig Army Court
      Agents
      But They did get it There was a great
      Deal of Drinken and men dying every
      Day from the Effects of Drink although
      we were Charged 1 rupee 12 Anna for Bottle
      Bass Stout or Burton ale 3/6. But only
      one anna for Dram nearly a quartern
      which was 3 pints one Dram for 2s
      of Strong rum and you Could
      have as much as you Like to Drink
      Carry none away to Barracks but we
      had a woman named Paddy Burns

60   3 Company 4t Battalion of Foot artillery
and 2 Troops horse artillery Europeans
the rest was Black Troops 1st Native Cavalry
71 & 64 In fantry in all we were 7000
Strong we now begun to get the place
into order the mens Boxes who had
been killed were taken out of store
and the kits in them sold by auction
by a Sergeant there was a Lot in my
Troop I had bought 6 Dozen of Shirts
a mans kit in India in quarters is 6
pairs of White Trowsers 6 prs of Draws
3 Flanells 6 Shirts 4 White Jackets
4 Puggerees 6 prs Socks 1 pr Setteren Trowsers
for water order 2 pairs Blue Clothen overalls
one Blue Stable Jacket 1 Dress Coat 1 Shacko
one Cloak 2 pairs of Boots besides these
we had many Fancy things not regimental
The dead mens things were sold for
a meer Nothing as men didnot want
them. We had 14 or 15 widows in the regit.
and most of them was married in

62   Called the old tin kettle. She had a
Tin Baby made with a wax Face. this
she would taken into the Canteen at Evening
and mimick a Cry and then give it a
Little Grog the childs body held more than
a Gallon. she would get the men to get
many rupees worth for her and she used
to then fill the Child when Full she would
mimick the Cry and say are I must
take the young Devil to its Mother I
suppose and she would go by –
the Sentry . and this she would sell
at 4 annas pr Dram in the night –
when it only cost her one anna –
When men had been drinking in the
day they would pay any amount for it
in the night.her and husband save
a Lot of Money he got his Discharge
Came to England and took a Public
house near London when he Failed and
afterwards we was told he went to
Australia to work herd. When the

April 1846–September 1848

63   Child trick was Discovered she was
taken before Colonel *White*, with
the Baby in her arms when the poor
thing had to Vomit which mak the old
Coln Laughd but he punished Both her
and husband it was this that made
him Leave the regiment. Then we
had Plenty of men who made Bishops
a sort of Blader to Fit into their
shirt inside the Trowsers a sort
of Bladder to hold 8 Drams
and smuggle it out of the Canteen this
way these men sold it to the other
men mostly at Gun Fire in the
Morning 5 AM this they called
Gun fire tots and got as we turnd
out to Drill these men would save
a Lot of money and Drink nothing
for some time This was called to
put the bag on. But when they
did Brake out.they would Drink
to such an Exstent that they had

April 1846–September 1848

65   when the Hot weather set in they
like us Left it off only sending a
mounted Party to follow the Blacks
carried the dead in Dullies
a sort of Covered Strecher. Our regiments
was made up to 700 Strong. The
16th Lancers was Broke up to be sent
to England after 24 years service
in that Country there was one man
went home who Come out with the
regiment. We got 200 horses from them
and 240 men Volenteers these men
received 30 Rupees to Volenteer the
14 Light Dragoons only got one man
named Self this was because they had
to do their own work or part of it
and they were very tight in the
Canteen Rules the men marked
off When they had 3 Dram each
of rum quite Enough 3 quarters
of a Pint nearly. I thought it
a very good Rule the men were

64 mostly to go to Hospital from the
Effects. At the time the Batta –
money was served out there were
about 30 men in Hospital from Drink
Regtml Sergt Major Died Sergt Major Kelly
Died Sergt Jones and many of the
Privates the Drink did more for Death
than the Fever or other Complaints
Soon After our arrival in Umballah
the 14th Light Dragoons came Also they
came from (Kerkee Bombay) and was
to Late for the Campaign and got
no Batta or Medle. This regiment
was Commanded by Lieut Col Havelock
and had to do part of their work
and brought on Fever they Burried
2 or 3 men Every week out of about
600 men which told on their Ranks
When they first Came to umballah
they Burried there dead with Military
Honors the Band and Sauls Dead
march the men in full Dress. But

❧

66 more Sober than our men. But in these
Day Drink was the rage in India. The
next Cold season the two regiments the
14th and 3rd use to Brigade togeather we
were Dressed alike only their Buttons
said 14th Lt Drag. round them and ours
said 3 Light Drags. We very offtimes
had 13000 horses on Parade Both regit
all alike a pretty Sight when in Line
we had also the 1st Native Cavalry 600
strong which would give us 18 or 1900
horses on Parade. The Strength of the
3 regiments would be 2000 horses
3rd Light Dragoons 701 – 14 Lt Dragoons
700 Native Cavalry 600. This number
would make 7 or 8 regiments at home
The Extra one in ours was a Sergeant
and Beat the Silver Kettle Drums a
Honor Granted us for taken the –
Drums in Battle some were in Spain
our time was now spent very idle
as all Drill was in the morning

April 1846–September 1848

67   and Dismounted Drill in the Evening
and as it was very hot in the Day
we sat on our Charpoy or Bedstead
and Plaid at Cards, Back Gammon
or Chess or anything that took our
tast in this way our time was –
past and at othertimes I would
read Books or set at the Needle
In the winter months I mostly went
out with my Gun with a Comrade
named Danl Larnden. This was after
Morning Drill was over as I was very
fond of romeing about the Country
and Converseing with the natives –
a people I Always found very kind
if properly treated by us But I
am Compeled to say some of our
men used the Poor native very
bad I recollect one day when out
we Came in Sight of a very Large
sort of Deer The Ellgie There were
10 or 12 of them and not more than

April 1846–September 1848

69   tuch them or come near the Flesh
of the Suah or swine it being –
unclean and would Break his Cast
But the white man eat anything do
anything. But serve God. our *Cast*
is never *Broke*. And one thing I
was very sorry to see oftimes when
out on night Patrolle in the officers
Lines and our Barrack we would come
across our Parson dead Drunk we
would have him carried to his Bungalow
or Dweeling house the Blacks would
Laugh and say as they Carried him to
his Bunglelow White man Potturee
Bote uteh ah adamy) Good man and
very nice Bibby (wife) She was
very Pretty and fond of Life and this
Couple never mist a Dance or a
Spree at the officers Mess and it
was at these times we used to find
him Drunk. He would have been
better away at Length he was sent

68   100 yards off we Both fired at them
and killed one a very fine Female
But it was no use to us as we were
8 or 9 miles in Jungle and nothing to
Carry it home so we Left it where it
Lay it was nearly as Large as an Alderny
Cow on another occasion we saw a
Wild Sow and Pigs and knowing they were
very spiteful we got into a Low Tree
and Fired and killed one of the pigs
and wounded 2 or 3 more there was
such a noise with the pigs and the
old sow you neverad heard she would
not Leave the dead pig and Kept
runing to the Bottom of the Tree
and then the pig we became
alarmed for our Safety but after
a time more than an hour she
Left Leaving us 2 pigs one dead
the other we killed and we took
them to Barracks and Cook them
ourselves as the natives will not

꒰

70   to another Station and we got an –
old Parson a very good man a Mr
Whitehead the men were very fond of him
as he would set in the Hospital for
hours with the sick and pray with
them and never find any fault with
our ways only exhort us to pray to God
he had the good will of us all this
Parson took the next Campaign with
us that is our Division of the army
I shall again have to speak of him
The drinking continued as Long
as the money Lasted and at the
beginning of Each month there was
a seen of Drunkeness as the men
were paid the Back pay for the past
Month and then that had to be
spent in Drink. about this time
the Steady men and non commissioned
officers started a Library and
Each member to pay 4 annas each
month and the Colonel Gave us his

April 1846–September 1848

71   Support and all the officers and
a number of Books to start with
and sent us newspapers a very great
Luxury in those day and the Coln
Caused a Coffee room to be opened
at Gun fire 5 AM and hot coffee
was ready at that Hour a Capital
thing for the men as we turned out
to our feild Drill at Gun fire –
beside Coffee you could get anything
to eat you mite want this was when
Lieut Coln Lockwood Commanded the
regiment The Library had a good
Effect and in a few months Half
the men belonged to it. They were
alowed to take the Book to there
own Beds where they Could Lay and
read and this kept the men from
Cards and Drink and very much
improved the Conduct of the men
we remain at umballah for 2 –
years and 6 months. There had been

〘〙

April 1846–September 1848

73   the Chapel and when the Blue Lights
were going in up went Chapel and
such a Smoke and dust. well of course
no body did it. and it was never found
out. I must say these men called Blue
Lights were some of the worst men
in the regiment and had made away
with there all for Drink and then
would turn Blue Lights a term for
men of this stamp. The Natives said
the Blue Lights were *Mud Wallah Cast*
Drinking religion We remain in this
way at Umballah for some time
I spent most of my spare time in
the Jungle and small Bush wood –
with my Gun and our enjoyment
in Barracks was such as any young
man Could Like. We had Books to
Read. Cards to play. Draught Boards
Chess Boards. Back Gammon and
outside the Barracks. we had skittles
and Cricket and once a Month

72   a Stone Laid for the Foundation of a
Church and a number of Coins and
papers placed under it but as we
went on a Campaigne the Church was
not got on with and some of the
Brave Lads who had been sent back
with wounds of Different regiments
took a Liken to the Bottle that Containd
the Coins. and its contents so they got
some Gunpowder and raised the stone
and when the Troops came back they
found it gone and the Stone some
few hundred yards off. While the
Drinking with the Batta money was
going on some of our men took it into
there Heads to turn *Blue Lights* that
was ranters and had a small –
Chapel built and made more cry
than wool in it. Well some other
Holy Boy took it into there Heads
that the Chapel stood in the way
and Laid some Gunpowder under

✎

September 27, 1848

74   We had a Bon Ton (Dance) and all
the Females of the Station invited to
it Half Cast and all so Long as they were
Wife of a Soldier. Well things went
on in this way. Until September 1848
when there were rummers of the –
Bengal Army taken the Field for a
Campayne as the Native Force at –
Moultan under Shere Sing had Deserted
our side and gone over to the enemy
who was in the fortress of Moultan
which place the British Troops had
Laid Seige to for some months all
the hot Weather But now had to
Entrench themselves as this 6 Thousand
had Deserted our side with there
General (Rajah Shere Sing) on the
27th September 1848 as we set in our
Barracks at Umballah about 11 oCk
morning a Camel Come Troting into
the Cantonments and in a great
Hurry inquired for the Brigadedare

September 27, 1848

75   quarters and was directed by the
sentry at our Guard and as this
seldom took place it put us all on
the Look out at 1 oClock it sounded
orders and then Come the news so
Long look for. The 3rd Kings own to
pack their Boxes and take them to
store rooms and our kit and horse
in Marching order. The regiment to
March at 3 oCk afternoon. Women
and Children to take up one Barracks
and several sick men Convelesants
to be Left with them poor Children
and Mothers some of them took the
Last Look at their Fathers & husbands
But they Bore it as a Soldier wife
should. Well 3 oCk Came and there
we set as fine a regiment of young
men 697 Strong as England could
wish for. we gave a Loud Hurra
to the women as we march off to
Chear the poor thing and off we

&

November 5, 1848

77   the town of Rannuggar on the Chinab
In the
morning we all march about 8 A.M.
and now to find the Enemy and
as the Boys would say to get Batta
or Prize money. Rajah Shere Sing was
with his army at the Town of Wuzerabad
about 60 Thousand men. and we made
for that place which is on the Bank
of the river Chanab about 70 miles
north of the City of Lahore. our army
at this time was under the Command
of Lieut General Curton on the 5th

September 27–November, 1848

76   went at a Trot not pulling a rein
until we was several miles off for
fear the women should follow and
two of them did although we march
15 miles and stoped that night in the
tents with their husbands. how they
got Back I Cannot say we continued
our march Untill we came to Moodkee
here we halted 3 day for the Infantry
and some foot artillery our camp
now came up to 7000 men. We then –
march to Ferozepoor where we joined
more of the army and we had to
Cross the river Sutlej and took
our route to Lahore – which we reach
in the First week in November and –
now we was 20 Thousand Strong all
arms. We then Crossed the river Ravee
and made for Jallunder
and then Direct to river Chenab to

November 20, 1848

78   November we come in sight of a
small party of the Enemy that had
been sent to look out for us and
we had a Smart Gallop after them
our Horse Artillery Keeping a long side
of us – But as their horses appeared
Fresh and we had made a Long march
we could not come up to them there
was one of their men killed. We
Formed our Camp here and waited
two days for General Sir Joseph Thackwell
But the enemy Changed there Camp
and went about 30 miles down the
river Chanab to a Town Called Ram
nuggah. Our army then Changed its
Front and took ground to the North
West and Halted about 10 Miles from
the enemys Camp and here we remaind
for the main Army and the Commander
in Chief Sir Hugh Gough who came in
on the 20th November 1848 and we was
not Left idle Long when he Came he

November 20–22, 1848

79   had an Inspection of the whole army
on General Parade and spoke a Lot
of Stuff to us of Laurals to gain
for our Country and honor to the
regiment But not a word about the
Pension you would get if you got
Cut about. and to say the Truth
we had not been idle before he
Come for we were on our horses half
the 24 hours. We had a double Chain
of Infantry Verdetts and in advance
of Them The Cavelry two men every
100 yards with orders at night to fire
on any one Coming from the Front
and when we were be lying Piquet
we never took a thing of man or horses
and the whole army turned out one
hour before Day Light Every morning
The Infantry to stand to arms The
Cavelry mounted the artillery with
Guns Loaded and match Lit and
we remained Like this for an hour

November 22, 1848. Battle of Ramnagar

81   Columns the Guns in the Centre
about 8 oCk we Came in sight of
the enemys out Post. The Sun had
risen and got Bright through
the Dust. The 3rd Light Dragoons was
ordered to Advance and Drive in
the Enemy out Post it sounded Trot
and we had to Jump a Nollah and
then down the deep Bank it then
Sounded Gallop and at them we
went But they showed us their
Backs Leaving the Tent behind them
down to the river and us after
them neck or nothing but they
took the Ford and joined there
army which Lay quiet enough but
was soon on the alert we halted
on the Bank of the river about Half
a mile from the Enemy the river
between us and waited Some time
until the remainer of the Division
Come up genl Cureton Came with

November 22, 1848. Battle of Ramnagar

80   after Day Light and then file into
Camp and after the horses had been
feed and ourselves we had that is
a Part of us every few hours to Patrole
and reconnitre the Enemy So we
was not very idle. We now begone
to Look forward for a General –
Engagement. And on the morning
of the 22 November 1848 we were very
Comfortable in Camp and all off duty
I should think asleep. At 4 oClock in
the morning an order was given that
the first Division of the army would
Dress immediately and turn out without
noise to reconitre the Enemenies Camp
and their Possirtions under the
Charge of Major Genl Cureton the
1st Division were about 8 Thousand
Strong most of it Cavelry and 12 Guns
it was very dark when we march
and the Dust made it worse so
we went very Slow in two small

82   then When he gave the order for
our first Squadron to Brake Ranks
and Gallop up the Bank of the river
to see how many Guns the enemy could
bring to base on us as went off
we went Broke up like a Lot of Sheep
only further apart we had not gone
far when bang went their Guns at
us as we Galloped for about 3 miles
we were told they fired 67 Guns at
us we had 6 or 7 horses but down –
but the men was not hurt I see Sergt
Woods horse shot and Pt Pooles and
Wooders in about 3 minutes and as
Jack Alder was in front of me 20
yards I see the Gun ready and they
was Lighting the match I said Look
out Jack but a round shot came and
Cut the Pouch from the Belt at his back
but didnot tuch him at this time
we were rideing over quick sands
and some of the horses got set fast

November 22, 1848. Battle of Ramnagar

83   up to the Belly the men had to leave
them by this time a Party of the
Enemy horse with Lance Came in
our rear one was behind me my
horse was nearly beat but I formed
a right rear Guard with my Sword
to Parry of his Lance should he
point as he was only about 6 feet
from me but we kept Like that
some Distance my horse at this time
Could only go about 6 miles an hour
But he did not Close up with me
Private Wm Hacken was behind him
and he put his sword through
him and put a Stop to his Gallop
he was well mounted and Come
alongside of me and said Jack
that Chap meant to have got you if –
your horse failed at this moment
a shot struck me in front of us
and nearly brought us to the –
ground but Better Luck on we

November 22, 1848. Battle of Ramnagar

85   Nullah we again form Line and
made two faint Charges but could
not get them out we now went back
to the Trees again as we see the 14th
Light Dragoons Coming Down their
horses being fresh not haveing done
anything but the Steady march in
the morning They was Led by Lieut
Colonel Havelock a very brave officer
and they Come on in Pretty stile
so Steady and Strate but the Colonel
knew nothing of the Nullah in their
Front full of the Enemys Infantry our
Colonel Michael White Called out Havelock
Havelock and pointed to the Nullah
but on they went. and then came
a Volley and Smoke. But the 14. Lt Drags
had gone down it and over them
but the poor fellows had some hard
worck I saw David Todd come back
I knew him he was covered with blood
and then more come back poor Todd

84 went and as soon as we were Clear
of them we brought our horses to a
walk and most of us got together
again and took ground to the Left
and in about half and hour found
our 3 Squadrons of the regiment
Drawn up near an Nullah and very
Close to a Tope of Trees we called the role
of our Squadron and 17 men and horses
were missing. The Enemy had now
Come out in great force and Crossd
the river to our side. and the Battle
begun in right Earnest and here we
set for nearly an hour their Infantry
fireing at us but didnot do us much
harm although the Shot went tit
tit round and by you very fast
several men were shot and many
horses wounded our right of the
regiment was now feel Back near
the Trees to try to Draw out the
Enemy but no go they keep to the

86 didnot go far a Shot come and knockd
off his head Colonel Havelock was
killed and between 20 + 30 men. and
soon after Gen G Cureton came down with
the Staff and went to find Coln Havelock
when a shot struck him he threw up
his arms and Life was gone also
Colonel of the first Native Cavelry on
the Staff was shot at the same time
We buried thm next day like Soldiers with
their Cloks around them all in one
grave at the Village of Ramnuggar
our Artillery was drawn up near
the Nullah and was makeing good
Practice on them The Infantry had
Also got at work and Death was
gathering in his Harvest in good
Earnest I could only see now and
again what was going on. But as
the Enemy out numbered us we had
to Change our Position very often
and when the Horse Artillery were

November 22, 1848. Battle of Ramnagar

87   Changing ground two of their
Guns stuck fast in the quick sand
so they were spiked and Left to
the Enemy The day was now geting
advanced and the sun showed signs
of puting an end to the Dreadful sight
so the army formed itself into –
Battle order for the morrow and come
to a Bivoact for the night at the
same time the Sikhs cross the river
having had enough of it themselves
and we had a very hard day and
man and horse wanted rest but we
had nothing to Eat the Horses had
been without food or water from the
night before and nothing for them now
and we dare not give them water
as they had nothing to Eat. I had
some Arack or rum in my Bottle
so I made a Drink and myself and
horse Shared it. (It *was* so *Dark*)
and the men begun to Look after

November 28, 1848

89   fire to them they were burnt down
I dont know what became of the people
as the men fell asleep they Let their
horses Loose which made great Confusion
and Caused us to get up and Swear
Jest as we had Droped off to Sleep –
Morning Came and with Daylight
our Tents Cooks and Commissery so
we got corn and feed our horses after
36 hours fast and rode for 16 hours
and then feed ourselves put up the Tents
watered the horses had our grog and
Lay Down and soon forgot all in
Sleep the Horses had been 36 hours
without food or water. and wanted
much looking after but our Blacks
servants took to them well I had
a good man very fond of the
horse and when he see he was not
hurt he patted and made much of
him and the poor Brute seemed
to know it for he squeeled and Seemed

November 22, 1848

88   anything they could get to eat I gave
my horse to another to hold so did my
comrade (Wm Makepiece) and we went
to Look for something the artillery had
found a Dead man of theirs in a house
near Ramnuggar – about 60 or 70 houses
in a Lump Clear of the Large Town and
this we Looted. Myself Makepeice
and Dick Curtis got a small Bullock &
took it to our Bivioact and we killed
it with a sword through the Body and made
a fire and it was soon eat The men
taking a bit as they could get it and
Cooked it at the Fire. Bread we had
none But I made a good meal on
the Half Cooked meat so was much
better off than my poor horse I lay
Down on the ground to try to Sleep
my horses reins over my arm I had
snatched a few winks when some of the
men Called out the houses are on fire
some of the artillery it was siad set

꠸

November 30, 1848

90   to thank him for what he got In the
morning we went over the Battle Field
and Burried the dead. Duty now –
became very Hard on us on Duty at
Morning on Duty again at night and in
the Day we had to Patrolle the Enemys
Posistions About midday on the 27th
November we had to turn out in a hurry
the Enemy had Stole a march on us
and taken several Thousands Camels
belonging to us that were out to feed
in the Jungles in Care of their Keepers
We Galloped many miles after them
but they had them too far and a
small army between them and
us and all we got was a few
shots for our trouble and returned
to Camp tired but none the worse
on the 30th November 1848 Lord Gough
came and took Charge of the Camp
He being Commander in Chief which
at this time was between 20 and 30

December 1, 1848

91   Thousands strong 64 Guns. 12 of them Heavy ones
The first Division of the army to which I belonged
Received orders to March a one oClock morning
1st December 1848. To Wuzzerabad a Large Town
on the Banks of the river Chenab about
30 miles from Ram nuggar our strength
was 8 Thousand men and 34 Guns with
orders to Cross the river and come up on
the other side of the river so as to steal
a March on the Enemy. We arrived at the
Town of Wuzzerabad at dark on the night of the
1st having march on the 30 miles we had
no Tents and we Lay that night on the
sand on the river Edge near the Ford
and When we had got our Grog ½ pint
arrack and some Cold meat and Bread
We Lay Down to rest. but not to sleep
for the water came through the sand
and made our Cloaks wet which made
us very cold. But we Dozed off at
times and had Little sleep we were
very Glad when daylight came when

✑

December 2–3, 1848

93   as we went Halting at times and
sent out small Parties to Look for any
of the Enemy that mite show themselves
at night we Lay among some Turmots
Carrots fields of which we Eat and gave
our horses got cold meat and Bread ½ pint of
Arrack and Lay Down for the night
after placing our Guard and outPost
at Day Light got our Grog meat & Bread
and Commenced the march and about
Midday we Lay Down to rest sending –
out some Guns and our Grey Squadron
or Left Squadron to Look out for the
Enemy. We must have Laid Down
nearly an hour. I was fast asleep my
Head on my Shako my horses reins in
my swivel on the Belt. When a Private
Jack Alder shook me and said Dam
you Corporal Wake up here Comes the
Enemy and at that moment 2
round shot past very playfully by
us and away they went We were

December 2, 1848

92   we got our Breakfast Cold Meat & Bread
and ½ pint Arrack and plenty of Water
about 8.30 AM 2nd December the Enemys out
Post came out to reconnitre us but kept away
from the river They werre only about one
regiment of Them we received the order
to undress take off our Boots Draws and
Trowsers tie them round our necks and
then Mount our horses to take the Ford
which we did in file or by twos a row
of Camels above stream and a row below
us. so into the water we went and cold
it was most of it snow water from the
Cashmere mountains the river was about
1000 yards wide. Some of the horses lost
their Line and had to swim We got over
without any Lost. Drove away the Enemy
and then the Infantry Cross in Boats
with the Guns by 10 AM we had all of
us on the Enemies side of the river
and Commence our march up the side
until it got Dark feeling our way

December 3, 1848. Action at Sadalapur

94   soon into the saddle and into Troops in
a few minutes our Infantry on their feet
and in Close Column of Companies the
Artillery moveing very quietly to the Front
the Guns sent out with the Grey Squadron
had now open fire covered by the Grey
Squadron and was slowly Falling back
to us but in such Lovely order like a
feild day. Our Little army now formd
Line to meet them although we Could
see they were 4 times as many as us
We were under the Command of Major
General Sir Joseph Thackwell with his
one arm. our regiment commanded
by Lieut Col Yarbury. old *Black Jack*
as soon as the Grey Squadron joined the
regiment the Guns Formed in our Line
and continued the Fire the Infantry
Laying down in Line to escape the
Enemy Long Shot. the Left of their
Line at this time begun to outflank
ours and we were ordered to try a

December 3, 1848. Action at Sadalapur

95   Faint Charge which we did. but it had
no effect to turn their Flank we were
then ordered to throw our right back
by Echellon which was done at a Gallop
and when our Line Came to front. It
was a great supprise to the Enemy for
our right now out flanked them by Half
a mile which caused them to Halt
they Had a great number of Cavelry on
their Left which Fronted my regiment
at this time our guns was doing a
good practice. there was in our Left
front a Sugar Cane plantation which –
was filled with their Infantry and
into this our guns fired Grape and
Canister and killed a great number
as we see them Lay dead after the
Battle. our Line now begun to –
turn the Table on them for we had the
order to advance and I Could see the
9th Lancers had got across the river
Also some of the Infantry which made

❧

December 3, 1848–January 11, 1849

97   with several others . Dick Curtis. Topley
Makepiece. Baxter and one or two more
went in search of Something to Eat we
Left our horses with our comrades we
went to the Village where the poor people
put up their Hands and beged of us not
to hurt them we had our sword blades
Drawn. we didnot mean to hurt them
we only wanted food. and at Length –
we found a young cow about half
grown and drove it towards our
horses but the fool would not go so
we tied its Legs and put a pole
through them and carried it back downwards
to our Troop. The Boys had made a fire
so now came the Tale how to kill it
and cook some. But while this was
going on Ike Stag run his sword
through the Best and before it –
was dead he was cuting a Slice off
its rump we soon all fell to and
some got sticks and we toasted it

December 3, 1848. Action at Sadalapur

96 the enemy turn and retreate the sun
was jest going down. so we gave them
a few parting shots and Let them go
there were the village of So dullapore be
tween us and the enemy and the people
stood on the top of the houses to see the
Fight although the shot and shell went
over their Head backwards & Forewards
from theirs and our guns) We were told
that while the Fight was going on Lord –
Gough was Left on the other side of the
tiver with the main army about 7
miles off and could not get Boats to
get across. and it was said that he
stamped and swore and run too and
throw Like mad until they found a
Ford in the river and got to our –
relief the Battle lasted about 4 hours
our Loss was but small at night we
Biviacted on the ground nothing to eat
Nothing for our poor horses we could not
get the water.) About 9 oCk PM I

98 at the Fire and eat it half done as
so many got round the Fire with peices
some other men got some fowls some got
a goat and a sheep so in a short time
we had made a supper on meat and
we had got our grog so we took our –
horses reins put them on our belt
swivle and Lay down to sleep. I can
say I sleep well nothing desturbed in
mind or body about stealing the young
Cow. at day break next morning we
was on the move after the Enemy. Leaving
a few behind to bury the dead and
see to the wounded but when we got
near the Ford at Ramnuggar the enemy
had all moved off and was a days
march in advance of us but we con
tinued to follow up their rear and
annoy them with our skirmishers the
whole day at night we encamped about
10 mile from the Enemy but they got
on the move in the night and in

December 3, 1848–January 11, 1849

99   the morning they were all gone and
there rear Guards out of our sight
our army continued to Advance until
we came to a place named Haillah
and here we pitch our camp and
the next day Lord Gough came up
with the main army . and then we
had a Standing Camp for a Month
Duty rather hard a Great many on
Duty at the time out Laying Pickets and
in Laying Pickets and a Squadron to
reconitre Every Day for several day
the whole army to sleep in arms
But when off duty we had plenty
of Sports such as races jumping in
Sacks jumping the High Leap and
any kind of Sport that was to
be thought off the officers and the
men mixing together the officer do
not have so much pride on Service
while we Lay in this Camp we got
every thing Comfortable and plenty

January 13, 1849. Battle of Chilianwala

101   Pied & Skew Ball horses A Troop Black horses
this made the 3rd Squadron B & D
Troops all Grey horses this was the 4th
or Left Squadron which was 8 Troops or
4 Squadrons Each Troop sent out 6 men
to Skirmish from the Flanks of the Squad
ron our regiment numbered at this
time about 600 men on duty but some
of these was on rear Guard in Charge
of the Treasureres the Squadron would
be about 120 Rank and File Each when
we were in the Front of the Enemy this
day. We march until about 10 oClock in
the morning when it Sound Halt and
stood as we were when it sounded
the Halt some of us got off our horses
I had been out skirmishing and it
had not sounded for Skirmishers to
Come in although we could see our
people puting in the small Flags for
our camp ground a man named
Dick Brown had been a Little way

January 11–13, 1849

100   of it and occasionally some Bottled
Beer we march from this camp Haillah
on the 11 January 1849. and Encamped in
a pretty place plenty of Pea Fowl and the
ground well looked to and the people seemed
happy on the 12 we march again this day
most of the day in a jungle but now &
then a small village at night we encampd
on a plain and Could hear the Guns of
the Enemy as if they had been at Drill
in the Evening before sun down) On
the morning of the 13th January 1849 never
to be forgot we march at 5 AM and
with a Strong party of Cavalry
Skirmishers to the Front I was at this
time attached to the Grey Squadron although
I belonged to A Troop the Black Troop
The 3rd Kings own Light Dragoons was
as Follows that is C and H Troops were
all Bay horses the 1st on the right Squadrons
J Troop Chesnut horses G Troop Dun horses
this was the 2nd Squadron E Troop was

⁓

102   farther into the Jungle then the rest
of us and came back and said there
were a Lot of the Enemy behind the
Village but Sergt Small came out with
our Bread and grog at this time so I
told him what Brown had seen and he
went back to tell the Colonel of the regit.
but he had not Left many minutes –
when two 6 pound shot past over our
head and in the Direction of the
Staff and Lord Gough. and this got
the old mans Irish out. For in a few
minutes more Bang went the Gun at
his Lordships side in return for theirs
we not got into our Saddle when it
sound skirmishers in and the whole
army prepared for Battle we took
ground to the Left and then we see
plenty of the Enemy who had been
all the morning waiting for us
and they Came down very Close to us
not farther off than 4 or 5 hundred yards

January 13, 1849. Battle of Chilianwala

103   off most Cavelry in Front of us but
we Could see their Infantry in their
rear by this time we had been at it
about an hour it commenced about
11 OCk AM but the artillery had done
a Lot of work and still kept it up
the right of our army near 3 miles
from us had most of it at this time
but 1 oCk PM they prest one Left
centre very much and come down
in Columns of 3 or 4 Thousands strong
about ½ mile from us on our right was
HM 24 Foot next to them the 15 Sepoy
on their Left between them and us
but between these two regiment was
Captan Christies Troop of Bengal horse
artillery and the whole was in
a thick Bush in our Front was
the most plain ground, but that
had plenty of Low Bushes. The enemy
had Chose a rare place for us to
work we Could not Combine one

✺

January 13, 1849. Battle of Chilianwala

105   the 3rd nativ̆e Cavalry was on our Left
which was our Left regiment was ordered
to support the 4th Squadron and then
to retire into Line again which they
did well) The 3 Squadrons of our regit
also went into Line and covered the
24th Foot or what was Left of them
I was attached to the Grey Squadron
Well away we went Capt Unett in
the Front and Lieutn Stisted and Cornet
Gough Capt Unett Shouting come on
Boys now For it. But he was soon cut
down and so was Lieut Stisted and young
Gough was also on the ground the 2 &
first Badly wounded. the enemy Formed
a complete Wedge and we had to cut
our way through them for quiet 100
yards before there was any Clear –
ground I believe the Colonel & regit.
didnot think of seeing any of
us again But as it was 46 were
killed and wounded) of the men Rank

104   regiment to the other. so close was the
Jungle in places about 2 oCk PM there
was a Great deal of Fighting about the
centre H M 14th Light Dragoons went 3 ries
about and went back into the rear right
by and over the General Hospital and one
wing of the 9th Lancers but they came
about again and back into the Line
this left a great opening in the entre
and the Enemies Cavalry come down –
on 24th Foot and poor fellows how
they did fight with the Bayonet but
the regiment about 450 men and 19
officers killed and the Queens Colours Taken the
Troop of Guns of Capt Christies was –
also taken from us and nearly all killed
Captain Christies was killed and the
poor 15 Sepoys stood until they were
nearly all killed at this time my –
regiment was ordered to advance the
4th Squadron to Charge the enemy right
Flank which was geting round us the

❧

106   and file 26 killed and 20 wounded in
the Charge and most of that 20 died I
had a Bayonet wound in the right arm
as we Cut our way back to the rgit
a Slight Flesh wound near the elbow
I have no other belief but that the Fellow
would have shot me as my horse was
plungeing and my sword in the Fellows
shoulder but Sergeant Wild Coming up
he cut off the Back of his head and
down he went Wild said come on
Jack and away we went about 7 of
us and got safe to the regiment when
I got a Bandage put round my arm
and joined the regiment what men
got back got Back 3 or 5 or 6 & 7
at the time some one way and some
Came another I can never forget this
charge such a mass to get through
how many of us did get back was a
wonder. Capt. Unett and Lieut
Stisted was Peesented to the Queen

January 13, 1849. Battle of Chilianwala

107 After they Come to England for their
Gallant Conduct. The Battle Lasted
until Dark at night when both armys
Stayed on the ground and the killed
and wounded Lay were they Fell
our small army Lost about 2 Thousand
and the Enemy it was said Lost near
5 Thousand so what with men and
horses the place was coverd with dead
and dying that night I prayed to
god that I mite never see that sight
again In the night it came on to
rain which did not improve our very
nice Condition but we had to put up
with it and I am proud to say the
men didnot grouble about it some
times they would wish they had some
Grog. I forgot to say above that we
took 12 of their Guns and they took
6 of ours Capt Christies Troop was nearly
all killed I believe 2 or 3 men and a boy
were not killed. The 24 Foot suffered

January 14–17, 1849

109 All the rain which had washed the
wounds as White as Veal some had
died but we could do no more than
what we did. Some had to be Left
to their fate about 10 oCk AM we come
Back to the regiment and got our –
Breakfast Bread & Coffee and then we
Mounted our horses to reconitre the
Position of the Enemy so as to know
how Matters stood after which Lord
Gough order a few of the regiments
to Change their Position and the –
Infantry had to throw up intrenchment
to watch the Enemy as we were but
a Short distance from Each other
the rain continued to come down for
Several Day which made the Camp
in a very bad state mud in every
place on the night of the 17th there was
such a stire in the Camp about
midnight a Elaphant had become
unmanageable and got Loose and

108   very much I believe their Loss was
450 men 19 officers and one of the Colours
of the regiment. the 2nd Bengal europeans
regiment Also suffered very Badly their
Loss was nearly as bad as HM 24th Foot
The 15th regiment Sepoys was nearly cut up
few men Left one of their officers come
to us and asked the Colonel to Send some
Help but he dare not move the regiment
without an order. Well as I said night
Closed the sad sight and the rain
Come down as if to Cleans us from
our past Sin. for I verily believe
man was not made by God to Kill
his fellow man. It has become the
order of man since by our Artifical
Life and keep the Rank of Nations
The next morning I went out with
James Regan to find his Brother twin
who was killed. We burried him and
many more that was found some of
the men had lived the night through

110   run through the whole Camp which
Caused great Trouble to the Soldiers
our horses broke Loose and so did horses
of other regiments and some of the –
artillery and the night being very dark
we could not get them but morning
came and most of them was got to –
geather at Daylight I was on main
Guard and what with the uproar and
the rain the main Guard Tent fell
down on us that was inside and
the men swore the Camp had gone
mad and would not put the Tent
up again so we sat and Laid –
about until all was wet to the skin
the new Guard Came on duty at
9 oClock in the morning. so we got
to the lines of the regiment and
at 11 oClock we had to start and
bring in a Convey of Corn about
3 thousand went on the road to
meet the Corn as it was thought

January 17–February 6, 1849

111   the Enemy would try and interupt it
on the way but we got it in safe
duty still continued very hard the
Infantry suffered very much as they
had to Lay in the intrenchment
and as there had been a great Lot
of rain it made it very uncomfortable
But when the Weather Cleared up
and got Dry it made the place
much better but it never was a
very Clean Camp so many dead
Laying about not Burried and
Dead horses and Camels all made
it worse. True the Birds and
Jackals Eat up a Deal but then –
there was a Lot Laying about
to make a very bad smell we
got our rations regular and I
must say very good under the
circumstances on the 6th February
we went out to reconitre the Enemy
and Changed a few shots but

February 7, 1849

113   Carbines at the advance I met Sir Genl
Joseph Thackwell walking in the
Jungle his Black Size Leading his
horse. When he said Sergeant you can go
go further into the Jungle as I
have jest come up and see nothing
of the Enemies out Post I think
they have been taken in so I gave
the order Left incline and we
went about 150 yards farther into
the Jungle towards the Enemy but
we had not got more than Half mile
before we came right to the Enemies
out Lying Picquet and between them
and their 2 Verdettes on the Look
out but at this point the Jungle
was very thick. But the enemy
showed the White of their heels to
us they jumped on their horses
and road off at a gallop W. Taylor
wanted to fire at them but my
orders was not to fire at them if

February 7, 1849

112   only with the mounted Party of
our regiment I dont think there
were anyone killed or wounded
on the 7th February I had to Patrolle
the front of the Virdetts of the Enemys
Lines and when a short way down
we had to go about 3 miles in their
Front to see what we could and –
report the same to Coln Foredice of
the Staff corp as at times their sentry
would Fire at ours in the day time
they were only about 2 hundred
yards from the Virdette of the
9th Lancers the Jungle in which
we had to go Through was very thick
in places and we had to march in
single file I had 4 Privates with
me William Taylor 1st Called Little
Billy Taylor as we had 4 Wm Taylors
in the Troop Richard Brown 2nd and
Julias Cooper 3rd and Thomas Thornit
Last I was on the left we had our

❧

114   they fired at us we was not to return
the fire but to march slowly on our
way and report the same to Col. Foredice
on our arrival at Coln Fordice Camp
I found he had been watching of us
with a Glass and asked me why I
went so Close to the Enemy and
into their outpost when I told
him what Genl Thackwell said but he
only Laughed at the mistake I then
return with the 4 men to my Camp
But I found on Conversation with
some of the 9th Lancers that their
verdetts was fired at very off
during the time they were on out
post duty. Camp life now became
very hard on duty night and day
and had to reconnitre the Enemy
which kept us always in the
saddle and our boots on our feet
and sword and Belts on) our feet
swoled very much as we could not

February 7–17, 1849

115   be allowed to change our boots for
only a short time before we was
mounted again as we had to take
Charge of the Camels while they
feed in the Jungle on the Bush
and as there were several Thousand
it took a Deal of Trouble there was
parties of other Cavelry regiments
as well as ours Native Cavelry &
all took part of this duty the
Infantry was worse off as our
Camp was partly entrenched round
they had to lay in the entrenchment
on Duty which got half full of
water when it rained which –
made it bad and caused a great
many Deaths with them and
the Camp near the tents was
very bad and the smell very
offensive more so when the Sun
come out they continued in
this way until about the beginning

February 20, 1849

117   Town I believe it to be the finest
Town in the Dooab We closed our
Line in his Front about 1½ miles
apart and here we waited until
part of the Moultan army joined
us on the Evening of the 20th Febrary 1849
the men of the 10th Foot and 60 Rifles
and some artilery men and they
all had plenty of money and gave
it away to us as if it was of no
use we got grog some way or other
and had a jolly Evening had a
Song told Each other of our Late
Battles. But at 10 P.M. all our
Comfort come to an End an order
Came round the Tents for the men
to join their own regiments as the
Camp would move at 5 oCk in the
Morning to Atact the Enemy so we
had a parting Glass shuck hands
and parted some of the Brave Lads
for ever. there was but Little sleep

February 17, 1849

116   of February 1849 when it was reported
that the Fortress of Moultain had been
taken by the British Troop and that
part of their army had been driven
out and was making towards us this
Caused Shere Sing to move his army
more to the Left. When we put our
right wing back and extended our
Left for about 2 miles so as to
Cover their movements on the 17th Feby
we went out to reconitre their –
Possition when we Come against
a Party of the Enemy when a Sharp
Fire was opened on both sides but
to very little good as a Lot of
ammunition was waisted and only
to end in smoke But one of the
Enemys Match Lock Balls struck my
Saddle which was a Little to Close
to be pleasant. Shere Sing now alterd
his plans and moved his Army
to the Town of Goojerat A Large

February 20–21, 1849

118   that night we Lay on the ground –
talking of home old Comrades dead
and the Coming day and who –
would see the Sun again set I.
fell asleep but had not slept long
when it was down with the tents
and get mounted which took us
about 20 minutes. The Army soon
got together and at day light there
we was face to face with the Enemy
The line of our army covered about
6 miles of the Front in a zig-zag
sort of order the 14th Light Dragoons
on the right with the 4th Native Lancers
The 9th Queen Lancers on the Left with
Capt Jacobs native Bombay Irregulars
and Infantry and Artillery filling
up the Intervals 3 Light Dragoons
Left Centre with the Scinde irregular
horse who carry machlock Guns and
very Long Lances a Brave Lot of men
in our Front Lay in ambush in a

February 21, 1849. Battle of Gujrat

119   Corn feild that was about 2 feet
High Jest Enough to cover them was
the 60 rifles. The Fine Town of Goojrat
in Front of the Centre of the army
About 7 AM our Line begun to
advance towards the Enemys Line and
we very shortly could here the Guns
on the right hard at work on both
sides we closed up to about 800
yards. about 10AM I took a dispach
to the Colonel of the 10th Foot with orders
to advance and take the Town in
Flank they were about 3 miles from
us I found them all Lying down
waiteing for orders they told me that
the 14th Light Dragoons had charged
Led by Lieut Coln Lockwood 3rd Light
Dragoons he was a acting Brigadedier
that day of the right Cavelry Brigade
As soon as I gave the Dispach to the
Coln of the 10th Foot he Looked at it
and called out Fall in 10th we got

Ǳ

February 21, 1849. Battle of Gujrat

121   is no use ducking if there is one
for you. I think you will get it
which made us Laugh. But Draper
was a nice Little officer and a perfect
gentleman he replied I cant help it
Colonel. Jest at that moment a 9 Pound
shot struck the ground at the Colonels
horses heels but Coln White did not –
move or Look round his Brave old
Face never moved with his White hair
round it he only said stiddy men stidy
make much of your horses men. I
think there was not a man or a
officer who knew Colonel White
that didnot Love him such a happy
Face and so kind to all. But he
could be sever if he Liked. Jest
at this time we was ordered to advance
covered by skirmishers which we did
and close up to the enemy and
some of our boys Fell. But we were
Laying a Trap for some of their –

120   something to do at Last. I turned to
go back to my regiment. When I heard
the Colonel give the order forward 10th
and away they went in Line but I
had not got Half a mile when I
heard the Enemies Guns at them and
the Sepoys was following up to their
support when I looked back I struck
my horse into a canter as so many
of the other regiments asked me
questions I could not tell them
but by the time I got back to my
regiment the Fireing was coming
up the whole Line and in a very
few minutes the round 6 and 9
Pound shot and shell was flying
over our heads. Captain Draper of
of ours every shot that went over
his head made him duck down his
head. When Colonel White who
who had seen the Peninsular fights
and at Waterloo said Captain it

122   artillery who followed us back as
we retired back by alturnit Squadrons
covered by Skirmishers their artillery
followed us and unlimbered about
150 yards from the Corn feild were
Lay the 60 rifles on the ground as
soon as they got the 6 guns to practice
on us we halted and showed a
Front and sounded Skirmishers in
up got the 60 riffles and killed every
man of that Troop and then we
went up and spiked the Guns and
Left them. The Battle was now
at its Highest and the air had
become filled with shop shell and
smoke. Trumpets were sounding Drums
Beating Bugles sounding Colonels and
other officers hallowing when all
of a sudden came the order for the
3rd Light Dragoons to Charge I could
see the 9th Lancers and the Black
irregular Cavelry doing the same

February 21, 1849. Battle of Gujrat

123   But we did not get much at them this
time as they made a quick movement
back into their Line we got among
some of their horse and killed a
few my horse run against one
of theirs and knocked him down
it hurt my Leg very much as it –
struck his horses shoulder. I put my
Sword into the man and went on
with the rest. we come to an halt
on the Left of the Town of Goojerat
When their Guns began to give it us
again hot. But in a Short time we
advanced again at a Trot. and
in Front of us was a Long hedge
of Prickle Pear a sort of Cacktus plant
about 5 or 6 feet high this plant grow
very Large in that country the Enemies
Guns was behind the Hedge and it
was very thick but at it we went
and through it too the pricks stucken
into man and horse. Jest over this

✒︎

February 21, 1849. Battle of Gujrat

125   we went I got on the raskle again
one of my reins was broken I tied
them togeather it sounded skirmishers
to the Front and we Changed our
Direction to the Left and the men
out skirmishing had some sharp
work for about Half an hour when
it Sounded Skirmishers in and
back they Come. I could now see
that the whole of the Cavelry
was to the Front as far as I –
could see right and Left it now
seemed as the Battle was drawing
to a close as we Could see the enemy
in Full retreat and Lord Gough
Came down the Front with his staff
his Leg was bleeding a Little below
his knee a piece of shell had struck
him afterwards I heard. The old
man said thank you 3rd Light
a Glorious Victory men. As soon
as he had been down the Cavelry

124   about 40 yards was a Large hole made
for their cooks to put slush into and
my horses Fore Legs went into this hole
and turned completely over with me
and I lay with my right Leg on my
Carbine and my horse lay on my right
Leg I seased my Pistle for the Enemies
Foot was all over the place. I heard
Tom Taylor say Pearman shot but I
knew better. My Comrade William
Makepiece came back to me as the
regiment halted about 200 yards off
and said shake the dam reins and make him
get up Jack) he kept Cantering round
me with his sword and kept off the
Straglin Foot of the Enemy at Last my
horse got up and Let my Leg Loose I
found I was not hert much. Makepiece
said here is one of their horses out here
and I made for it but Captain John
Sullivan came and said my horse
was caught at the regiment so off

✎

126   Front we got the orders to advance
in Persueing order the whole of the
regiments 6 or 7 Thousand Covering
8 or 10 mile Front when in Persueing
order 3 yards apart. When we Persued
the Poor Flying Devels to the Banks
of the Indus river. It was now
nearly Dark but the right Division
of the army was ordered to Cross the
river which they did in the night
and Followed the routed enemy
as Long as there was any Left
they then continued their march
as far as Pershore where they Halted
my regiment with the remainder of
the army returned to Goojerat where
our Tents was Left But was to
much worn out to pitch tents so we
got something to eat from the Cooks
and Lay down for the rest of the
night I had been 20 hours in the
Saddle and cannot say the miles

February 22, 1849

127   we rode the next morning we was
so stiff we could not do anything and
I was very sore from my Fall and
my right Leg was very much bruised
but we were to have a standing camp
and Live in Clover as the Enemy was
entirely Cut up and peace was to
be settled at Lahore as soon as the
Dobar could be held by the Govenor
general who had been sent we remain
some weeks at Goojerat until the Enemy
had been sent back and had to surrender
the Guns and all arms of war to the
Commander in chief Sir Hugh Gough
we had very Good times at Goojerat
in the afternoon after the Battle 22
February 1849 myself Privates Makepeace
Fke Stagg. Wm Penfold and one or two
others went into the Town where was
many more Soldiers of other regiments
to Look at the place But we come
accross an old money changer and

February 22–24, 1849

129   White Body a Beauty) Makepeace said
you cant ride him Sergeant I said
I could the Black Size or Groom said
nay nay saib nay puckerroe. (*steal*
But I got on his back for a ride and
the rascale run away with me but
I managed to get him to our Camp
Captains Draper and Overy of C & H
Troops see me ride him in and said
Pearman where did you get the arrab
I told them we found it on the edge
of the Jungle. Overy said what do
you want for it I said two Flask
of Grog and 100 rupees £10. after some
time he gave us one Flask of Grog &
the 100 rupees and I am sorry to
say we spent the money in more
grog which did us much harm
on the 24th February my Birth day
I had been out mounted to reconnitre
which we did when on picquet when
we see a man with a two Bullock –

128   made him tell us where he had put
his money but he would not say until
we showed him our pistols when he gave
us a Bag of Gold about one quart with silver
Stagg put it on his shoulder and we
was marching off with our Loot when
we was met by one of the officers
belonging to our prize agents
he said what have you got there Soldiers in
that Bag. So Stagg droped it on the
ground and said Look Sir. When he
marked a ↑ Broad arrow on it and –
said bring it along but we walked
off and Left him to do what he liked
with it when we heard no more about it
he could not tell to what regiment
we belonged as we were in White
shirts & Draws and puggerie Cap
we went down a street to the Bazzar
where we see a Fine arab horse tied
down with Head and heel ropes
with pink main and tail and

130   Hackney and two chest of rupees
Johnny Grady ask him where it come
From he said it was sent from the
Town so we took it and filled our
Holster pipes on the saddle and collected
some Gun powder that was Laying
about Left by the Enemy in Lumps
when in retreat and blew the rest
up and when the Bullocks and man went
awaywe heard no more of him this
was the only way to get prize money
for the Company only gave us Six
months Battle £3.16." in all But
we made what we could and done
very well if we had not spent
it in a very foolish way I mean
Drink which Take away the reason after
a few Days the Prize agents had got
all that was worth having but never
the Less the Division of the army that
came down from Moultan Fort had
Plenty of Money. Belts round their

February 24–April 7, 1849

131   Body and the waist of their Trowsers
Lined with Gold and Braces Lined up
and over the Shoulder and although
the 10th Foot and 32 & 60th Regiments had
been searched many times by the Prize
agents and there officers still they had
plenty of money and the men robed
one and another when Drunk very much
which Continued some weeks even after
the army had been removed to Meen
Meer the Great Parade ground and
Barracks at Lahore belonging to Ranjit
Sign and about 2 miles from the city of
Lahore the Captical of the Paunjaub
The 3rd Company of 4 Battalion of Foot
artillery Bengal Troop had to bring down
the Treasure and they Burried a
Quantity of the Treasure near unto
Lahore and begun to sell some when
it Came to the Generals Ears and a
Search was made a woman of the
14th Light Dragoons split Counsel and

February 24–April 7, 1849

133   I knew the man well he was afread
to keep it for fear of being Flogged so
there the things remain. Poor Williams
after he was Flogged got an Exchange
into my regiment 3rd Lt Dragoons he gave
100 Pounds to a man named Wm Walker to
Change regiments which they got done
Walker had a Black Wife and wanted
to stay in the Country. When we came to
England Williams was Promoted to the
armory Sergt 3rd Lt Dragoons and Died at
Exter in Devonshire from the Effects
of Drink he always had plenty of
money and spent it very freely with
his Comrades he was well beliked by
them I fired over his grave poor Fellow
Many an officer as taken more in other
ways and not got Flogged our own
Commander in Chief had many things
given to him by Marah rajah Gooloob
Singh and I think as they were our
enemy that was anything but right

132   the 3 company of artillery was all placed
under arrest officers and all as all had
a finger in the pie the 14th Dragoons and
some Sepoy soldiers had to do duty over
them for some time but they never found
the Treasure and I have no dought it is
there to this day as we were taken away
from Lahore and no one was Left and
the men of the 3 Company never split
The 10th Regt of Foot had the most money
Armery Sergeant Williams of the 10th was
supposed to have got the Gold Hilted sword
belonging to the Marah Rajah of Moultan set
with Dimonds they search for it but
never got it They tried him for Plunder
reduced him to a Private soldier and
then Tried him again and sentenced
him to 100 Lashes which he poor Fellow
got every one of them. The Fellow Gold
Hilted Sword was broaken from the
Sword and Gold Hilt and Dimonds
Threw in a Well at Lahore by a Private

134   the Poor Soldier must not take anything
from the Enemy. After a Short time
the arms of the Enemy were Collected and
sent away under an Escort to Lahore and
the rest of the army followed and we
arrived at the old Sikh Parade ground
Meen Mear a fine Flat place would Hold
50,000 men in camp at this place we were
halted for some time and Genl. Gough
Left us and Genl Sir Charles Napier took
the Command of the army and we
were reviewed by him after we was
drawed up in Close Collum of Squadrons
also the 14th Light Dragoons. When Genl.
Napier said 3rd Light Dragoons I am
Proud to see you. you Look a fine
Lot of young men and the Charge you
made this day was similar to one I
see made by the regiments when at
Salamanca I say again I am Proud
to have Command of such men. he then
turned to the 14th Light Dragoons and

February 27–April 7, 1849

135   said 14th Kings own I am proud to
       see you for with the regiment I served
       in Pictons Light Brigade and I see
       in Front of me men with Soldierly
       Faces Broad Chest and Long and power
       ful Limbs and if you had been
       properly handled on the 13th January
       the Disgrace that now hangs over the
       regiment could not have taken place
       at this a young Trumpeter by name
       John Springit about 18 years old
       rode up to the Genl and said General
       our Colonel is a Coward. Genl Napier
       said make that man a prisoner
       which was done. and after a
       Little more talk we was dismissed
       to our Tents. about an hour after
       this as we set in our tents we heard
       the report of a Pistol and in a
       few minutes Came the report that
       Colonel King of the 14th Light Dragoon
       had blown out his Brains which

∽

April–September 20, 1849
December 6, 1849

137   So weddings went on merryly as they
       are articles that would not keep
       4 or 5 a day some women in that
       Country have several husbands before
       they are very old. I knew one that
       married the six husband in the regt
       to which I belonged. she had been in
       several regiments she came from
       the 75 Foot to us. We remained at
       Umballa until September 1850 When we
       received orders to march no one seemed
       to know were we was going to at this
       time at Last on the 20th Sepbr we march
       out of Umballa in the Direction of
       of the Sutlej river having very easy –
       Marches and enjoyed ourselves much
       on the way never very tired but we
       soon found we was distined for
       the Paunjaub which we came on the
       6th December and Crossed the river at
       Ferrozepoor and then marched to Lahore
       were we remained several day to

April 7, 1849

136 was True. we were all very sorry that
he did that as we got no explanation
what made the regiment retire in the
way it did. how ever John Springit
was released from being a prisoner
he afterwards died at umballa from
the Effects of Drink. Soon after this
our division march in route for
Umballa which place we reached
on the 7th April 1849 our regiment
taken the 4 right Barracks the 14th
Lt Dragoons the 4 Left Barracks the –
centre Barracks was Left for the married
Sergeants and the Sergeants mess room
and the temprey Stables was made
also into married quarters and the
Canteens. There was many widows
and some young unmarried Girls
14 years of age. who had to get married
or go off pay at that age and the
widows to go off pay at 6 months
from the Death of their husbands

❧

December 1849

138 refresh the horses we then crossed
the river Ravei into the Jellendar doab
and when we arrived at Jellender we
stayed 3 day with regiment 29th Foot and
played a Cricket match and the non
Commissioned officers gave a ball to
us as our women and Families were
with us. and a Splendid supper &
altogeather it was a good turn out
But one of our married men named
George freind had a very narrow escape
of his life as he returned to Camp at
about 2 oClock in the morning and
about ½ mile from the Barracks he –
was Caught in a Lassue by a Tug –
or Highway Robber but he put up his
arm and the noose went over his head
and arm so he slipped it off the next
day we again Commenced our march
towards Wuzzerabad and then on to
Seal Cote an open Jungle about 20 Miles
from Cashmere. Majah Rajah Goolob

December 1849–May 1850
[May–August 1851]

139   Sing came to see us and we escorted
him back to Cashmere were we staid some
14 or 15 day . only one Squadron I went with
it and a very fine country Cashmere
is. We went back to Seal Cote and then
begun to clear the Jungle away and the
24th foot began to build Barracks and the
native Soldiers also. I had some good
Sport at this place with my Gun as
there was plenty of wild fowl of all
sorts. and such a quantity of small Snakes
some to be found in the tents every
Morning. in May 1850 We left Seal Cote
to go to Wuzzerabad where there were
some tempery Barracks which we were
to occupy and about the End of May
I was taken with a pain in my right
side which got worse every day one
morning I had Paraded the men for
duty and took them to the Guard
Mounting as I came back I
got nearly home when I had to set

❧

[May–August 1851]

141   blood tingled what people call having
the pins and needles I felt quite –
helpless. but I felt two sharp pricks
one in Each arm. and in a short
time I opened my eyes and see Doctor
Trousdel leaning over me with is Gold
Lace Coat and Gold Epuilettes on he had
run from a Dress mess dinner to
attend to me. When I opened my eyes
he said Pearman dont speak dont
move. I again shut my eyes and lay
very quiet he had bled me in both
arms. he didnot Leave me for an hour
the next morning he came and I was
Cuped and he had on my side many dozen
of leaches and the day after that a
Blister over the whole of the sore places
I then remained for about 12 day my
side a little better but still very bad
the Blister had nearly healed up when
our head Doctor came Dr Henderson by
name and they both Examined me

140   down I was so ill after a short time
I got to my room and Laid down. Sergt
Cooper came and asked me what was
the matter with me I said I was very
ill he then sent me to the hospital and
I was seen by Mr Harding an halfcast
then compounder for the regiment and
he gave me some medicine about 5 oCk
PM Doctor Trousdel see me and gave
me more medicine. When about 7 oClock
PM They all thought I was dying and
sent again for Doctor Trousdel at this
time the men was standing round
my cot and several said I was
dead but I knew better Micky Caughlin
said I shall send word to his Troop
which he did stateing that I died at
7 oClock PM. I didnot think I was
dying although my sight was nearly
gone I could see the men as if I were
looking through a thick fog I felt no
pain my body felt all over as if the

142   and Came to the conclusion that to
save my Life my side must be opened
and a small apsess cut away they left
me with this consolation the following
day Doctor Trousdel asked me if I was
willing to have my side opened as he
said my life could not be saved without
doing it and perhaps not then he
was a Scotch-man and a very plain
spoken man four days after this I
was taken into a room at the End
of the Hospital where Doctors Trousdel
and Dr. De Arsy perform the opperation
which Lasted about ¼ of an hour
I was then Carried to a bed in the
Hospital with the other men a Silver
pipe was in my side for some time and
served to carry off the Discharge from
the Liver. When the pipe was taken
out I had a Seaton put into my
side under neath the place were
the pipe was. the Seaton was as Large

October 1852
[May–August 1851]

143   as a tobacco pipe and this was
kept in for several months. four
months I was Laid in my back and
Eight places Came through my skin
which had to be dressed by lifting me
up on Doubled up Sheets when I was
able to walk about I was allowed
to Leave the hospital for a walk in
the morning and Evening and as I
got better I had to ride on an Elephant
and at Last on a Camel and then
I had my horse to go out where I
liked in the Cantonments they were
very kind to me and gave me every
endulgence I was Eleven months –
from my duty about the time I
got well the regiment got orders
to return home to England and –
we commenced our march as soon
as the Cold season set in of 1852
about the beginning of October we had
our horses for about 3 weeks march

✤

October 1852–February 1853

145   Some sport the officers Shooting wild
fowl which we got our share off we
had a Gun on a Swivel a gun with
a Large Mouth carried two or 3 pounds
of shot and this was at the Head of
the Boat on the Swival and when
we came across a Lot of water Fowl
which are very numerous on the Indus
this Gun was fired and then the
officers got into the Boat and killed
with small Guns what was wounded
and got them into the Boat and
when we stoped at night we had
a feast on these occasions we see
many sights on the Indus some of
the old places Left by Alexander the
Great at one place there were a plain
a sort of raised platform of Lime
and Earth beat together and in
good preservation said to be his
Counsel table in his Standing –
Camp when on the Indus with

October 1852–February 1853

144   and then they were taken away and
sent to other regiments in the country
and we staid in tents Several day
until two Flat Bottomed Boats were
got ready and these had to be towed
along by two Steam tugs into these –
Boats we were packed Like pigs at a
market in a pen at night on the Boat
I was in 25 men had no room to
Lye down on the decks no beds was
alowed as they would have been to
hot some times in the day we were
alowed to stretch our Legs on the
Banks for an hour we had made
about 200 miles in this way. when the
men grumbled so much that the officer
in Charge got a tent to hold 30 men
and this was put up every night
for that number to Lay in as we
didnot travel at night in this
way we Came 800 miles down the
river Indus. Some days we had

$\sim$

3 February 1853
[5 February 1853]

146   Fleet at Last we reach Kurrachee in
the Bombay Presedincy on the 3rd February
1853 and about the End of the Month
we embarked in the Ship the Duke
of Argyll an old wooden ship very
slow but very comfortable she could
stand rough weather without your
being much tost about the regiment
took 3 ships to bring us home our
ship called at the Cape of good hope
where we took in more fresh water
and Stores and I went on shore –
with others and to Change our rupees
into english money but at the Cape
they were 2 pence Less Value to us
then in India but we had to Loose
it in India a ruppee is to the Soldier
2s/½ but at the Cape they would only
give us 1/10½d for the rupee and in
England 1/9½ for the rupee so they had
us always but it did not matter
much as Soldiers are like the Sailors

February–June 1853

147   when they come home what they
       dont spend in drink the sharks
       steal that are always on the Look
       out at Chatham the last place that
       god made and that is why it is
       peopled with such a sort on our
       arrival in the Channel I was on
       watch and when near Dover it was
       geting Light I saw what I thought was
       the stars going out but the sailor
       on watch at the port Cat head said it
       was the Lamps being put out at Dover
       I went to the ships ganway and
       hollowed down the hole to the men
       in their Hammoks. There is Dover
       in sight when up they Came in
       their shirts and there was no geting
       them Down again until they had
       seen dover at Dover we Lay too as
       we had to be medically Examined
       before being allowed up the river
       and then the arbour master

✒

June 27, 1853

149   Children poor things – on the 27th
       1853 Monday the Custom house
       officers came on board to see what
       we had got they made a search of
       the ship and then the officers and
       then the men and all our Kits also
       but we took them in after all as we
       Exspected it would be so. But the
       Custom officer Brought most of our Cigars
       themselves I sold one 300 Cinsurah
       Cigars at 1 penny each they only Cost
       me 1 rupee 12 annas about 3s/6 in
       English money. by the time this was
       over it was 11 o'clock and Gravesend
       was full of Fathers Mothers Brothers
       Sisters Sweethearts and hundreds
       of Girls and thives we commenced
       to Land and got on shore but it was
       hard work to keep the men from the
       drink so many people kept bringing
       it to them at Last we got into the
       Train for Chatham all standing so

June 25, 1853

148   allowed us to proceed to gravesend
which place we reached on the night
of the 25 June Saturday 1853 we Lay
there all sunday as we were not allowed
to Land on Sunday it was a fine day
but seemed very Cold to us I thought
I never was so cold and with my Cloak
on but the pleasure steam boats from
London came down with the roses of old
England Dressed in White they threw
their Pocket Hankerchiefs to us and some
flowers as the Boats went round us
and kissed their Hands but they were
not allowed very Close. The Bum boats
Came along side and sold us things
a Lot of roughs if you Let them
have your money before you got hold
of the article you never got it at all
I gave a man in a boat nearly a new
Coat and trowsers made in Cashmere of
Camel hair for a Loaf of Bread & about
one/lb of Chees and most of that I
[added later] Gave the

❧

June–August, 1853

150   many friends and all as Close as we Could
stand women Girls and all and when
we got to Chatham we were taken to
the Casemates for our quarters and
then Left to our selves to be robed
for on that very night several of the
men Lost their medles and money
we remained at Chatham about
6 weeks which was a continual seen
of Drinken from 70. 80. or 90. prisoners
to be taken before the Colonel every
morning for being absent and
Drunk while at Chatham the
regiment being nearly 700 men with
the Depot from Maidstone it was
opened to give Volenteers to any of
the Light and heavy Cavelry for the
men that Volenteered they were to receive
51.10.0 and about 360 volenteered and
that kept up the Drink most of these
men Volenteered to the regiments going
out to the Crimean. We at Last

August 1853–April 1854

151   got the order to go to Exeter in
Devonshire I was sent with 3 others
to Bath to get Billets for the regiment
which Came by Train But a many
of the men had gone to other regit
to Collect horses as the regiments at
home and at Ireland gave us so
many each as they could spare to
give us a start we got about 150
horses in this way the remainer
we got young ones and trained
ourselves while at Exter the Crimear
was was Declared and the 8th Hussars
Came to Exeter to us and we played
them off to Plymouth to embark
we now recevied orders to march to
Manchester and when there the Scotch
Greys came and stayed a week with
us and then Embarked at Liverpool
at this time our duty was very
hard training recruits and young
horses we could not get them ready

❧

March 1856–March 1857

153   any more staff appointments made
as there would be a reduction in
the armt of 20.000 men. When I
heard this it made me very much
dissatisfied with the army after
the hard work I had so I
made up my mind to Leave if they would
Let me which they did after a great
deal of Trouble by my paying to them
£5–"–" after all my hard service
But I Left the regiment in disgust
in February 1857 and on the 16th
March 1857 I joined the Buckinghamshire
Police at Aylesbury and on the 7th may
I was ordered to a Station and went
out as Groom and Lockup Keeper
to Superintendent Bragg at Steeple Claydon
where I remain until June 1859
when I was Promoted to Acting Sergt
and sent to Long Crendon Bucks until
in September of that year I was sent
on Detective duty to find the writer

1854–March 1856

152   fast Enough I went to Burnley and
had 60 old soldiers with me and we were
Drilling all Day and then we Could
not get Enough plenty of Recruits but
we had to make Soldiers of them in
Six weeks poor Boys they went out to
Turkey like Lambs to be Sloughtered as
they Could not ride but they had to
go in March 1856 I had to go to Sandhurst
College to assist to Drill the Gentlemen
Cadets and soon after I got there
the Riding Master Captain Ward broke
his Leg and Left me in Charge of
the Riding school altogether a Lance
Sergeant of the 9th Lancers Mathews by
name Came from Canterbury to help me
I worked very hard in the Riding
school at Sandhurst and was there
Promised a Staff appointment but
when the Crimear War was over
the Duke of Cambridge the commander
in Chief said there would not be

——

154   of a Threatening Letter sent to PC
David Flinn Stationed at North
Crawley in which Letter it stated he
would shoot him also a Magistrate
named Devid Selve Lowdes of Bucks
I Dressed ragged and had a small
Parcel of writeing paper to sell and
some times I beg but was 3 weeks
before I could get a Clew but in
october I found a Gipsey by name
Thomas Saunders was Sleeping in
a stable at the Swan Public house
at Sherrington Bucks. and with the
assistance of the Police Constable at
that place I got the Landlord to
Let me also sleep in the stable by
makeing him believe I was hard up
in the morning we both got up when
it rained and was very cold and
we went into the Tap room and
I called for a pint of Beer which we
had together near the Fire we began

155   to talk of various things when I asked
him if he could write me a Letter
to a comrade that had deserted his
regiment and was then at Buckingham
he said he would we then both went
to the Windsor Castle Public house at
Sherrington near Newport Pagnell –
the Landlady supplied me with the
Paper & ink and some more Beer &
Bread and Chees which I Paid her for
She had a baby in her arms which I
wanted her to sell to me but she was
very Indignant. I only did this so as
to draw her attention to Saunders while
he was writeing the Letter I Thore the
paper in half sideway and raged
and gave her the half I did not want
then and asked her to keep it for
me as I should want to have another
Letter wrote. But realy that she mite
Produce it as a Witness that saunders
wrote the Letter for me on the other

157   Many a Soldiers tale of India and the
Campaigns I had been in After the
Trial was over they made me go to
the Bull Inn Aylesbury and have
Dinner with them and they Laughed at
my wanting to bye the Baby and
so did the Judge smile. After this I
was made a full Sergeant. I was then
stationed at Long Crendon. I went on
several other Cases as Detective and
was very successful and in January
1862 I was Promoted to Second Class
Inspector and sent to take Charge of
Great Marlow which place I become
very fond of it was a nice home &
a good Garden In 1863 I went as a
Detective with Sergt. Story to Stoke Goldington
where Lord Carrington had a Farm Burnt
and all the ricks the young man that
did it enlisted for a Soldier and
gone to Tilbury Fort he had been home
on Furlough he was apprehended

156   half when I should want her evedence
then I put the letter in my Pocket and
went to Newport Pagnell & See Inspector
Shepherd and the Magistrate it was
bench day and they made out a –
warrant for his apprehension and I
took it to Finn Police Constable at North
Crawley for him to find Saunders and
apprehend him which he did that
night at Bedford when Saunders –
see me and Found I was a Police
Constable he opened his eyes and looked
at me and so did the Landlady when
she brought the half sheet of my paper
and gave her evedence – Saunders –
was Committed for trial and had to
wait 5 months and Some day before
it Come on when he was sentenced
to 9 months more. A Great number
of the people of North Crawley come to
hear the Trial as I had Lodged at
several Public houses and told them

158   [added later] in the Fire case I got 5£ reward
on our evidence by a warrant and
brought to Aylesbury where he was
Tried and got 15 years transportation
After this I was promoted to 1st Class
Inspector in January 1864 and sent to take
Charge of the men employed at Eton College
and the Street and here I remained –
until I tendered my resignation to
the Chief Constable being 62½ years of
Age and at the October Quarter Sessions
of 1881 I was granted a pension
from the Supperannuation fune of
£69=6=8 per year I was 17 years
and 9 months stationed at Eton College
and on my retirement Presented me
with a Testimonial in Velom with
the words – To John Pearman of Eton
We the Inhabitants of Eton desire to
Convey to you on your retirement as
Inspector of Police for the past 18
years) Our appreciation of the faithful
manner, you fulfilled that office

159   and beg your acceptance of the
accompanying Purse of money
That your future be blessed
with all the good this world can
afford is the sincere wish of the
subscribers.
Thus ended my Public Service of
40 years in uniform but I must
confess if I had my time to see again
it would not be past in the same
way. As my sincere impression is
man was not made to Slaughter is
Fellow man. for any other man or state
although he may have ingaged himself
as an hired assassin in my mind
one man as as much right to the earth
as another But I know we must have
rulers But not as they now live in Luxury
and riot. God made animated nature
all ruled by a certain Law of its own
But man as Prostituted that Law and
made artificial Laws to suit his own

160   purpose and Aggrandizement which as
nothing to do with God, Look at the pride
of the Church the Bishops must have
his Coach to go to church on Sundays were
is the Commandment remember the
sabbath day and keep it holy thou –
shall do no manner of Labour.
But we must highly respect the founders
of many religions and one in particular
Jesus of Nazareth. He was a well inspired
man who wanted to free his country and
others from the abuses of Priesthood
and the oppression of tyranny of
Kings and Ceasers of the day. such
pure reform such simple definitions
of the religious Laws & amendments to
the existing civil Laws, they would not
accept. They accused Jesus of high
Treason and Condemned him to die
on the Cross which was not a special
Death invented for him, but Commonly
used by the Jews for criminals, the

and beg your acceptance of the
acompanying Purse of Money.
That your future may be blessed
with all the good this world can
afford is the sincere wish of the
Subscribers

Thus ended my Public Service of
40 years in uniform but I must
Confess if I had my time to see again
it would not be past in the Same
way. As my sincere impression is
man was not made to Slaughter is
Fellow man. for any other man or State
although he may have engaged himself
as an hired assassin in my mind
one man as as much right to the earth
as another. But I know we must have
rulers but not as they now live in luxury
and riot. God made animated nature
all ruled by a certain Law of its own
But man is Prostituted that Law and
made artificial Laws to suit his own

purpose and Aggrandizement. which as
nothing to do with God, look at the pride
of the Church the Bishops must have
his Coach. to go to Church on Sunday ware
is the Commandment remember the
sabbath day and keep it holy thou –
Shall do no Manner of Labour –
But we must highly respect the founders
of many religions and one in particular
Jesus of Nazareth. He was a well inspired
man who wanted to free his country and
others from the abuses of Priesthood
and the oppression and tyranny of
Kings and Ceasers of the day. Such
sure reform such simple definitions
of the religious Laws of amendments to
the existing civil Laws, they would not
accept. They accused Jesus of high
Treason and Condemned him to die
on the Cross which was not a special
Death invented for him, but Commonly
used by the Jews for criminals, the

161   Same as quartering, hanging and the
guillotine are used amongst us now
I am always astounded when I see
a *Cross* displayed anywhere it is –
after all, but the dirty exhibition of
a gibbot on which man was tortured
Disgusting to look at, I shall always
prefer a well inspired picture of
Jesus in all goodness and pious meditation
The Christians and their religious code
of Life were established. But the Leaders
of the present day terribly misuse
the so called Dogmus, which is not
the principles and meaning of the moral
Law of Jesus. They have been altered &
revised by Priesthood from time to time
to encircle and subject man through
the medium of useless beliefs –
founded on their unscrupulous –
principles to fill their Coffers with the
Body of the Golding Calf & imbrace
them with the pomp and vanity of the

163   world to be happy & joyful as all
other animated nature are it is the
artificial Law that cause so much misery
in the world and not the law of God
Let us look at how the Land is Laid
out by the Law of the people. In England
66 persons own two millions of acres of
Land; 100 persons own four millions of acres
710 persons own one quarter of the whole
soil of england and Wales.
Scotland as 19 million of acres of Land
12 persons own 4,346,00 or nearly one
quarter of the whole of the Land in
Scotland, 1700 persons own nine,-tenths
of all the Land in that Country, While
the remaining one tenth is left to all
the rest of the population. now –
Let us to go, Ireland we shall find
that out of 20 millions of acres 744
persons own nine and a half millions
of acres or nearly the half of all the
Land of Ireland.

162   world, by which means they distroy
      the work of Jesus, which was done out
      of pure and simple love of mankind
      we marvell his death which was
      only perfectly human.
      Jesus paid the penalty of the Law
      of his day as many as done since in
      England he wished to be the reformer
      of his day. but if we look at the middle
      ages Galilee was burnt for his discover
      ies in Science and astronomy it not
      being in accordance with the Scriptures
      of his day. But true Philosophy & Science
      will oblige Priesthood to lay down their
      Dogmus as the light of truth & Education
      enlightens the people with Gods Love
      for his animated nature of the earth
      Budda also Came to die and save the
      world centuries before Jesus. & so –
      Mahomit should have died but he lived
      to make many followers. My firm
      belief is man was sent into the

164   And to sum up we shall find that
      two thirds of the Soil of england & Wales
      are owned by 10–200 persons
      That two thirds of the soil of Scotland
      are owned by 830 persons
      That two thirds of the soil of Ireland
      are owned by 1–942 persons
      Now is not this a cruel monopoly of
      the Land given by god to us all
      so the great bulk of the population
      are thus divorced from the soil
      of their native Land
      And men calling themselves Christians
      make these Laws and take their oath to God
      as members of Parliment to do their –
      duty to God & man. how do they carry it
      out the above will show they make
      plenty of Show of religion But as to
      righteousness they shut their Eyes and heart
      would to god they would take a *Lesson*
      from Jesus the Nazerien for he said
      in his Eleventh Commandment Love
      yea one & another as I loved you

165   Now the Best Love we have for each other
is to Love him for our own advantage
For Instance when we find a part
of the world that would be of use
and a Profit to us. We at once Covit
the same. but then it is peopled –
with a dark skinned race Gods people
but what of that God as not made
their views to meet ours in this
he was not omnipotante, So we
wish to make Christians. *I.E. Covit*
their Country it will bring a good
return for the outlay – our first
step send out 6 or 8 missionary men
with many faces but one head and
such as will in a short time bring
about what is wanted. They meadle
with the ways and the views that
God as given them in his omnipotance
But the Christian do not consider that
he as given the right way of
thought. Well to bring about this

167   God made all things to Love the
earth and to enjoy it and be happy
on it for the time he as alloted
our stay on it and all animated
nature to do so until man puts his
hand to it and then it must
yeal something for him no matter
in what way. We should always
have in our minds eye the words
Thou shalt not Covit nor desire
But the Christian is much troubled with
Mammon Worship Gold is their God
Another matter I could never under
stand. Why do the Christian Cry at
a Furnial of the Dead when he say
the body is at rest from his labour
the Christian is told to rejoice. But
you see the Husband weep who as
starved his wife to death and
otherwise Illused her and you see
the Husband weep who as loved and
Cared for his wife. You see the

166   our next Step send a few soldiers they
will soon show the way to become
Christians. The next step is you must
pay for the Loss you have put us to
by being so stubbern as not to accept
our views of religion. So you must
pay the cost. now comes the grand step
Annexation of their Country and in
a short time a few years we send
them a Bishop and all his host
and you must pay for that likewise
O John Bull you are a great rouge
Thou shalt not covit, nor desire
Now let us look at our many views of
religion of Different denominations in
what way do they Love each other I
think the Love is envey. What an im-
mitation of Jesus. who saitheth Love
yea one another as I have Loved you
O the Tyranie of opinion. you must
not think, I.E. think to loud. or you
will be set down as an heathen

⚬

168   Children weep who as much illused
their Parents you also see those
weep who have loved them and been
most kind to them all seem to
weep at the grave it must be only
a Form In my duty as a Policeman
I had to part two Brothers from fighting
over the Bed taken by them from
under the dead body of their mother
to see which should have it they both
wanted the bed which they got out
of the window Both these Brothers
weep at the grave and well they
mite the one was a Christian Catholic
the other was a Methodist of Baptise
Why did they weep. Men weep at
the grave when they are to have
the Fortune of the desease or a part
in a short time Why do they weep
surely it is astounding to see such
weeping when by his acknowledged
Dogmus he is told to rejoice and be

169   of Great Gladness for our brother rest
from his labores But such sights are
see at the grave that would make a
free thinking man shudder. If we
only look at the Parsons of the
differents of Creeds how they fight
and Squbble for their gane in coin
not in righteousness Gold is God. –
Love thy neighbour as thyself and be
yea kind to all men. But did any
man know a Bishop on the Benches
at the house to Vote for any Cause
that was to benefit the poor man
I have looked for it from them for
the last 40 years but have failed
to see them Love their neighbour as
theirselves. Place Place is the word
But thanks to God few of them are very
happy. It is as easy for a Camel to pass
through the Eye of a Neadle as a rich
man to enter the Kingdom of God
and Why because they enjoy not the

171   is seting and the twilight closes in
that darkness of which no one can
tell he shut his Eyes as thou to sleep
Could we but keep this in our
mind and try to enjoy the great
gifts of god we should make an
heaven of the blessings god as gave
to us, True the poor man is robed
of his birth right by the acts passed
in Parlement and the acts of our
Great landed property men and
then again the poor is much robed
by the High profits Charged by his
Fellow man for gold is god and
man will do anything to get it
at least most of them. But thanks
to Death it ends there and let us
try to think less of gold and
live to enjoy this earth and be
as happy as the law of man will
allow us then there will be some
thing to live for and be happy

170   Earth (Cast Cast) distroy their happy
ness they love not their own kind
Another word in the Christian Dogmus
I could never understand that is the
word Omnipotent . which he saith God
is and I also think he is but why send
away men to alter the law of God when
it must be his will that all men shall
be the same or why a difference –
of Languages if it was his wish they
should all be Christians he is Omnipotent
and donot and never did require
an Adjutante. Let us look at his mighty
ways and then be happy for all his
kindness see at the earth how Lovely
with all its Trees and Flowers and
the Birds) and Fishes of the Water all
for us to enjoy the earth, that is if
we will only be Content. The man
who is Content is in Paradise he is
in heaven before death for that as
no sting for as the Sun of his life

≈

172   The Archbishop's war cry
Our Great medicine man has once
more sent his Instructions to the
God of Battles, our army in Egypt.
He begins, – O Almighty Lord God–
King of all Kings and govenor of all
things that sittest on the Throne judging
right; Now if the archbishop believe
in this god who governs all things
and judges right; Why does he presume
to instruct him. The he says, We
Commend to Thy fatherly goodness our
men etc. But as if doubtful of this
fatherly goodness he teaches god his
duty to the British section of his Family
Forgetting that his fatherly goodness
might have an equal interest in our
Egyptian brothers for if god be father
the Soudanese and Aribs are our brethren
Does he not preach we are the children
of Shem. Ham & Japheth after the Flood
He ask god to protect our men through
all the dangers But what are the dangers

173   are we not hired assasins, They are
       the effects on us the invaders of the
       self protecting efforts of the Invaded
       He invokes divine help to the mighty
       army of the oppressors and divine hin–
       –drance to the feeble crowd of the
       oppressed; The *medicine M*an, also
       says, Grant also that we may evermore
       use thy mercy to thy glory to the advancement
       of thy Kingdom and the honour of our
       Sovereign, – What mercy, Mercy to the
       British As Sir Hugh Gough said at
       the Battle of Goojerat when we was
       about to pursue the Flying enemy
       no prisoners men (I.E Kill) Yes
       but what is its results, suffering
       and death to the Egyptians, But
       of course that is nothing to us we are
       pious people (and they believe the
       False Prophet (*What is Sin*)
       Then again do the advancement
       of Gods Kingdom and the honour

175   the tenth of that tenth that is
       the priesthood of the Jews had
       but the hundredth part the rest
       was for other uses of the rest of
       the Levites and for the poor
       the Stranger the widow the orphan
       and the temple. But supposing
       the Jewish priesthood had the
       tenth which they certainly did
       not the Christian priesthood does
       not claim under them Christ was
       not a Levite nor of the tribe of Levi
       nor of the Jewish priesthood but
       Protested against the priesthood
       their worship their ordinance their
       passover and their circumcision
       Will a Christian priest of the now
       Church of England say it was meet
       to put down the Jewish. But meet
       likewise to Seize on the spoil as if their
       riches were of divine right. Though
       their religion, was not as if a

174   of the Sovereign run in parallel
lines. If gods kingdom be the ultimate
good of mankind there his glory
would be enhanced by the obliteration
of the last trace of Kingcraft.
But most strange of all this
Empurpled and fine linen'd High
and haughty (medicine man) of the
meek and lowly. Tries to hoodwink
the Omniscient by saying,, We seek
always the *deliverance* of the oppressd.
The Archbishop must know that the
whole history of his church proves
his words to be False. If there be
such a thing as *Blasphemy* surely
this prayer is a specimen of it
Again Let us look at the Tithes of
the Church. The Jews took not the
Tithes. The Priesthood of the Jews had
not the tithes. The Levites had the tenth
because they had no other inheritance.
But *Aaron* and his sons had but

176   Christian disinterestdness might
take the *Land* and the tithe given
in lieu of *Land* and posseion of
Both and devisted of the Charity
exclaim against the avarice of
the Jews. The apostles had no tithe
they didnot demand it, They and
he whoes mission they preached
protested against the principle
on which tithes is founded. Carry
neither scrip nor purse nor shoe
into whatsoever house ye go say peice
Here is Concord and Contempt of
riches not tithe, Take no thought
what ye shall eat or what ye shall
Drink nor for your Bodies what
ye shall put on, so said Christ to
his Apostles. Does this look like a
right in his priesthood to a tenth of
the goods of the Community
Beware of Covetousness seek not
what ye shall eat but seek the

177   Kingdom of God. Give alms and
provide yourself with bags that
wax not old, a Treasure in heaven
which faileth not This do not look
like a right in the Christian priest
to the tenth of the goods and the
produce of the land. One should
not think that Christ was laying
the foundation of the tithes but
Cutting up the root of the chain
and admonishing some of the –
modern priesthood if these precepts
are of divine right Tithes cannot be
so The precept which orders a Contempt
of riches, The claim which demands
a tenth of the fruits of the earth
for the ministers of the Gospel
The peasantry in apostolic times
had been the object of Charity
not of exaction; Cyprian the
Bishop of Carthage tells you the
exspences of the church are frugal

179   Necessity required them Justly
to have food and raiment be
there with content. What is the
meaning of the Church they starve
one part to feed with Luxuriance the
others They hang one man who as
Committed a small Crime and
Praise other men who has Committed
Large ones. Marlborough his 1000s
and so did Wellington and so as
many others and Alexander his
Millions they are all Famous
in history for Great men. But say
Kill one man) are for what there
is the rub) say Plunder or what
ever it may be he must be Hangd
he is a little Murderer, Marlborough
Alexander Plundered Countries. But
they were Great men) How many
men were lost in Italy & upon the
Rhine for settling a King in Poland
Both sides could not be right

178   and sparing, But her charity
      great he calls the Clergy his
      Fratres sportulentes a Fraternity
      living by contribution.
      Forsake says Origan, (The priest
      of Pharoah who have earthly
      possessions and come to us who
      have none, we must not consume
      what belongs to the poor we must
      be content with simple Fare and
      poor apparel, Chrysostone, in
      the Close of the fourth century
      declares that there was no practice
      of tithes in the former ages, and
      Erasmus, Says that the attempt
      to demand them was no better than
      Tyranny. At the council of –
      Antioch in the fourth century which
      declares that Bishops may distribute
      the goods of the church But must
      not take no part to themselves nor to
      the priest that live with them unless

                    ༄

180   But these are Great Crimes) only
      Kill one solitary man and you must
      be Hangd. The Great man is Clothed
      in Purple and it is not a Sin so
      say our Great Medicine man at
      Canterbury and so say the church
      The Arch Bishop and the Clergy
      send up prayers for our armies
      in the field (Oh what Cant) were'
      is their Charity none in the soul
      and but little benevolence in the
      Pocket Gold and power is the God
      of our Great Christian race
      The Sernity of nature we should
      consider) the impassive serenity of
      nature through all the struggle and
      Anguish of Life. There are times
      when this Serenity becomes dreadful
      and Maddens men is this mans indifference
      they ask themselves wildly the mask
      of the Indifference of God; Nature
      knows no Sympathy. Our sadness our

181   Gladness stir not a pulse Claim
not a sigh (our struggle in life
makes man a selfish animals.)
She attends our gay occasions with
Flowers and festal music. *what*
Joy. She breathes the same music
and scatters the same Flowers over
our graves. Let us thank God
that it is so. Pain and storm
strife and anguish birth and
death *are for time*; order beauty
life are for eternity. Nature is
right she will not bewail our
calamities as though they were
irreparable. She smiles and sings
as she reweaves for us the threads
of our broken purposes or heals the
leading trendrils of our hearts Why
should nature weep and moan –
and stay her benign and beautiful
processes, when she knows that
the stroke of Death which we think

❦

183   of Crushed humanity for Gods sake
let it be a reality and not
a humbug. I write with full
cognisance that all men are brothers
in the Flesh and if some are criminals
by the artifice Law made by man
they will be coequal in the eye of God
or if not so our Criminal Class
must have been borned to sin by
the omnipotence of Gods will oh
what is sin)) (*The Question*) was
Adam & Eve when made in a Savage
state or was they in that State called
Barbarian or was they made in a State
of Civillization. To me it appears they
were in a naked and Savage State
for at the fall there eyes where opened
and they sewed fig leaves together to
hide their Nakedness here to commence
the First act of civillization althow
we have no knowledge of their Stone
or Bronze age) Looking at Cain

182   is crushing us in a benediction
Nature is so constant because God
is so constand – so Constant in
his purposes to transmute suffering
into Glory and moan into Song
of this the sunlight and the
Garden of the earth with all its
animated nature and the calm
procession of the Seasons are his
Witnesses. Do we not Prostitute thies
Comforts for a vain Glory and the
Vanity of Power. I will say with the
true musleman or Fire worshipers
God is Great (and what little
trust we put in him) man attends
his worship his Church. But in his
race for wealth he forgot both God
and Church and only keeps the
sembleance. I do not touch the question
whether religion is good or bad. But
what I do say is if we are to have
religion and flaunt it in the Face

184   and able or the First Jealousy
cain murdered his brother able
this as the appearance of the Savage
age and nothing is spoken as of
any kind of Manufactory of Tools
or Buildings Therefore had they not
have fell as we are told in the Book
of Genesis God intended that they
should remain in a State of Nature
as many Thousands are at the present
time in Lands unknown and this is
the will of God without any Doubt
and is to this day. if his will was
otherwise it would be altered at
one without the aid of men sent
to Preach religion to them but the
Christian race ignor the will of
God and say they must be made
Christians God Cannot be right
to keep them in a State of nature
But here is the rub if they were
Left as they are we should not
be able to take posession of their

185 Land and then *Tax* them to
have a piece of it again and
in a few years we can send
them a Bishop and make
them pay for him also. Oh John
Bull you are a great rouge.
Thinking of the Commandments
given to Moses in the Burning bush
Shurley there had been some before
as the world had encreased to
such a large number so as to
keep in Bondage the whole of the
Isrealites Shurley this was a rouse
by which moses was able to command
the many and get them under
his subjection for the sake of gain
or why was the Egyptians so many
years without Commanders this
is a neglect I cannot understand
But it made a good opening
for his Brother Aaron who made
a good thing of it and was the
first of his race to collect Tithes

187 Looking at the treatment of Ireland
conquered by the sword 700 years
back and kept in Bondage all
those years. I think they are in
want of a Moses very much for
if we read right we can see that
they are more Taxed than the
Israelites was by the Pharoah and his
Oast. If we read well the different
scripture histories we shall find that
the Isrealites was much better off
then the Irish at the present time
What we want is righteousness not
religion. But Landlords must
have their rent. no matter what
the Value of the Crop this is the
rub money is the God of the –
Great) The is life worth the
liveing for The rich live for Wealth
and immorality at least it is
all they Study or the Greater
part of them a few think

186   Shurley this must be Blasphemy
       as to his meeting with god in a bush
       as he gave us no fact of such a
       thing. Looking at the present as
       to the State of things when the Com
       mandment thou shalt not covet
       nor desire. Why if we only look at
       the several acts of Parliment of
       the last 50 years there as been
       nothing but covet & desire by the
       Great and more so by the members
       of the Church and still they cry
       we are poor and the Church is
       in want *oh* the *poor* Clergy I
       pity them. And then do they not
       help to keep the whole of the poor in
       Bondage see the hours they work to
       feed the great. This is not the
       Charity Taught by Jesus he gave
       Them the Eleventh Commandment
       Love yea one another even as I
       have loved you) and he gave up
       his life but the rich think otherwise

188   for the Poor – Now the poor is the
       Child of the Soil and borned to
       labour and thanks to God they
       are Content there with if they Can
       get it to do. But the temptation
       of Break the Law or what is called
       sin is very great with the poor
       I Cannot but think if there is
       such a thing as Sin. The cause
       are not been the same with the
       rich as lay at the Door of the
       Poor and yet they sin but very
       little Compared with the Rich
       They may break the Law many
       ways and often but that is
       the Law made by man for his
       own ends not the Law of God.
       The Rich break the Laws they have
       made for their own ends and
       the Lawyer will Drag them out
       of their own Dirt for the
       Golden Calf) or money – (God)

189   What is life. if we look at it as
poor men we cannot find much to
live for ours is a life of heavy toil
to get a bare living and to amas money
and Whealth for the great men of the
day. True we have some hours of rest
from labour. But should you have a
Family that is taken up for them –
But should you be so unfortanate
as to be out of work you and the
Family have much to suffer. But I
must be very thankful I have never
been out of employment or without
a Shilling since I first took to Keep
myself at the Age of 13 years & 9 months
I have been very lucky. Had good
health and always careful, and
could not make away with much
Money as my Nature was not to
take pleasure. But to watch the
way and doings of Mankind
and to learn if possiable what

191   We oftimes had to face Death in
the worse form. But there is a
pleasure in that for it places
the great man and the poor on
a footen. I have oftimes put my
foot on a Dead officer as we put
his body under ground and said
to myself were is your Rank
now and then Mr Officer was
not the same *Tyrant* as in england
Dead men tell no tails they know
that out there – And at the time
I am speaking off India was to
the White man a free Country we
Could go where we liked no Trespass
out there and John Company behaved
well to us shared some of the
Plunder with us Soldiers I mean
in prize money not so the Queens
Government and then John Company
didnot make us work found us
plenty of servants plenty of Grog

190   he as to live for. Working at my
Trade (Sawyer) until I was 21 years
I thought it time to give up such
hard work which brought little
more than a liveing for myself but
much for my employers. The Railway
started and Joined the Great Western
and was employed as a Guard &
remained at it for two years but
not likeing London I was far from
being settled although we made –
good wages and not worked hard
But I felt I should like to travel
and see other Countries. Well one
day I had a tiff with the Supperintendent
and we got to word and my temper
very hasty we got nearly to blows
so I made up my mind to be a
Soldier and enlisted at once
and soon went to the east Indies
Now of all my life this was the
most worth liveing for although

192   and good living if they were
Thieves and stole the Country I
must say they gave some of it to
the Blood hounds (i.e. soldiers) who hunted
down the rightful owners
Well with all the faults
of a Military life there is more to
live for then the poor man who in
England is a free paid Slave. I
Cannot say much for the Policemans
life he must be a special man &
Look after other mens faults and
shut his Eyes to all is virtues I
must say I done very well in the
Police Force. But as I said before
it is not a happy life. But what
am I thinking off how much of
happiness is the lot of the poor
the more he thinks the less is his
happiness my Idea is the less
a poor man is taught the more
happiness he will enjoy as he

193   is more content with his hard
life for the Laws are so made to
keep 3 fifths of the people poor and
to hard work to keep the other 2
fifths and to make them content
with their hard Labour. Well man
is but an amable after all But
a thinking Amniable. But we have
no facts as to the state after Death
if there was the so called great
men would do different to what
they do at the present time. They
would not so Covet and would
be more Moral in their ways
It is this uncertainty of the –
future that make the difference
But if we look to past history we
find the poor was always the same
The Nazarene called Christ tryed to
reform man but they would not
have it then and now they are
somewhat worse they Care less
for righteousness Gold the word)

195   I have offtimes laid and
tried to reason in my own mind
Beleiving in God to be Omnipotante
why is the Cause that so much
and many temptations to do wrong
are at the door of the poor and
the Rich can revel in Luxury
and sin yet and live to the
Alloted age of man and their
Children follow in their foot
steps) Can religion then
be only Cant if so to whom and to
what Can we trust I once Said
to an Indian Black man why do you
trust and put such faith in the
water of the Ganges. He replied I
act as I was taught. You do the
same. I could ask you why do you
put such faith in Jesus you would
say I was taught to do so) Now
both are but theiry. There is the
Rub we only do as we are taught
But he enlightened me on one

194   If one man rule he will rule for
his own benefit, and that of his
Parasites. If a Minority rule, We
have mant Masters, instead of
one. All of whom must be fed
and served: And if the majority
ruled and wrongfully ruled why
the minimum of harm is done
and then Comes a Oliver Cromwell
If we could see man Just to his
fellow man. we shall look
for the end of things and the
end of the world. I do think
we should be thankful that we
are of the poor Brotherhood for
if there is such a Thing as sin
we then know that the poor are
with all their Temptations the
most just and the most –
rightous and the most happy
that is if their poverty is not
to great for them to bear

196   thing that I could not deny
he said you have a trinity in
Unity the Father Son and Holy
Ghost) Now he said I can tell
you in that you are right you
have the Gun Sword & Bayonet
in unity and in them you put
your trust and you should do
so for they have made your nation
Great and brought you all you
have surely these are your God
in whom you put your trust see
how your nobles worship them
all they have as been got by
this trinity in unity the
Gun is the Father the Sword
the Son and the Bayonet the
Holy Ghost of the white man.
Yet said he we a Great deal in
common you have a religion that
teaches more Love than you
Practice. I have a religion that
teaches more Morality than we can

197   Manage with. But we have
all our Idols and we are very
much alike after all
The people who worshipped an
Oliver Cromwell would never
tolerate a George the fourth
A True Musselman not a Mehomitian
a Fire worshiper put me right on this
Subject, Were I an Englishman he
said I would worship the gun
Sword & Bayonet only. See what it
has brought your country. All her
possessions. all her liberties all
her money, all her commerce all
her advantages, Do you think we
gave you the Concessions you
enjoy in our country of our Free
will, Not at all. Your soldiers and
sailors with their united arms was
the argument that prevailed with
us did you persuade the Sikhs
to accept your rule or did you
force them to do so at the point

๛

199   Socialism – V – Atheism
Jesus was a Socialist he preach
it from first to Last and such
is pure Christianity. But how
many Christians may I ask practize
their Dogmas they Prostituet it
Thank God the veil of the temple
is rent in twain and we can
observe the people in their war
paint. And with the eye of reason
we are able to detect the frauds
set up in the guise of Parsons
Jesus. said. Go ye into the Highways
and byeways. Take neither purse nor
scrip but say peace) John Parson do
not say peace when he Seize the
tithe to revil in his debauchery
Jesus took no tithe or his followers –
Take from Jesus words in St. Matthews
Even so ye outwardly appear –
righteous unto men. But within
they are full of hypocrisy and
Iniquity. Ye serpants ye vipers can

198   of your Guns Do you make
a footing all over the world by
peaceful Means or do you do it
with the Gun. Is not your Gun
your great civiliser your great
persuader your one argument
Why then are you not honest
enough to make it your Idol and
worship it) Gold is your God
I was ashamed to say we only
went out into the world to be
a Blessing to others and if
we Chastised others it was –
because we loved them I.E
their wealth) Now when I see
a Gun I take off my hat
to the National Idol and say
Salaam (oh Allah) The Zulas
can tel in what the Christian
as done for them and then
again at Burmer and now we have
granted another Charter
in South Africa to Christians

200   ye escape the damnation of hell
in Luke the 14th V 15 his Master says
But God Knoweth their hearts for
that which is highly esteemed
among men is abomination in the
sight of God. This will show that
socialism is the very essence of
Christianity. By Socialism I mean
a Just and comparative equal –
Division of Capital. Property and
Labour. and the right of the people
to the land. Read their Masters
words Jesus said Sell whatever
thou hast and give unto the poor
and come and follow me. Give
unto every man that asketh of
thee Acts 4th V 32 & 34. And whoso
ever doth not bear his Cross Cannot
be his disciple. Let us imagine as
well as we can the manner in
which an Omnipotent Deity would
regard the Iniquties of poverty

201   Caused by *war*. and property
stolen with the prayers of the
great medicine man at Canterbury
the Omnipotent Eye darts down
upon such Cant. Then an angry
frown Knits the Godly brows of
the Omnipotent creator. why
do yea say (Thy will be done) –
Did I not Command, thou shalt
do no murder) who commanded
you to thurst you Bloody Steel
through the hearts which I have
Created. have I not said. Thou
shalt have none other Lords
but me, Why then do they call
themselves Kings & Dukes & Lords
And have I authorised you
to monopolise the soil while poor
be starving in the Vale and Shadow
of Death and the parson
mockingly exhort them to pray
Give us this day our daily Bread

203   The question was asked was there
any Virtue in the Oath as it stood
and not one in the house attempted
to answer the question. If that is
so were is the Value of all our religion
of so many sorts. If there is no virtue
in the Oath. And now let us search
for Justice in Man. If we Commence
at the Crown and go down step by
step until we arrive at the Lowest
state of man we Cannot find him
Just for Civilliseation as made self
the first law of Nature and the
Gold.Rank and Power and such like
as take all the mercy from the noble
heart. But we have many Benevalent
people. But then what do Jesus say
in his Socialism to the rich man
who we are told said Lord Lord what
must I do to be saved. What was the
answer. Give up all and follow
me. did he do so no, then I should
presume he was not save) What

202   But yet have stolen it ye titled
thieves and hypocrites. Then
what doth God require of thee
O man. But to do Justly and to
love mercy and to walk humbly
and love thy neighbour as thyself
Now if God Exspects Justice & Mercy
from man we shall never see it
rendered to man and if that is
the Conditions on which we get
to heaven I am sadly afread that
none of us will reach that place
if such there be. But all mankind
have some Idear of a future State
But there is not a religion on
the whole earth that Give a fact
of this future state all is a
Theory. Now the whole of the Clergy
and our learned men know this
and the same was as good as said
in the house of Commons when Mr
Bradlaugh refused to take the oath

204   would in the present day be the
case if asked to do the same. The
result would be the same they would
their way Sorrowing and the Clergy
from the Arch Bishop to the new
borned Curate would do the same
they would go their way sorrowing
and realy Dought the Strength of
his word and this is the Christian
faith. Well may the Black man
Call the Christian (Barra Cultha)
I.E Great Dog) and really he is such
his Liveing, habits of blood thirstyness
and Plunder Justified the name
What of the Commandments Thou
shalt not Covet. Thou shalt not steal
Though shalt not murder) What do
they even think of Moses. But I
supposed the Pherrows had Laws for
the people before Moses wrote his
God had shuly not neglected his
people for so many Thousands of years
for they must have been a very great

205   People and very numerious as they
are said to have had 6 hundred of
Thousands of Troops in the field
and that would be at the smallest
Calulation take a Nation of some
40 Millions of people to feed that
number in the field at the small
rate of rations on which a Eastern
soldier can live. Shurly God had
not neglected the people so long in
want of law were with to be governed
No – no there is some fable work here
The old soldier Cannot understand
this the Soldier must be supplied
and so must the Cattle. If not
they will soon find a way to do it
for themselves. This kind of religion
should be made more Clear when
we are told to *Read Mark & learn*
the man that think much must
Dought this Cant. What Unionety
in there in the Church Laws and

207   offend against the law of man
that is not sin) Sin must be som
thing against God. and here we
come at the word Justice where that
is not found there is Sin in all
its worst form. I donot think but
that much of the immorality of man
is sin for that is handed down to
the third and fourth generation
But in this kind of sin the Rich
are the greatest offenders as they
are in everything else with which
they have to do. I s Murder a Sin
I believe it a Sin but Can man make
a Law for Soldiers to Murder each other
and that sort of murder not to be sin
no man Preist or Peasant Cannot say
it is not sin although our Military
law make such Murder not punishable
but such cannot be the Law of God
or else away with the word justice
war and military murder is only for
the agrandizement of Kings and the Great

206 the Laws of the Parliament made
by man they are both to keep order
in this world of Civiliation God do
not acknowledge these Laws all he
ask of man is Justice. But then
the Deplomicy of the Parliment is to
Keep 3 fifths of the Population poor
and to keep them Content with being
poor and if Distress is to severe
why make a subscription for them
but they must be kept poor or they
would not work to keep the other two
fifths in Comfort and most of them
in pomp and splendour. and what
do these two fifths think of what
God Exspects from man (*Justice*)
they laugh at the word and live
on in their Luxurious immorality
Well what is the meaning of the
word of sin. As it anything to do
with Justice I cannot understand
the word sin. I know when we

208 What is Marrage but a life of
trouble and Care and in most cases
of the Poor a Great deal of poverty
My own married life as been a life
of much care haveing to raise eight
Children out of Eleven borned. well
I have always been a very Careful man
never making any wast of money or
anything else by which means I was
able to save a little money to meet
any trouble in old age. And then
I always had in my mind the chance
of geting a pension which I did &
a very good one. Well the early part
of my married life was I suppose
much the same as other peoples
some times a few sharp and hot
words with the Wife but soon over
mine being a very hot temper and
my Wife being of a very different
Disposition from mine it would
lead to words but on the whole we
got on as well as most people I

209 would always be Master of the
home and I spent the money as
I found my wife was not up to the
mark in laying out money to the
best advantage but this never
led to any words it was always about
the Children a Wife can be to much
of a mother and indulge the children
to every folly I must say this was
the case with my wife. She is a
most hard working woman and in
the whole a Careful woman. But
she as a very bad fault that is
Ingratitude. she was always ungratful
thinking man had nothing else to
think of but her and then it
didnot matter what you gave her
in the way of money she never
was thankful for it. I never spent
a shilling from the home but
that she never took into account
Perhaps had I been a man otherwise
I mite have been better thought of

❧

211 other kind of food and when
all had been satisfied we went
on our Journey and this we
did for many years and it lives
in my minds eye and I can even
enjoy the Sight now when I think
of it and picture their happy
young faces and that I think is the
real blist of a married life
But no affection ought to make us
blind to the faults of the Children
or the mother. We may accept them
as part and parcel of the beloved
but we ought not to ignore them or
Call them good or only the ways of
other peoples faults may soon turn
to evil and the Children loved
beyond reason is a lasting fault
of the Parent. We must do our duty
in order to love them. such love
is passionles. Duty gives neither
kisses or caresses I have always
tried to do my duty to my God ´

210   as then she would have had to
work to bring something to help to
maintain the Children. But I
knew she had enough to do to keep
the house and the Children straight
and this she did much to her great
Credit for the Children was always
clean and fit to be seen and I
must do her justice the Children
was taught no bad ways or did
they see any. And I must say the
early part of my married life was
mostly happy I used to save some
money every year so as to give them
a days outing somtimes 2 day and
go to Sandhurst and this gave
me more pleasure than anything
I ever had about half way to
Sandhurst we used to stop on the
side of the road put the nose bag
on the horse for him to feed and
then take out the Children and
give them Cake wine and some

212   Without any show of religion
My Wife also without any show of
any kind mine was not a Boyish
love it was the love of a man to
do my duty and take Care of her
when I took her from her fathers
house I swore to god to do my best
to maintain her in Comfort and
this I have done up to now and with
the help of God I will continue
to do so and if it please God
to take me first all I have in this
world or comeing to me is hers and
for her own disposeal I am not
afraid she will go wrong with it
Although I know my wife never
had much affection for me but
I swore before god to do my best
by her and I will try to do so until
my life ends) When I married her
I was aware of the difference of
our ages and she knew the same
and it should not make any

213   difference as to our duty to each
other I will do my duty to her
though she may not see it clearly
I must make no alteration on my
part God will be my Judge I was
a man never given to much pleasure
and money never was anything to
me as I was a man that could
not make very much money if
I had the Chance but with eight
Children an Inspector of County
Police as not much to spare I
could have spent more than I –
did if I had followed my own
wishes I was always very fond of
Birds and when I was first
at house keeping I got some but
my Wife found much fault with
them so as to get to hot words so
I gave them up at once and here
was one of my home comforts gone
but I had enough to think of soon
in the Shape of a Child my Rose

215   was a sort of persons that wanted
but little looking after my worst
duty was seeing to the College
Students but I did not make a
trouble of that the Head Masters
seldom say much if things were
alright they knew what the
students were they had been at
College themselves as Boys. Take
the thing in the whole I was very
Comfortable at Eton But I had many
trials as a father in the year 1866
my Children took Gastric Fever and
Arthur the Baby was nearly Dying
and I lay by the side of his cradle
all my spare time by Day & night
for 17 Day Exspecting it to be his
last we got over all that and
paid a good sum to Dr Gooch
all went well until the end of
August 1867 when one morning after
Breakfast John Could not stand
and was very ill and in a little

214 then I changed my station
as a Constable and my second
Child John was borned and now
more want of money. But I worked
hard and was rewarded with
Promotion and more money and
another Change of Station to
Great Marlow with rank of
Inspector. I continued to work
hard and was sent out on
Detective duty and was very
successful and got another step
of Promotion when my 3rd Child
was born Elizabeth and a Change
of Station to Eton College and
with the Rank of 1st Class Inspector
and here I remained until I
left the Police force with a pension
of £69–6s–8d per year in October 1881
and I must say I was very much
better off as my Pay was better &
my Duty much lighter and nearly
my own master and the people

216 time after Lizzie was the same I
went to Dr Gooch and when he
Came he said they had got the
Scarlet Fever and in a few day
more Arthur was also taken with
it Rose was poorly but not ill my
Wife had a baby 4 months old
and the Wife was ill and not
able to give the Baby the Breast
and it was weaned at this time
the Students was at home on their
Holliday and would return on
the 18. 19 & 20 September. I lived near
the College in fact almost in it
Docr Balston was the Head Master
he sent for me when he said he
should like me and my Family to
leave the College until we were all
well as he could not have the
Students back while such a bad
case of Fever was in the College
he said the College would pay any
Extra Exspence I mite be put to

217   Dr Gooch and Pearle both said I
must not move them but a few
miles as the Children could not
stand a Journey of long distance
Dr Balston the Head Master said
I could go to the Sea Side But the
Doctors said I must not be on the
road over an hour. Now here was
a trial for a man to move my
Wife and Children, Almost said
Death to some of them But again
I thought of the tradespeople of
Eton it had been the long Holliday
and people no work had become
short of money. So I made up my
mind to do my best to get the
Wife and Children to some place
and for 3 day I Drove all round
the place for miles and William
Harris went with me I had his
pony & Cart. No one Cared to
take me in and then they Pay
under the Law for Taken me in
but at last a Mr Cam a nice

✑

219   and my van shall take what
other things you want I could
not thank him Enough. But
he said no thanks I may want
the same or somthing of some
one some day now set down a
bit and then let me know at
what time you will want it
it was arranged I should start
at 10 the next morning & True
to time he was at my Gate with
the Close Trap & his Van. I got my
Wife in with the Baby and the
2 years old one in her lap also
John I put into a Blanket and put
him in the corner by his Mother
I then got Lizzie into another
Blanket and put her in and
her sister Rose who was well to Hold
Lizzie on the Seat I got on the
Box with Driver but Prior to
this I had put my Bedding into the
Van for their use at Winkfield

218   man and his wife said they
       would take their Chance and
       take us in as they were in want
       of money. He was the Landlord
       of the   a Public House
       at Winkfield Berks. I then felt
       a little more light hearted and
       Drove home. Now came another
       Fix I could not get a Conveyance
       to take us they said no one would
       ride in it after us and the students
       was to come back in two days Mr
       F. Bunce of the Turks Head Eton see
       how I was fixed when me & Harris
       put the pony into his Stable and
       went to the Bar to have some Gin
       he said what is the Matter Mr
       Pearman I told him the whole &
       he acted a man he said I am
       not a Rich man. But you can
       take my Broham for your Wife and
       Children and if they wont
       ride in it after I will burn it

                    ✦

220   We started at 10 A.M and had
       got through Windsor to the foot
       of High Standing hill when my
       wife taped on the Fly window we stoped
       John was taken worse. I looked at
       him and he poor Boy was like
       Death the motion of the Fly had
       made him feel sick I rolled the
       Blanket round him & took him
       out when he was very sick at
       this time a Gentleman Came up
       on Horseback and said do you
       know whats the matter with
       that Boy. I did not answer him
       as the Boy was Vomiting he said
       he as the Scarlet Fever I replied
       I know that. He then looked
       into the Fly and said (Inspector
       I had my uniform on) they have
       all got the Fever were are you
       taken them I replied unto
       Winkfield he said no that you
       shant I replied that I shall and

221   Put my son in the Fly again
       and was about to get on the
       seat myself when he said what
       is your name I am the Doctor
       of Winkfield and must know
       he gave me his name when I
       showed him the paper for their
       removal signed by Dr Gooch &
       Pearl & Ellison and told him
       to go and see the Head Master
       of Eton College which he did and
       when he came Back he was in a
       better Temper. I supposed the
       Head Master had Tiped him
       For when he Called on me at the
       Public house I was staying at he
       said it was alright & I could
       get anything I mite want at his
       surgery I remained at Winkfield
       until the 5th November when I
       returned with my Family again
       to Eton & thank God they con
       tinued to do well & again got strong

227   work scarse and many are
       out of employment why make
       a subscription for them so as
       to pass the bad time over
       but dont alter the Laws so as
       the poor could rise out of their
       poverty oh no that would not
       do they mite be above the work
       if they did. That is what they
       Call Political economy both
       sides of the house do this some
       times they are Drove by the will
       of the people to a little for them
       but they rangle for a long time
       and then they leave some hole
       or corner to themselves. Now
       if God gave out the Justice as
       the parson so much talk about
       He would strike these men from
       off the number of mankind
       so this retched poor live on
       until the end without having
       to thank God for anything or

222   Returning again to the will
of God I offtimes think what
as he done for those poor people
that live in poverty of the worst
sort from birth to Death and no
Cause of their own Now what
have they to thank him for they
have never known a comfort from
the begining to the end with no
fault of their own in any way
Compare this with our Queen
and the Great people and also
the Middle Classes and then
think were the thanks should
come from) Well again we
will look at our Parlement
men they make Laws so as to
keep 3 fifths of the whole people
very poor so as the very poor
may work and keep the other two
fifths some in Comfort and some
in splendour and should there
be a very bad winter and the

224   their fellow men this is the
Called Civilization or a Civil Law
the few to live in pride and go
to Church and Kneel and they
come out and rob and starve
or nearly so the poor. If there
is a God shourly this must
greave the Spirit of God and
call fourth his vengeance –
But the rich man take no head
of that and the Bishops and
his satellites look up to the rich
man as their liveings come from
them here is a mockery and
God donot stop this sin if
their is such a thing as sin
But the *Great* and *Rich* donot
Care much wether this is sin
or not they take it as it comes
and the devil get the Last as
the old woman say when she
and the world was at logerheads
however let this be as it may we

225   all think more of this world
      than we do of the next the Parson
      included. Now if we look things
      up in Calm thinking way we see
      that the Established Church and its
      Laws do distroy very much the Liberty
      of the Subject for all men have ⸱
      to support it directly or indirectly
      and that too in all the Pomp & pride
      and Vanitity that the earth produce
      and yet these very Bishop and their
      Satilites will tell you that if you
      wish to be saved you must renounce
      them all (here is humbug) No no
      as I have said before the faith
      hope and Charity of the Christian
      is the Cannon. sword & Bayonette
      we depend on them for all our
      Grandisement and when they have
      done their work and we have
      annexted their Land we are content
      that is if we can make them slaves
      indirectly for they must then

227   After this fashion or if so
      he did. Where and when will
      the very poor look for Justice
      oh what is Sin (what Bosh)
      to preach to the thinking mind
      There is a Myth in all this we
      Cannot understand. Then we
      have another Great Question
      to ask ourselves why as God
      Given to some people the pleasant
      parts of the Globe were all is
      sunshine and happiness and
      left some on parts of the Globe
      were there is no sun or happiness
      Shurly this is not a fare start
      for next world. then again
      if the Christian faith is the
      only right faith why in the name
      of God are we not all of the
      same Cast here is another myth
      The whole thing must be of
      Mans own creation so as
      to make a Law for himself

226 work for us to help to keep up
the Dignity of our Great empire
Then were is God with his
Justice he dont Chrush this dambed
peice of Iniquity for if there is
a God it must greive the Spirit
of God and down his wrath
Let us go bak six or seven thousand
years or a few thousand years –
before england was discovered
and look at the Laws of Egypt
and Rome we find there was
but a small difference in the then
Laws. Civil. Military or religious the
Great object was then to keep the
poor to work for the great in power
and to keep them contented the
same is our Laws now in a
Lawlised Nation wherever it be
three fifths of the whole people –
must be poor and very poor to
work to keep the State. Shourly
God did not devide the people

❧

228 Now let us look at the Church of
Rome and the Popes dreadful
curse upon Heretics when he
Excommunicate them from his church
The Curse –
1st May the father who created man
curse him or them (2) May the son
who suffered for us curse him
or them (3) May the Holy Ghost who
was given to us in our Baptism
curse him or them (4) May the
Holy Cross which Christ for our
Salvation triumphing over his
Enemies ascended curse him or
them May the Holy and eternal
Virgin Mary Mother of God
curse him or them. May St. Michael
the advocate of Holy Souls curse him or them May all
the angels and archangels Principalities
and Powers and all the Heavenly
Hosts Curse him or them May
St John the Chief forerunner
of Christ Curse him or them

229   May St Peter St Paul St Andrew
and all others of Christs –
Apostles together with the rest
of the Disciples and four Evangelists
who by their Preaching Converting
the whole universal world curse
him or them. May the holy and
wonderful Company of Martyrs
and Confessors who by their holy
works are found pleaseing to God
Almighty Curse him or them –
May the holy Choir of the holy
Virgins . who for the honour of
Christ have dispised the things
of this world. Curse him or them
May all the saints who from
the beginning of the world to
ever lasting ages are found to
be beloved of God Curse him or
them. May he or they be cursed
wheresoever they be whether in
the House or the feild of the
Highway or the Path or in the

231   in their Shoulders in their wrists
in their arms in their hands
in their fingers in their Breast
in their heart in the –
interior Part of their Stomick
in their Reins in their Thighs. In
their Genitals. in their Hips in
their Kness. in their Legs. in their
feet in their Toes. in their Nails
May he or they be cursed from the
Crown of their Head. to the sole of
their Feet. may their be no Soundness
in him or them. May the son of
the living God, with all the Glory
of his Majesty curse him or them
and may heaven with all their Powers
That move therein rise up against
him or them to Damn him or them
unless they shall repent, to make
Satisfaction. Amen, Amen, so be it

Never was heard such a Dambed
Relation so. Shocking as this is

230   wood or in the water or in
the Church May he or they be
Cursed in liveing and dyeing in
Eating or Drinking in being
hungry in being thirsty in
fasting in sleeping in slumbering
in waking in Walking in standing
in sitting in resting in p=ss=g.
in shxtt=g. and in bloodletting
May he or they be cursed in all
the faculties of their body.
May he or they be cursed inwardly
and outwardly. May he or they
be cursed in the Hair of his or
their Heads. May he or they be
cursed in his or their Brain
May he or they be cursed in
the Top of his Head or their Heads
in their Temples in their Foreheads
in their Ears and Eye Brows
in their cheeks and their Jaw bones
in their Nostrils in their teeth
in their lips in their throat in

232   I should think this very
Unpolitical as well as wicked
this is Blaspheme and Shurly –
must greive the Holy Spirit
of God or then what is Sin
What can the Godess
Victoria think of this
Cant she being Defender of the
faith and Head of our Land
for which she receives 85.000£
pr year beside other Large wind
falls and what she makes of her
Farms Parks and her private Bank
Now this 85.000£ is paid from the
Civil Survice money to which every
person pay a part. Now as
Victoria being Defender of the
Faith should have a Conscious
and Knowing that the Harlot
the rouge the thief the murderer
all pay their part towards it
she should through back the 5000£
as Conscience money from this people

233   But no she takes the whole and
grumble for more and live in
all the pomp and Vantity of the
Great (This is the Defender of the
Faith) More Bosh) Now I –
think of Faith. Hope. & Charity
was the root of the hope of the
Christian race, they would make
Charitable Laws so as the poorest
of the poor would have a Chance
to rise from their Humble State
and live in Comfort by their
toil. But no say the men at the
Helm of this Great ship we must
not Let them rise they wont
work for us then we must not
let them Starve but make a
Gathering in Bad times so as
to keep them Contented what
more can they want (They do
that much for their cattle
they dont want one or the other
to die, it Both is a *Loss*

☙

235   their is one unhappy on
the Earth oh the most Great God
make my Brother happy and
they try to do so. Whatever
the Christians say to the contrary
let the Christian live among
them and see for hisself
I donot mean the *Mehomit* I
mean the Musselman who donot
follow that Prophet I mean
the Pure Musselman or Fire
worshipers who bow down to the
Face of the Sun these people
pray with a pur heart and
donot Covit the Pomp and Vanity
of the earth. And I have always
found them to have peace of
mind and no doubt that is the
much talked of Heaven. But
we must build up a hope of some
kind the wild Blacks have the
happy hunting grounds to go to
there is their heaven

234   an as a Half Bread Welshman
I must hate the English as
the Irish Hate them and I
have long time wished that
some thing would turn up
with england & America so
that England mite get a
sound beating by them
the Irish would then be able
to get back their own Country
again. There is no unity for
there is no Love and the Scot
and Welsh are much the same
The Gun sword & Bayinet is
the unity of the whole
And there is not a Bishop
or Parson dare say a word
although he preach of the
Faith hope and Charity no
if he did where would they
be. He Cannot say as the
Mussleman Preacher saith oh
God I Cannot be happy while

꧁꧂

236   British Soldiers
Twas early one morn at Windsor
Equiped in fighting costume
Gave three loud ringings cheers
Three cheers for Queen & Country
For Albert Edward Three
With helmets high on rifles
The men Cheered Lustily
Smiling the gallant Edward bowed
And bade the Troops God speed
Brave Fellows Always ready
For any daring deed
Willing for Queen and Country
To suffer and to die
No thoughts of fear come nigh them
Though tears dimmed many an Eye
Sadly from Windsor Barracks
Came fourth a mourning band
of women whose brave husbands were
Bound for a foreign land
The wives of British soldiers
by orders turned adrift

237 With four and Eightpence weekly
  Left for themselves to Shift
  The Children of brave fellows
  Have two pence each a day
  Allowed for them to live upon
  While fathers are away
  This the reward of valour
  This the result of Fame
  Think on this fact. oh – Britishers
  and blush to hear the name

  God save the Queen
  for Britons never shall be
  Slaves.
  Now Play rule Brittaner
  For a Paltry sum of Gold
  when my brain was fired with
  drink life and body both
  I sold for a soldier dare
  not think
  Amen

239 and have burnt each other at
  the stake for their Cast and all
  this God see and know, his being
  Omnipotent Well then again look
  at the difference of the Start in
  life our Queen had a noble start
  compare that with the Gutter Children
  of the earth and look at their
  start they surly have nothing to
  thank God for. Now by a Close
  Calculation of the birth rate it would
  take about 65 generations from the
  time of the Christian era to the
  present time to produce our Queen
  that is if each Female of her
  race commenced to generate at 20
  years of age one with the other
  thus you see the whole of that
  65 generations had no cause
  to Commit any sin. Now it
  would take the same number of
  generations of 65 to produce me
  and when I look back for only

238 The Justice of God.
Looking Justice strait in the face
I cannot see were it begins or were
it ends. If we look at all the ways
of man. We will begin with the
most humble of our race as there
is only about 35 pr cent of the people
of this earth in a state of Civilisation
and 65 pr cent not Civilized but are
in Different state of Habit some
are in a Savage state no Law some
are in a Barbarous state and have
a few Laws. Now were can be Gods
Justice with these people there must
be a reason why it is so. and should
be explained away if possiable &
then again in the 35 pr cent that
are Goverened by law there are
about 3000 different Cast of a
religious belief all saying each
other are in the wrong and are
ever ready to Slay each other
for there way of Worship to God

✒

240 the past two generations of
my Family what an amount of
temptations we have to endure to
avoid and to look at if what
our parsons Calls sin to git
a chance to live while our Queen
and the Lords & Dukes fare of the
best, the poor Children of this –
Carrupt earth can get for them
and then they cry moor moor
Why do God stop this King
Craft as we pronounce him
God & King of Kings the only ruler
of princes Were is Justice) But
I have made a Great Mistake for
France can rule Kings & princes
why should not other Nations
Can the Poor look for Justice from
their Rulers. *No* there is one
Law for the poor and another
for the Rich if God was Just
to all alike he would put an
end to this King Craft at once

241 And then again look at
our Labor market see how our
Rulers make Slaves of us for the
sake of Wealth. Well may Dan.
De.foe) in his work put man Friday
neck under Crusoe. Foot we see
this every day and yet these
very Christian men make a very
Great Cry about the Slave .oh
were is Gods Justice Well then
again let us look at the price
of Food these very men if they
have a chance make a ring
and raise the price to get
Wealth and Starve the poor
and then attend prayers on
the Sunday at Church and
say though shall not covit
or desire Now I think such
men should be struck by God
from Mankind as we read
of in the Book called the Bible
at Sodom if such is truth

243 Where shall we find God
Justice shourly this could not
be if God was Just to all alike
I think we must forget Justice
and go with the Black Warrior
to the happy hunting grounds
But as I have said in another
part of this Book the pure
Mussalmen are the nearest to
God that is if there is a God
I donot mean the Mahomet he
is like the Christian a
follower of man and Can
turn any way he likes to
Prostitute the said Dogmas
Can our Great Rulars ever think
Morally on this great Matter if
they do how they must shuder
for what is to come if they
think there is a future but
they must think otherwise or
or they could not carry on
in the way they do though

242   God took vengeance on those
Can we see a Reason why
he should not now for our
modern Babylon is filled with
every Curruption and Sin—
But what is Sin who can
state when we find 65 prcent
of the whole earth know nothing
about it or God) oh were is the
Justice talked of to be found
not in England that is certain
What as been Stanleys Game in
Exploring affraca but to get Wealth
and in a few years to send the
White Man's Faith hope & Charity
to them I.E The Great Gun the
Sword and Bayonet for in them
we place our trust and when
they have done their work with
England's hired *Assasisers* I.E *Soldiers*
with a few Missionary he will then
send them a Bishop and Build
them a Church and make them
pay for it a little more

244   life if they only once thought
of such and end and Gods
Justice. Then they say there must
be rulers. That we know in a
Lawlised nation or as we are
told a Land of Civilization but that
donot meat that every poor man
shall put his neck under the
foot of the rich and powerful
no the Lawlised Nation of the
Earth are to make the poor man
slave and toil while the power
ful live in immorality and
sin (If there is such a thing
as sin) And should not our
Parson shake with fear when he
flaunts this Dogmus in the face
of a suffering humanity knowing
as he do that he donot follow
out one word of it in practice
he going the way of all men
he to as to submit to the powerful
man who as his living in their

245   in their Hands and should
he so dare to say a word so as
to offend one of them they would
soon seal his fate with the
Bishop) No the parson must
shut his Eyes. and open his
mouth and see what God
will send him. England
boast of her freedom to the
people. Why they have none if
you want to see Freedom you
must leave England and look
out some were else. And yet
as I said before they must and
will Flaunt their Dogmus in
the Face of suffering humanity
But still I like Law and have
always tried as a Soldier and
a Policeman to maintain it and
to keep up Disciplin. but when
we think of God. and then our
Rulers we look for the reasons why
it is so maintained and God

247   Ladies continualy bringing the
Brimstone to trim the hearts
burning in the Kings hands
in the centre of the hall stood
a Great mas of people makeing
fun of the Kings. Dukes. Lords
and their Lady loves. Who in
their turns went into hell to
stir up the furnises which opend
at the Back of each King while
the hot ashes burnt the Brimstone
in the Hands of the Dukes. Lords.
and their Lady loves as they
applied their task to fill the
Kings hearts. In a Gallery round
the Hall Danced the Devil imps
and in a sort of Pulpit at the
end sat the Devil surrounded by a
Grand Band of Imps playing
the most Death like music
in the most Discordant sounds
such is the Fate and the future
of Kings Dukes Lords and theirs
after that let us pray –

246   donot put an end to it as he
is Omnipotant. Looking all this
in its face how can we make
our way for a further we must
go to the happy hunting grounds
Now a Book I was reading the
other day of the Inhabitance of
Hell It said there the entrance
led into a Great Hall in which
was a Large number of Pedestals
on the top of each stood a King
of the earth holding in his hand
his own heart from which blazd
Cauldering fire which gave out a
great red light. Their Eyes were
roling from Side to side as if
in search of more subjects
to their number as there was lots
of spare Pedestals Beneath them
ringed the Dukes and lords
in their turn had to trim
the Fire in the heart held
by the Kings of the Earth the

✺

248   Population of the World
      Savage & E.T.C
   Lives in Asia   800.000.000
      " Europe   320.000.000
      " Africa   210.000.000
      " America 110.000.000
The Isles of the Sea 10.000.000
Of these it is Estimated that
500.000.000 are clothed & live in houses
700.000.000 In imperfect dwellings and
250.000.000 are wandering barbarians
Now What as God done for the last
named Barbarians shourly nothing
Europe is composed of many *Cast*
and so as America well Africas
the greater number are Savages
why didnot God send a Son to
one and all and not leave it
to the Crafty Christian who are
the men or people who worship
Gold and have a trinity of Gods
I.E the Gun Sword & Bayonet
these have brought them all the

249   Wealth power and also maintain
the pride of the Church . Oh
when I think of God and *Justice*
I think Why do he not do away
with all King Craft what rot
somthing like Justices. Justice
and now let us Moralise on mans
Justice at home one man one Million
of acres for Game preserves alone
in Scotland and Let us look at the
wealth some of the Dukes hold in
London. How will all this when
Compared with the Commandments
the one that say thou shalt not
Covit and another saith thou
shalt do no murder. Why these
Great so called men indirectly
murder thousands by the pent
up poor dwellings in London what
brings fever and such like but
these poor Hog styes. Away with
religion with wealth is god

✧

251   Copy of Letter by me Corpl
Pearman writen on Battle Field
Camp Goojrat 24th Febrery 1849 –
My Dear Mother
I take up my pen to address
these few lines to you and I hope this
may find you in the injoyment of
good health as thank god this leaves
me at present & I hope all my Brothers
and sister and all the Children are
also in good health. Give my love
to Jane & to Bobs Wife. Ann & to Sellwood
& little Frank & Kiss all Janes Children
for me. For those was happy days I –
spent at home with them. Ann Maria
said she was going to write to me again
but I have never got the letter. I hope
Little Louisa is still at service and
will do well. she was the little thing
that was fond of work when I was
at home. I hope some of the Boys are
able to work by this. And let me know
how my Brother William Children

250   What is a Soldier
A man forced down under
the Brutalising machine of
military life which presses out
nature from the very veins and
bones of its victims and shapes
from the warm living flesh
a puppet a tool a thing a
Creature without eyes or ears
or sence or will of its own –
a plaything for death a –
missile in the merciless hand
of the State for pomp and
Vain Glory. were is the Jutice
of God so much talked about
by the Great Medicine man at
Canterbury and all his crew
why do they flaunt this dogmas
in the face of the suffering
humanity away with Kingcraft
and all this cant the Idols
are the Cannon the Sword and
Bayonet mounted with Gold

꙳

252   Are geting on & Give my best respects
to Mr & Mrs Hayzell I hope they are
doing well & Give my best respects to
Joe Barnham & his Sisters and to
all enquiring freinds
My Dear Mother I will now Give you
an Account of the late Campayne as
well as my Memory will alow me to
do. But you will most likely have seen
all about it in the newspapers but
I will give you as true an account
as I can for the papers dont at all
times speak the truth. We march from
Umballa last September the 27th of the
month to form an Army at Lahore –
which is about 200 miles south East
of Umballa and after a deal of delay
we reached Lahore on the 30th of October
and Formed an Army of about – 7000 –
strong & 3 Troops of Guns .18. in all
The Enemy under the command of
Rajah Shere Sing was then laying at a
Town Called .Wuzzerabad on the Bank

253   of the River Chenab about 70 miles
north of the City of Lahore. On the
2nd of November we crossed the river
Ravee north side of the city of Lahore
under the command of Genl Curton and
on the 5th Novr we had a gallop after
a small portion of the Enemy but
could not come up with them I believe
there was one man of the enemy killed
on this occasion. We halted here for
a day or two to allow a Force to come
to join us under the Command of Genl.
Sir Joseph Thackwell. But the Enemy
moved from their Possion to a Town
much Larger and 30 miles down the
river Chenab our army then took
ground the Westward and halted –
About 8 miles from the enemy who
was Laying at the town of Ramnuger
We were now to wait for reinforcements
which didnot join us until the Evening
of the 20th inst. All things now appeared
to be going on very Comfortable and
we was looking forward for a General

255   was ordered to advance along
the bank of the river to find out
the possition of the enemys Guns
So away we were ordered and off we
went for about 5 miles at a Gallop
in Loose file like a flock of sheep
The Guns of the Enemy rattling at us
all the way. My horse was dead beat
& so was most of the other mens horses
It was such heavy ground all quick
sand which broke in. We had 5 horses
shot. but not a man on the Gallop
We now retired to find the regiment
which was formed up in Front of the
Enemy under a very heavy fire of
Match locks & here we sat & was fired
at for near an hour. at Last we was
ordered to take ground to the rear
We had one man killed many more
wounded but may horses wounded
The 14th Light Dragoons was now ordered
to Advance their horses being Fresh
they Came down in very good order
and Charged the Enemy but most of

254   Engagement Lord Gough was now
at Lahore. On the morning of the
22nd Novr onst We was laying comfortable
on our small peice of Gutteree or Bed
when an order Came round the camp
at 4 oCk in the morning that the first
Division of the Army would get ready
immeadiately and turn out without
noise to reconnitre the possition of
the Enemy Under the command of
Major Genl Creton this Division was
about 8 Thousand strong most of it
Cavelry with a few Guns. About Eight
oClock AM we came in sight of the Enemy
out Post the 3rd Light Dragoons was now
ordered to the Front and the word was
given to Gallop and away we went
Neck or nothing and Drove there out
Post away without any loss to us we
sounded a halt to let our Guns and
Infantry come up. We took the Town
of Ramnugger. The Enemy was on the
other side of the river Chenab looking
at us. The first Squadron of my regiment

256   the Enemy was in a Nullah and
Could not be got at. Their Colonel
Poor Havelock was killed a good
and brave officer 17 men killed and
29 wounded & 30 horses Genl Cureton
went to look were was Havelock and
he was shot also & Coln of the 1st Native
Cavelery and several more officers we
Burried the General & the two Colonels
in one Grave. There were little more
done this day a little sharp fireing
of the Infantry & Artilery. We had
one of our Guns got fast in the sand
& we could not get it away it fell
into the Enemys hands. our loss was
very heavy in fact we got the worst
of the day but we held the ground
Night now came on us & Nothing for
our horses to eat. After a hard days
work and us on their backs for 16
hours. the night was very cold and
lots of our horses got loose and caused
a great deal of Confusion. We made‾
a fire got a Bullok & killed it —

257   which we cut up and cooked at the
fire & eat it half raw. A small Village
was set on fire & burnt down. Day
light came . but no corn for our poor
horses near five oclock the rest of the
Army came & brought our Tents & our
Cooks & the rest of the camp followers –
And now we fed our horses for the
first for 36 hours. All through bad
management We Pitched our Tents got
the Cooks to work. Burried the dead &
at night we forgot all our troubles
over a Glass of Grog & went to sleep
as sound as tops as if nothing had
happened. Duty now became very hard
On the 27 Novr we had Another Gallop
After the Enemy they had taken some
of our Camels. But we didnot over
take them they got Safe away with
them and we got a few shops for
our labour but no one hurt. On the
30 inst. Lord Gough took Charge of the
Army which were about 20 Thousand
strong and 64 Guns & 12 heavy ones

259   of the river we was laying Down
on the ground in the hot sun
most of the men asleep. I was myself
we were waiting for orders from Lord
Gough. When the Enemy Opened a heavy
fire from their artilery upon us &
soon woke us up & made us jump
into our Saddles we soon formed line
and got into Battle order when
a General Engagement took place
about 3 oClock in the afternoon &
by Dark we had well beat them &
caused them to retreat to the river
Jellin Our loss was but very little
in this Battle My regiment lost
but one horse. the Enemys loss must
have been very great as I saw many
dead on the Battle field next day
This was the Battle of Soo.do.lipore –
We now marched to a place called
Hailah and was Joined by Lord
Gough and the main Army – we
formed a Camp of 20 Thousand &
men and remained here until the

258   My division of the army were ordered
to March at 1 oClock A.M on the 1st
of December to Wuzzerabad 30 miles
up the Banks of the river Chenab
8 Thousand strong & 34 Guns with no Tents
or Camp & Nothing to encumber us –
Cross the river & Come down on the
other side as the Enemy was on that
side of the river. You would haved
Laught to have seen us at day light
We took off our small Clothes and
made them fast round our necks and
got into the Saddle so to Cross the river
some of the horses had to swim
3 native Soldier was Drowned it was
on the morning of the 2nd December the
water was very Cold melted Snow
from the Mountains it was a very
heavy Day march on the 1st December
after we Cross the river we Marched
towards the Enemy but none in Sight
On the 3rd December we was halted
about 5 miles from the Enemy &
our main army on the other side

260   11th January 1849 and we were very well
off in this Camp and very Comfortable
and got everything we wanted & had
plenty of Sports when off Duty when
on Duty it was very hard for Cavelry
so oft to reconnitre the Enemy Camp
on the 11th we marched 3 AM from
this place and on the 13th we came
to the main camp of the Enemy it
was pitched on a hill about 2 miles
from were the Battle was Fought
which was a thick Jungle near the
Town of Chillian Wallah About 11 am
we Drove in their advance Parties on
their main Army and about 2 oClock
the Battle raged very hot our artilery
with that of the Enemys kept up a
Continual roar of Thunder. This was
a very hard fought Battle in the
midst of a very thick Jungle and
we could not get at them our fourth
Squadron the Grey Squadron Charged
a Mas of all arms like a Wedge and
our loss was great 25 killed 21 wounded

261   and our Capt & Leut I was attached
to the Squadron & got a slight flesh
wound in the arms we did a great
deal of Execution in this Charge
but how we got back none could tell
HM 24th of foot lost a great number I
think it was 410 men 19 officers and
the Queens Colours of the regiment
The 15 Sepoys was cut up and so was
Capt Christys Troop of horse artilery
and the Guns taken but we took
12 Guns from the Enemy in the Charge
Our loss altogeather was about 2000
killed & wounded. The Enemy Loss
was about 5000 killed & wounded
There was some Confussion in our
line by the 14th light Dragoon going back
At Night we retired to a Town or
Large Village in our rear and lay for
the night the next morning we
went over the Battle field to bury
the dead and get in the wounded
it was a Dreadful sight to look
at so many Dead also the horses –

263   until they had crossed the Indus
and on to Pershaw. We took the whole
of their Camp and Carrage & Guns and
many Thousands of small arms. Our loss
was but small in this Battle and
I hope this will be the last and the
end of the Campayne which I think
it will. About 15 Thousand of our Army
and 60 Guns as gone up the Country
under the Command of Genl Gilchrist
who I think will settle things
there – There is a great talk of
some of the army returning to
quarters very shortly before the hot
weather set in. I think my regiment
will return to quarters this season
this was the Battle of Goojrat –
There as been great riches taken by
the Solders at Moultan the 10th foot
& 32 foot & 60 rifles as made a great
deal of Money some of them several
hundred Pounds I shall now
Conclude for the present and I

262 It began to rain it had a little on the
night and it Continued to rain for
several days which made every thing
very uncomfortable We now began to
entrench our Camp as we had to stop
here to wait for the army from
Moultan under the command of Genl
Wishe who had Just taken Moultan
Our Duty now became very hard we
could not take our things off and
oftimes had to sleep in our arms night
& Day. About the 15 Febrery the Enemy
shifted their Camp to a Town Called
Goojerat and on the next day we
moved after them and was then
Joined by Genl Wishe army on the 19th
inst when we saw some old Camp
Comrades and had a Glass togeather
On the 21st inst we had another –
Slap at them the Battle Commenced
about 8 oClock AM and by 12 oClock
noon we had beaten them and put
the whole of their army to Flight
which was followed by part of ours

264 hope you will answer this as
soon as posseable so no more
at present from your affectanate
son
Corpl John Pearman
HM 3rd light Dragoons

PS Tell my Brother Robert
I got his letter but could not
answer as it is a great deal
of trouble to get letters sent
away Give my best respects to
him and all inquiring friends
Direct to
Corpl John Pearman
HM 3rd Light Dragoons
Army of the Sutledge
India

265   Is Marriage a Failour
      Well with most people it is they
      build castles in the air or their house
      upon the sand which the storms of Life
      sweap away and they are lost for ever
      very sildom man & woman come togeather
      of the same Temper and of the same
      Disposition. The Rich are mostly immoral
      and oft comes to Divorce. The Middle
      Class oft comes to straife by living up
      to and some times behond it and then
      Bankrupsey follow. The Mechanic also
      wish to look up and live beyond his
      income. In my mind the only people
      to whom marrage is not a failour is
      the very poor in country villages.there
      both seem more to pull togeather their
      Children's feed scant and Clothed the
      same but they seem happy therewith
      and as Children grow up they only
      look for the same life as their Parents
      In Towns and Particular Large ones the
      Poor take up to pleasure. True it was

      [three pages cut away]

      ✐

267   Bucks Constabulary
      South Eastern Division
      26th May 1869
      Robt Tolladay v Murry —
      Forged a Cheque on a Banker of Sir
      Edward Sherlock Gooch. Baronet
      Information laid by Rt Tolladay
      10th May 1869 who sayeth on 7th May inst.
      Reginald Temple Strange Clare Grenvell
      Murry Late of Eton Bucks did Forge
      the said Cheque of £10–"–" which was
      Cashed at Neville reid & C Bank Windsor
      on the Bank of York. (Murry Gazetted
      Prisoner apprehended in London and
      Brought to Windsor the White Hart Hotel
      at 10-30 PM 25th May by two Police Officers from GSG
      26th May 1869 Charge withdrawn by Rt Tolladay
      at 11A.M at Capt Farrer house Willow Brook
      Eton. Warrant torn to peices & Distroyed
      by Capt. Farrer. Prisoner was kept at the
      Crown & Cushion Eton in Charge of Police
      Constables Critchlow & North from 11 PM
      25th May until 2–40 PM 26 May when

266   Names of Men in the Draft
of Recruits of 1843 = 3rd Lt. Drag=

S. M.	Baker	Pt Foot	Pt Nichols
Sergt	Darling	Gorham	Potter
Trump	Tinsley	Goodman	Roberts
" "	Russell	Harding	O. Regan
	Thompson	Hamilton	G. Regan
	Miles	Hazard	Rogers
	Robinson	Hawkins	Rockliff
	Pearman	Hill	Robson
	Cox	W. Joy	Steele
	Barnyard	F. Joy	Tayler
Privates	Alexander	Jones	Topley
	Baker	Kettle	Wolfe
	Brion	Livermore	West
	Blake	Louch	Wright
	Coe	Locket	Williams
	Curtis	Middleton	Reeves
	Cooper	Mouse	Robinson
	Cumber	McGee	Godfrey
	East	Monday	Capt Forbes
	Elderkin	Miles	Cornet Colt
	Friend	Makepeace	

268   I took him to London by the GWR
Where he was Examd by several Doctor
I then took him to Paris in France
Where I arrived at 7.30 AM 27 inst
and took him to an Asylum where I
left him. Left Paris at 7.50 PM the
same day. Arrived in London 8 AM
28th May and at Eton at 9.30 AM
Cockshut V Murry 24 June 1876
Forged Cheque £15–"–" on Farquar & Harris
Bank St James Street London was
Committed for trial at Quarter Sessions
Aylesbury October 1876 from Slough Court
5th July 1876) Witnesses in the case
Lord Kensington Revd James Evans
of St Pauls H. A Feeind . Banker A Cockshot
Prosocutor Jane Lauridge cashed Cheque
PK Keep & Inspr J Pearman
Got four *months* Imprisonment
Carrington .V. Murry the supposed
Father Charged with assault & Pergery

269   Buried at Ealing & Brentford Cemetry

Elizabeth Pearman
Died August 1st 1866. Aged 88 years
Jane Pearman
Died December 19th 1865. Aged 63 years

Thomas Pearman Son of Jane
and Thomas Pearman
died Febry 25 1872 Aged 37 Years

John Pearman Son of Rbt & Elizth Pearman
Borned at Kingston in Surry Febry 24 1819
Robt Pearman Father of the above was Borned
at Nettlebed Oxon
Died & Burried at Kingston Surry
Married at Hampton or near there to Miss
Elizth Woodham Mother of the avove Jn Pearman
John Pearman Enlisted in 3rd Light Dragn Augst 26 1843
Joined the Bucks Police 16th March 1857 and resigned
18th October 1881 On a Yearly Pension of £69.6.8

෴

To Be Burried
Put me into the Earth as
I have come from it so
that I return what I have
taken Let there be no Kind
of Sorrow for I am at rest
Let no foloowers be there more
than those who dig the earth
up and cover me in & Those
who may Carry my body let
no mock Service be said over
me by paid servants But lay
me in and Cover me in Level
down the earth at the spot
that I may be for gotten and
no kind of rayment worn
by my relative But I hope
and trust they will learn to
know that this is the end of
all men for in my travels
over the Globe I find that
is the end of all and they

270   War Service East India
      Sergt John Pearman 3rd Lt Dragn
      Was present at the Battle of Buddewal
      21 January 1846 and Mirat 28th January
      1846 and Sabroan 10th February 1846
      for which he was awarded a medal
      and one Clasps
      was Present with 3rd Light Dragoons
      at the Battle of Ramnugar on the
      22nd November 1848 at the Passage
      of the Chenab on the 2nd December
      1848 and at the battle of Sadoolapore
      on the 3rd December 1848 and at
      the Battle of Chillian Walla and
      Charged with the 4th or Grey Squadron
      Slight wound in right arm on the
      13th January 1849 and at the Battle
      of Goojerat on the 21st February
      1849 for which he received a medal
      and two Clasps [was also in a Sharp Skirmish
      when in Charge of a Convoy of Corn
      when under the command of Capt
      Overy of C Troop 3rd L Drago –
      17th February 1849 –

                    ✒

      are soon forgot by man
      the man who eat his fellow
      man is jest the same Cast
      as nothing to do with it
      we live only by and with the
      liveing so I hope and
      Trust this may be the –
      wish of all I leave behind
      Lay me down and then
      forget I was ever here this
      is the Last wish
              of John Pearman

Notes to the Transcript

When Indian place names appear in the notes below, the following convention has been used: Pearman's spelling is reproduced, followed by the conventional British spelling of the word as found on British maps and in gazetteers of the mid-nineteenth century. It was usually this spelling and pronunciation that Pearman was trying to remember and reproduce. The modern Indian spelling is then given, and it is this that is used on the maps to which the reader is referred, and which is current on modern maps of India. Sometimes the spelling of place names has remained the same over the last 150 years, and so the last spelling given in these notes will always be the modern Indian version. In general throughout the notes, I have retained the spelling of battle names as they are given in modern military histories.

For details of cavalry drill and field movements, the reader is referred to the standard authority, Marquess of Anglesey, *A History of the British Cavalry, 1816–1918* (3 vols), vol. 1, 1816–50, Leo Cooper, 1973, pp. 95–113.

Page 1 Her Majesty's or the King's Own Light Dragoons was formed in 1685. It had a distinguished and public history: action particularly remembered was in the Battle of Dettingen in 1743, against the French in the War of Austrian Succession; and at the Battle of Salamanca during the Peninsular Wars. The Regiment had left for its tour of duty in India in 1837: 'Its numbers were increased to the normal Indian establishment of eight service Troops with one recruiting or depot Troop left at Maidstone. The eight service Troops consisted of 44 officers and 702 rank and file.' See The Marquess of Anglesey, *Sergeant Pearman's Memoirs*, Cape, 1968, pp. 22–4. For conditions at Maidstone, see p. 275, note 18.

Page 2 'Fare the well Love . . .': I have been unable to trace this song.

Page 3 'Parade twice a Day once for health Clean feet and body': 'I took great pride in keeping myself clean,' wrote a staff sergeant in the Indian army of this period, 'which at all times is the principle part of a soldier's duty.' Thomas Quinney, *Sketches of a Soldier's Life in India*, David Robertson, Glasgow, 1853, p. 8.

Page 4 'Tiger Isles and Sand Heads': by Sand Heads Pearman means the inward ends of the banks of sand that lie beneath the water at the mouth of the Hugli River. It is less clear what he is referring to by

'Tiger Isles'. All the islands across the Sundarbans (see note to Page 9) were infested with tigers, and Sagar Island was the largest of them. In the 1840s the island was referred to by the British as Saugaur Sand, and it may be this pronunciation – misheard and connected in his mind with tigers – that Pearman is trying to reproduce here. The problem with this interpretation is that the Sundarbans are at some distance from the Sand Heads at the mouth of the Hugli, and would never geographically be spoken of together. The *Thetis* was not a naval ship, but rather a merchant carrier brought in for the purpose of transporting troops to India; therefore no log can be traced which would give an account of the actual negotiation of these waters.

Page 5 'Dimmond Harbour': Diamond Harbour. See Map I.

'Garden reach': Garden Reach. See Map I.

Page 6 Fort William. See Map I.

'Chinsurah': Chinsura. See Map I.

Page 8 'arrach': arrack. Liquor distilled from rice and sugar.

'Collerar': cholera. Cholera was pandemic in India after 1818, having previously been endemic in the Jessore region. See Michael Durey, *The Return of the Plague: British Society and the Cholera, 1831–1832*, Gill & Macmillan, 1979, pp. 7–9. Trading, and the movement of large bodies of troops about the sub-continent had played a role in the spread of the disease.

Page 9 'Major Mythyus': probably Captain William Mathias of the 62nd Regiment of Foot. In October 1845 he had served for 15 years. Brevet-major in June 1846. Fought at the Battles of Aliwal, Baddowal and Sobraon.

'the Sunderbuns or the Floating Islelands': Sundarbans. See Map I and note to Page 4. Common name for the tract of intersecting creeks, channels and swampy islands forming the part of the Ganges Delta nearest to the sea, and bounded by the mouth of the Hugli and the Megna – now the Madhumate – (the combined Ganges and Brahmaputra) Rivers. About 220 miles wide. Etymology obscure.

Page 10 'Gutteree': a quilt, usually made of cotton, that could serve as cloak or sleeping mat.

Allahabad. See Map I.

Page 11 'Dinnapore . Mongeah and Bannares': Dinapur, Monghyr, Benares.

For Dinapur, Munger and Varanasi, see Map I.

Page 13 'Cawnpore': Kanpur. See Map I.

'Major General Sir Joseph Thackwell': Lieutenant General Sir Joseph Thackwell (1781–1859). Served in the Peninsular Wars and at Waterloo. At the beginning of the Second Sikh War, he was in command of a division of cavalry, but after the Battle of Ramnagar, he succeeded Brigadier General Cureton as cavalry commander. See George Bruce, *Six Battles for India, the Anglo-Sikh Wars, 1845–6,*

1848–9, Arthur Barker, 1969, pp. 256–61, 283–6. See E. J. Thackwell, *Narrative of the Second Sikh War*, Richard Bentley, 1851.

Page 14   'Tope of Mango Trees': grove. 'The word is in universal use by the English, but is quite unknown to the natives of upper India.' Henry Yule and A. C. Burnell, *Hobson-Jobson: a glossary of colloquial Anglo-Indian words and phrases*, John Murray, 1903.

'Aekeres': 'hackeries'. Bullock cart used for the transportation of goods. From the Hindi *chhakyra*.

Page 15   'I was Lance Corporal': this is the first elaboration of the untruth John Pearman tells about his sergeantship. The monthly muster rolls return Pearman as a private soldier for September 1845. Public Record Office, WO12/592, Monthly Muster Roll of the 3rd King's Own Regiment of Dragoons for the three months ending 31 December 1845.

Lucknow. See Map I.

Page 16   'we had twelve stand of old arms with us the old Brown Bess': the Brown Bess was a flintlock, smoothbore musket. It was the regulation infantry weapon, until the general introduction of the rifle. On the general state of British unreadiness for warfare, and conflicts over equipping the army, see Bruce, op. cit., pp. 70–102.

Page 17   'Kurnaul Station': Karnal. See Map II.

Page 18   'shall we be there in time to get the *Medle*': with this phrase, Anglesey (1968), op. cit., p. 19, makes Pearman representative of all soldiers 'throughout the ages (except, perhaps our own)', attributing to him the valour of a simple man wanting a simple prize. He did win medals: two were struck, one for the Sutlej Campaign (First Sikh War), one for the Punjab Campaign (Second Sikh War). Photographs of them can be found in Anglesey, ibid., facing pp. 64 and 129. I think it is impossible not to read some retrospective irony into this reported desire for reward; but this indeed may be the response occasioned by having read the whole text, rather than John Pearman's literary intention.

'form Square': see above, p. 48 for the square as the basic organisational unit of an army in battle. See John Keegan, *The Face of Battle*, Penguin, 1978, pp. 185–6, for its psychological importance. See also Brian Bond (ed.), *Victorian Military Campaigns*, Hutchinson, 1967, p. 25, for how the square remained a valuable formation against non-European opponents until the end of the nineteenth century. The name was deceptive in fact, for squares took on various shapes according to the terrain and military situation, becoming sophisticated and flexible formations. See also note 57, p. 278.

'I fell my 6 men in under a tree': see above, note to Page 15.

'Bus . se . an': Busseean. Bassian will be found on modern maps near the town of Raikot, Punjab. See Map II.

Page 19   'Sir Harry Smith': Lieutenant General Sir Harry Smith

(1787–1860). Served in the Corunna campaign, and in the Peninsular Wars. In 1840, appointed adjutant-general of the Queen's Army (as opposed to the East India Company's Army) in India. After the victory at Aliwal in January 1846, he was made a baronet. See G. C. Moore Smith (ed.), *The Autobiography of Sir Harry Smith*, John Murray, 1903.

'in one colum': see Anglesey (1973), op. cit., pp. 102–3 for the 22 basic field movements of the cavalry, of which 'the most important was the ability to ride across country, keeping in line and maintaining correct spacing. The operational unit was the squadron, divided into a right and left troop. Each troop. . .consisted in theory of twenty four other ranks. The space between the front and rear ranks into which these were divided varied, depending on whether the squadron (of which there were generally two or three in a regiment), was in "Order" (twenty-four feet), "Close Order" (eight feet), or marching in fours (four feet). The normal interval between squadrons in line was twelve yards.'

Page 20   'Loodeanna': Loodheana. See Map II for Ludhiana.

Page 20f   Pearman calls this engagement at Badowal a battle. ['Memoir', p. 270] See an account in Anglesey (1968), op. cit., p. 34; Bruce, op. cit., pp. 162–3; and in Khushwant Singh, *A History of the Sikhs*, Oxford University Press, Bombay, 2 vols, 1977, vol. 2, pp. 50–1. Two battles of the First Sikh War had already been fought, at Mudki on 18 December 1845, and at Ferozeshah, on 21 December 1845. The Sikh army had been defeated and driven back across the Sutlej River, camping at Sobraon and awaiting reinforcements. Having built a bridge of boats, they crossed the Sutlej and entrenched themselves on the south bank, while a smaller force crossed at Ludhiana, some 60 miles to the east, thus placing the British siege train under threat. To deal with this threat, and to relieve Ludhiana, a brigade was detached under the command of Sir Harry Smith, and it was this force that John Pearman made contact with on 20 January 1846. The midnight march was undertaken to deal with what was believed to be a small force of Sikhs at the fort of Badowal. Discovering that in fact a force of 8,000 Sikhs under the command of Runjur Singh had camped round the fort, Smith decided to avoid Badowal and head for Ludhiana. Pearman is describing men marching in order of battle 'over ploughed fields of deep sandy soil, as the Sikh force moved parallel through a line of villages linked by roads. The head of the Sikh column, a large body of cavalry, outflanked Smith's forces by about a mile. . .'. Bruce, op. cit., p. 162. Bruce quotes Sir Harry Smith: 'the cavalry moved parallel to the enemy, and protected from the fire of his guns by a low ridge of sandhills. My eighteen guns I kept close together in rear of the cavalry, in order to open a heavy fire on the enemy. . . this fire, which I continued for some ten minutes, had a most auxiliary effect, creating slaughter and confusion in the enemy's ranks. The enemy's cannonade upon the column of Infantry had been previous to this furious. . . As the column moved on under this cannonade. . .the enemy. . .formed a line of seven battalions. . . I therefore. . .changed front on the centre of the 31st Regiment and of the 53rd, by what is a difficult move on parade even – a countermarch on the centre by wings. . . This move was executed as accurately as at a review. . . I now directed the Infantry to march on Loodiana in echelon of Battalions. . .the guns in rear of the Cavalry . . . the movement was so steady that the enemy. . . did not attack, but stood amazed, as it were, fearing to quit his stronghold of Budowal and aware that the junction of my force with that of Loodhiana was about to be accomplished.' Smith, op. cit., pp. 530–2. This was Pearman's first experience of battle, and he presents it as an extremely confusing experience.

Page 21 'he was my front rank man': See note to Page 15 above.

Page 27 'Elephants cakes': ' "elephants' cakes" – huge cakes, made from very coarse attah and bran, mixed with chopped straw for elephants! Each man had one of these issued, to last him for a whole day, no other bread being to be had.' N. W. Bancroft, *From Recruit to Staff Sergeant* (1885), Ian Henry, Hornchurch, 1979, p. 48. This was before the Battle of Ferozeshah, 21 and 22 December 1845. See also W. R. Bingham, *The Field of Ferozeshah in Two Cantos*, Charles Edward Bingham, 1848, p. 31.

Page 28 'Bud . de wal': Badowal. See Map II for Baddowal.

Page 31 'Jugron': Jugroan. See Map II for Jagraon.
'Coln Alexanders Troop Horse artillery': Brevet Lieutenant Colonel James Alexander (1802–88). Bengal Artillery, 1820.

Page 32 'Adjutant Smyth': Major General Sir John Rowland Smyth (1806–73). Commanded 3rd Light Dragoons from 1847 to 1855. Wounded at Battle of Aliwal. Lieutenant General in 1870.

Page 33 'skirmishers': to skirmish is to send out a small party of soldiers ahead of an army, to engage in irregular fire with an enemy. See note to Page 19.

Page 33f Battle of Aliwal. See Singh, op. cit., vol. 2, pp. 50–1; Bruce, op. cit., pp. 164–90; Anglesey, op. cit., pp. 40–7. Sir Harry Smith, learning that the Sikh force, joined by 4,000 infantry, was on the move to Ludhiana, attacked and defeated it in the tract of land between the villages of Bhundri and Aliwal. See Map II. The ground here was good hard turf, by way of contrast with the dry sand of Baddowal. Victory for the British at this point meant that their communications were secured. The Sikh army had now to evacuate all bridgeheads south of the Sutlej River, except the one at Sobraon (see Map II) which they proceeded to fortify. This entrenched army was about 30,000 strong and possessed 70 cannon.

Page 34 'unlimber', 'limbered up': to fasten together two parts of a gun carriage in order to move it away.

'an Nellar': a dry watercourse. 'Nullah' is the accepted nineteenth-century British rendering of the Hindi *nala*.

Page 37 'Fortress of Valore': Filor or Philour. See Map II for Phillaur. 'Calcutta Musaiin': Calcutta Museum.

Page 38 'Prince Waldemarr': Prince Frederick William Waldemar (1817–49), nephew of King Frederick William III of Prussia. He used the name of Count Ravensburg during his Indian tour, and was present at the Battles of Mudki, Ferozeshah and Sobraon.

'Lord Gough army': Lieutenant General Sir Hugh Gough (1779–1869). Served throughout the Peninsular Wars. Knighted in 1815. In 1822, given command of the Mysore Division of the Madras Army, and in 1843 was appointed Commander-in-Chief of the Indian Army. After the defeat at Ramnagar, Sir Charles Napier was appointed to take his place, but he had achieved victory at Gujrat before this actually happened. He was promoted to full general in 1854 and in 1855 became Colonel of the Royal Horse Guards. Lord Gough's relationship with Sir Henry Hardinge, Governor General of India from 1844 to 1847, caused problems throughout the Sikh Wars, though Hardinge waived his right, as Governor General, to command the field, and served as Gough's second in command. See Bruce, op. cit., pp. 118–19. Gough's engineers, from an army of about 20,000 men, were now reconnoitring the Sikh positions at Sobraon described above (note to Page 33f). Gough wanted to attack immediately without waiting for Smith's forces to join him from Aliwal, or for the artillery to arrive, which was making its way up from Delhi. See note to Page 44f.

Page 39 'Gutteree': see note to Page 10.

'Bright Boys': no dictionary of slang or colloquial usage that I have consulted offers an explanation of this phrase; its meaning, though, seems quite apparent.

Page 42 'Lieut Coln White': Lieutenant General Sir Michael White (1791–1868). Served in the Mahratta War and in the First Afghan War. Joined 3rd Light Dragoons in 1839. Promoted to Major General in 1854.

'in the previous Battles of Moodkee . and . Ferozeshah': see Map II for Mudki and Ferozeshar. For an account of the battles see Bruce, op. cit., pp. 103–41. See also Bingham, op. cit., pp. 43–4 for the extremely heavy losses sustained by the 3rd Light Dragoons at Ferozeshar.

Page 44f Battle of Sobraon, February 10, 1846. See note to Page 38. This place name was written as Sabroan and as Sabraon by the British. For Sobraon, see Map II. When consulting modern maps, the reader should note that the battle took place at Little Sobraon, south of the river and near the obelisk at Roda Jallewala. The first part of the artillery convoy arrived at Sir Hugh Gough's camp on 7 February, and Sir Harry Smith (and John Pearman on the 8th).

Conflict over method of attack ensued among the command, with Gough favouring heavy artillery bombardment, followed by infantry and cavalry assault. Heavy rain fell on the evening of the 9th, and the action that John Pearman describes was, in fact, shrouded in mist until mid-morning. Sobraon was an artillery and infantry battle, and the cavalry was used only once, in the incident described by Pearman on Page 51 of the 'Memoir', when the first entry was made into the enemy position. This complete victory by the British caused extremely heavy Sikh losses of about 10,000 men. Bruce, op. cit., pp. 173–91; Anglesey (1968), op. cit., pp. 50–2; Singh, op. cit., vol. 2, pp. 51–3. The savagery of the British towards their defeated enemy caused an outcry in Britain.

Page 45 'Clos Column of Troops': Anglesey (1973), op. cit., p. 103 describes 'Close Column of Squadrons' as 'a massing of all the troopers, with their officers on the flanks, and all the trumpeters and farriers at the rear'.

Page 47 'General Gilbert': Major General Sir Walter Raleigh Gilbert (1785–1853). Served in the Bengal Artillery from 1800 until his death in 1853. In the First Sikh War he commanded a division of the 35th Bengal Native Infantry, being present at the Battles of Mudki, Ferozeshah and Sobraon. In the Second Sikh War he fought at Chilianwala. Created a baronet in 1851.

'General Dick': Major General Sir Robert Henry Dick (1785–1846). Served throughout the Peninsular Wars, and was present at Waterloo. In 1838, given command of the centre division of the Madras Army. Transferred to the Bengal Army in 1842. Killed at the Battle of Sobraon.

'. . .and Smith': see note to Page 19.

'I see Abercrombies sappers': Colonel William Abercrombie (1812–58), Engineers, Bengal Army. Wounded here at Sobraon. At Siege of Multan, and fought at Gujrat. For the attempts made by the engineers to gain a foothold on the Sikh entrenchments at this stage of the fighting, see Bruce, op. cit., pp. 187–8. He quoted P. R. Innes, *History of the Bengal European Regiment now the Royal Munster Fusiliers and How It Helped to Win India*, Simpkin Marshall, 1885, pp. 400–3, especially p. 403 to this point.

Page 50 'from line to Echellon': a formation of troops in which the successive divisions are placed parallel to one another, but no two in exactly the same alignment.

Page 51 'sponge staff': the pole and sponge used to clear out cannon.

Page 54 'Aean Battalions': possibly from *aeolic*, of the wind, light. Courtly Persian provided some Sikh military vocabulary.

Page 55 'Batta din': *bhata*, from the Hindi. An extra allowance made to soldiers when in the field.

'the Exact Loss on our side': Bruce, op. cit., p. 190, gives the totals of 320 dead and 2,063 wounded.

'Bobagees': *bobachee*. A cook. 'This is an Anglo-Indian vulgarisation of *bawarchi*, a term originally brought. . .by the hoards of Chingiz Khan into western Asia.' Yule and Burnell, op. cit.

Page 56 'Khoonda Ghat': see Map II for Chak Kunda, where the main Firozpur–Lahore road and railway crosses the Sutlej River. A ghat is the sharp bank of a river that gives access to deep water. Campaign maps of the Sikh Wars show Khoonda Ghat near the villages of Khunda and Buggiawala, but these settlements themselves change location over the next 50 years, as the course of the Sutlej alters. It is therefore impossible to verify the exact location of this bridge of boats from maps alone. The reader should locate the Firozpur–Lahore highway, and see the bridge of boats serving the same function as it does nowadays.

'Kussoor': see Map II for Kasur.

Page 57 'on Verdit': vedette. A mounted sentry placed in advance of the outposts of an army to observe enemy movement.

'out Laying Picquet': Anglesey (1973), op. cit., p. 103. 'In bivouac or camp, picquets formed an encircling guard. Beyond these, just in sight, was a chain of vedettes, each generally consisting of two men.'

'Maharajah Gholab Sign': Maharajah Gulub Singh. Leader of one of the major contending factors in the Punjab after the death of Ranjit Singh in 1839. He was an acceptable negotiator to the British, having long been in contact with them, and having refused in the past to align to either the Dogras, or to the Sikh aristocracy. He had prevented the Dogra forces from joining the Punjabi army, and it is possible that some understanding about the future of the Punjab had been reached between him and the British, before the Battle of Sobraon. See Singh, op. cit., vol. 2, p. 55. Immediately to outbreak of war, he had administered the departments of revenue and finance in Lahore, and had been selected as spokesman for the military government in 1845.

'Fakir Nooroodan': Fakir Nur-ud-Din. One of the Fakir brothers, who had also steered a course between the Dogras and the Sikh aristocracy in the pre-war period.

'Bhzee Ram Sign': here Pearman apparently means to record the name of Ram Singh Bhai, though 'Bhzee' seems to be an attempt to render the word 'wazir' or 'vizir'. For Ram Singh Bhai, see Singh, op. cit., vol. 2, pp. 35, 59.

Page 58 'Meen Meer': Mian Meer. The shrine of Mian Meer, which gave its name to the parade ground, was surrounded by the cantonment, which has itself been absorbed into the city of Lahore. See Map II.

'the Great Dubar': this Treaty of Lahore was actually signed on 9 and

11 March, not on 18 February. 'Durbar' means court, in the courtly Urdu/Persian used in government circles. Jallunder Doab was ceded to the British (advancing the borders of British India by 100 miles). An indemnity of £500,000 was fixed on, but could not be paid by the Lahore government; instead, the hill territories between the Indus and the Beas (including Kashmir) were handed over. The British gained control of both banks of the River Sutlej, and the Sikh army was reduced to 20,000 infantry and 12,000 cavalry. The treaties of Lahore were replaced by a new one, ratified at Bhairowal in December 1846. The British government here undertook the protection of the young maharajah during his ministry. The Punjab was occupied, and a British residency was established at Lahore.

'Sir Henry Hardinge': Field Marshal Sir Henry Hardinge (1785–1856). Served at Corunna and in the Netherlands Campaign of 1815. Tory member of Parliament for Durham in 1820; Secretary at War, 1828–30, Irish Secretary in 1830 and from 1834 to 1835. Secretary at War again in Peel's ministry, 1841–4. In 1844, became Governor General of India. During the First Sikh War, he waived his right to command the army, and served under Gough. See above, note to Page 38. After the Second Sikh War, he was created Viscount Hardinge of Lahore.

Page 59 'the Young Maharajah': Dulip Singh (1838–93) was in fact sent to Britain after the Second Sikh War, in 1854, after his conversion to Christianity. See Singh, op. cit., vol. 2, *passim* and p. 87 for a brief account of his life after leaving the Punjab. See also Michael Alexander and Sushila Anand, *Queen Victoria's Maharajah. Dulip Singh, 1838–1893*, Weidenfeld & Nicolson, 1980.

'Umballah': Ambala. See Map II.

Page 60 '1 pr Setteren Trowsers': *satara* possibly describes a finely ribbed woollen cloth according to Anglesey (1968), op. cit., p. 60.

'Shacko': Shako: barrel-shaped cap.

Pages 62–3 'a Tin Baby . . . Bishops': for similar strategies for getting drink away from the canteen, see Arthur Swinson and Donald Scott (eds), *The Memoirs of Private Waterfield*, Cassell, 1968, p. 61.

Page 64 'Kerkee Bombay': Kirkee.

'Lieut Col Havelock': Lieutenant Colonel William Havelock (1793–1848). Served in the Peninsular Wars. In 1841, he became second Lieutenant Colonel of the 14th Light Dragoons and commander of that regiment in 1845. Killed at the Battle of Ramnagar.

Page 67 'The Ellgie': large short-horned deer; perhaps the *nilghau*, phonetically transcribed from the Hindi.

Page 69 'White man Potturee Bote uteh ah adamy': here Pearman is transcribing phonetically a dialect of rural Hindustani (Urdu). Roughly translated, this means 'some of these people are good people'.

Page 71 'Lieut. Coln Lockwood': Colonel Sir George Henry Lockwood (1804–84). Joined 3rd Light Dragoons in 1825. Served throughout the first Afghan War, during which he had command of the regiment. He commanded a brigade at the Battle of Gujrat. Bancroft, op. cit., p. 38 for a similar (and not uncommon) effort undertaken by a philanthropic officer. For this development in the cavalry in general, see Anglesey (1973), op. cit., pp. 143–4.

Page 72 'Blue Lights': no dictionary or glossary of slang that I have consulted explains this phrase. Partridge, in his *Dictionary of Slang and Unconventional Usage*, gives it as a term for 'a sanctimonious seaman', late nineteenth–twentieth century, which seems close to its evident meaning.

See H. M. Conran, *Autobiography of an Indian Officer*, Morgan & Chase, 1870, p. 94 for enthusiasm (and Methodism) among troops in India, and the high rate of conversion: 'It is there, in the far-off land, that the prodigal most frequently "comes to himself", and whilst all the early associations of childhood and home are flooding his heart with tenderness, you can cast in the good seed in hope of a welcome reception.' For Methodism in the British Army in India, see Owen Spencer Watkins, *Soldiers and Preachers Too, Being the Romantic Story of Methodism in the British Army*, Charles H. Kelley, 1906, pp. 144–51.

Page 73 'Mud Wallah Cast': again, Pearman is transcribing the uneducated Hindustani of British army camps in this period. See above, note to Page 69.

Page 74 'the Native Force at Moultan under Shere Sing had Deserted': this local rebellion of April 1848 is described in Bruce, op. cit., pp. 201–21. The siege of the fort that followed is described on pp. 222–50, 265–80.

Page 76 'Ferozepoor': Ferozepore. See Map II for Firozpur.

Three lines are scored through on this page of the 'Memoir'. After 'Jallunder' in the penultimate line in the transcription, Pearman originally wrote 'where we played a Cricket Match with the 29th regiment of Foot and Halted two day (We had a Dance at Night in'. Here, he simply corrects a mistake of memory. See also note to Page 77.

Page 77 'Rannuggar on the Chenab': Ramnegurh or Ramnuggar on the Chenab River. See Map II for Rasulnagar.

'Wuzerabad': see Map II for Wazirabad.

'Lieut General Curton': Brigadier General Sir Charles Robert Cureton (1789–1848). Served in the Peninsular Wars. Joined 16th Lancers in 1819. Served in the First Afghan War. Killed at the Battle of Ramnagar.

Eleven lines are scored through on this page. Pearman had originally written 'the 29th regit as they were then in there tents. One of our men George Freind was coming from the Barracks by himself when a

Tug or Highway Robber throwed a Lassoo over his Head but he put up his arm and it went round his arm as well as his neck so he got it off again. We caught the Fellow and made small meat of him he told no tales.' So originally this passage ran directly on from Page 76 (Pearman added the top line of the transcription when he revised this section). He tells this story later ['Memoir', p. 138]; but does not there mention the fact that they killed the Indian thief. This incident does not accord with the respect he showed for Indian people in the second half of the 'Memoir'; shame at the memory was the most likely reason for crossing it out.

Page 79 'Verdetts': vedette. See note to Pages 19 and 57. Pearman presumably means here a small group on foot, acting as scouts.

Page 80f For the Battle of Ramnagar, see Bruce, op. cit., pp. 251–64; Anglesey, op. cit., pp. 71–8.

Page 81 'about 8 oCk we came in sight of the enemys out Post': the Sikh outposts were on the south side of the river, and the Sikh army was on the north. Gough, eager to discover the strength of the enemy, and believing it necessary to deal with the force south of the river before the Chenab could be crossed, turned a reconnaissance into a battle. The cavalry were used on this occasion, but very badly, especially when Havelock led some of the 14th Light Dragoons into the quicksand that Pearman had earlier experienced. See the account in Anglesey (1973), op. cit., pp. 270–6.

Page 84 'an Nullah': see note to Page 54.

Page 93 'Turmots': turnips.

'Grey Squadron or Left Squadron': see note to Page 19.

Page 94 'Lieut Col Yarbury': Lieutenant Colonel John William Yerbury (1804–58). He commanded the 3rd Light Dragoons through-out the Second Sikh War.

Page 94f Action at Sadalapur, which Pearman calls So dullapore and, later, Sadoolapore (see 'Memoir', p. 270). See Map II for Sadalapur. Thackwell (see note to Page 13) replaced Cureton after the latter's death at Ramnagar. Gough's intention here was that he should march down the north bank of the Chenab, and attack what was left of the Sikh position at Ramnagar. The plan misfired, and Thackwell fought this minor and inconclusive action.

Page 95 'Faint Charge. . .by Echellon': see note to Page 19.

Page 99 'a place named Haillah': Heylah. See Map II for Helan. The small village of Helan is situated some ten miles to the south west of Phalia, which will be found on modern maps of India. It seems likely that Pearman (and others) was trying to reproduce the word 'Heylah' rather than 'Helan', and that a standing camp might be situated at this much larger settlement. Nevertheless, topographical detail in other accounts of the Sikh Wars shows that it was certainly at Helan, not at Phalia. See E. J. Thackwell, *Narrative of the Second Sikh War in 1848–9*,

Richard Bentley, 1851, pp. 103–5; and J. H. Lawrence Archer, *Commentaries on the Punjab Campaign, 1848–1849*, W. H. Allen, 1878, pp. 33, 38. I am grateful to Andrew Cook of the India Office Library for clearing this point up for me.

Page 102f   Battle of Chilianwala. See Anglesey, op. cit., pp. 84–93; Bruce, op. cit., pp. 281–97. Another battle in which the cavalry was little used, as the ground was close jungle in places. Pearman did not actually witness the events he describes on Page 104. The heavy losses at Chilianwala and the disastrous performances of some officers caused outrage in Britain. The Court of Directors of the East India Company was forced to recall Gough (though it took four months for this news to reach India) and to appoint Sir Charles Napier to command the Indian Army. See below, note to Page 134.

Page 105   'Capt Unett': Captain Walter Unett (1813 or 1814–60). Cornet in 3rd Light Dragoons 1833. Served with them in the First Afghan War. He commanded Pearman's Grey Squadron at Chilianwala. Lieutenant Colonel 1854, Brevet Colonel June 1857. It was he who was later to write Pearman's reference for the Buckinghamshire Constabulary.

'Lieut Stisted': Lieutenant Thomas Heathcote Stisted. Made lieutenant in December 1847. He does not appear in the Army List of the 3rd Light Dragoons after 1850.

Page 114   'Coln Foredice': Colonel John Foredyce of the 74th Foot.

Page 116   'Fortress of Moultain': Multan.

'Goojerat': see Map II for Gujrat.

Page 117   'Dooab': *doab*. Hindi, meaning 'two waters'. The land lying between two rivers which eventually flow into each other. Gujrat lies between the Rivers Chenab and Jelum.

Page 119f   Battle of Gujrat. By the time the troops from Multan had joined Gough on 20 February, the Sikhs had placed themselves in an unentrenched position on an open plain near Gujrat. Gough now had an army of over 20,000 men and more artillery than the Sikhs. The lie of the land and the weather allowed a sustained use of the cavalry for the first time in any of the battles of the Sikh Wars. See Anglesey, op. cit., p. 103. The British troops sustained very few injuries.

Page 127   'Dobar': *durbar*. See note to Page 58.

Page 129   'nay puckeroe': 'don't steal it'. The merchant here speaks the Hindustani dialect that Pearman transcribes throughout the 'Memoir'. His mother tongue was almost certainly Punjabi, but he would have used the language that he knew British soldiers were likely to understand.

Page 132   These stories of looting and treasure-taking were added by John Pearman's grandson in 1967. George Pearman to the Marquess of Anglesey [copy] July 15, 1967, in which he mentions 'two portraits painted on ivory, which had formed part of the screen of the Sikh

Maharajahs. These ivory miniatures were taken by my grandfather when the palace was looted and he kept them instead of handing them over to the Prize Agents. Some years later he returned them to young Prince Duleep Singh who was then living in England.' In a previous letter he mentioned Dulip Singh as a student at Eton. However, the maharajah was never a student at Eton, though his two sons, Victor Albert Jay and Frederick Victor attended the College in the late 1860s. The maharajah himself was a guest of the Queen at Windsor in the winter of 1854–5, and again in November 1865 and in early 1867. It is conceivable that Pearman made contact with him on one of these later visits, if the story is true. See Alexander and Anand, op. cit., pp. 56–9, 113–14.

Page 134   'Genl Sir Charles Napier': General Sir Charles James Napier (1782–1853). Served at Corunna and throughout the Peninsular Wars. In 1839, commander of the Northern District during the Chartist disturbances. F. M. Mather, *Public Order in the Age of the Chartists*, Manchester University Press, Manchester, 1959, pp. 141–80, and *passim*. Served in India during the Scind Campaign.

'if you had been properly handled': that is, at the Battle of Chilianwala, when the 14th Light Dragoons retreated at a crucial point. See 'Memoir', p. 104.

Page 135   Lieutenant Colonel King actually committed suicide in July 1850. See the account in Anglesey, op. cit., p. 109; in E. J. Thackwell, *Narrative of the Second Sikh Wars*, Richard Bentley, 1851, pp. 140–5, and in J. C. Marshman, *Memoirs of Sir H. Havelock*, Longman Green, 1860, p. 185.

Page 137   'We remained at Umballa until September 1850': 'Pearman's dates here are rather shaky. The regiment actually marched out of Ambala, in the course of periodical relief, for the newly formed cantonment at Sialkot, on October 22nd, 1850.' Anglesey (1968), op. cit., p. 110.

Page 138   'Seal Cote': Sealkote. See Map II for Sialkot.

'Caught in a Lassue by a Tug': see note to Page 77. Thug, from the Hindi *thag*, a highway robber.

Pages 138–9   'Goolob Sing. . . we escorted him back to Cashmere': for the Amritsar Treaty of 16 March 1846 which recognised Gulab Singh Dogra as maharajah of Jammu and Kashmir – a reward for his services to the British – see Singh, op. cit., vol. 2, pp. 57–8.

Page 139   Of this account of his illness, Gordon Everson remarks: 'as the Marquis of Anglesey points out, Pearman's memory of dates around this time is faulty. His near fatal illness must in fact have been in 1851, for the musters show him incapacitated from May to August at Wazirabad.' Gordon R. Everson, 'Sergeant John Pearman, 3rd Light Dragoons', *The Orders and Medals Research Society*, 20:3 (Autumn 1981), pp. 154–6.

Page 142 'a Seaton': surgical thread or tape, drawn through a fold of skin so as to maintain an opening for discharge.

Page 146 'Kurrachee in the Bombay Presidency': Karachi. See Everson, op. cit., p. 156: 'The musters show they sailed in the "Duke of Argyll" on 5 February, 1853, although Pearman recalled it was the end of the month . . .'.

Page 150 'Casemates': rooms built in the thickness of the ramparts of a fortress; used as a barracks.

Page 153 Family history elaborates the account that Pearman gives here. George Pearman to the Marquess of Anglesey [copy], 10 February 1968, in which he mentions 'the family tradition that he bought himself out to avoid a court martial. . . According to family gossip he had been promised a staff appointment but it was actually given to a protégé of the Duke of Cambridge. The old man was so infuriated that he waylaid the Duke and grossly insulted him, telling him that he was no gentleman . . . As a result he was threatened with a court martial, but Colonel Unett stood by his friend and managed things so that my grandfather was able to buy himself out. . .'.

Page 158 'a Testimonial in Velom': on these demonstrations of appreciation to local policemen, see Carolyn Steedman, *Policing the Victorian Community: the formation of English provincial police forces, 1856–1880*, Routledge & Kegan Paul, 1984, pp. 143–7.

Page 159 'God made animated nature': this is the first of several references to 'animated nature'. See also Pages 162, 163 and 167. Pearman moves from the use of this idea to a discussion of nature's indifference (Pages 180–2), then of a state of nature (Page 184). For a discussion of this conceptualisation of nature, see above, pp. 90–1 and 4–5.

Pages 163–4 These figures of land ownership in Britain are possibly taken from Charles Bradlaugh, *The Land, the People and the Coming Struggle*, Austin, 1872 (there was a new, revised edition in 1882), but are more likely to be from a newspaper that used this pamphlet as a source, especially during the setting up of the Land Law Reform League in 1880. See, for instance, Annie Besant, 'The English Land System', *National Reformer*, 11 January 1880: 'Five persons own estates exceeding 2,000,000 acres in extent, and twenty persons own estates considerably exceeding 5,000,000 acres. Less than 2,200 individuals own considerably more than one third, but less than one half of the United Kingdom.' See also *National Reformer*, 18 January 1880. This material was issued in a penny pamphlet in February. See *National Reformer*, 8 February 1880. There are echoes here too of Henry George, Book VII, Chapter iv: 'in Great Britain today the right of the people as a whole to the soil of their native country is much less fully acknowledged than it was in feudal times.' Henry George, *Progress and Poverty*, Kegan Paul Trench, 1881, p. 342. Another possible source is the first chapter of Arthur Arnold's *Free Land*, Kegan Paul, 1880, pp. 1–13. Chapter I, 'Who Had the Land', presents statistical material from which Pearman could have worked out these figures. This would anyway be familiar territory to him as a policeman: readers of *The Police and Constabulary Almanac and Guide*, Manchester, annually from 1858, knew exactly how many acres there were in each police division, what their rateable value was, and how policemen were thus distributed.

Page 168 'a Christian Catholic. . . a Methodist of Baptise . . .': what I have transcribed may be John Pearman's attempt to turn the word 'or' ('a Methodist or Baptise') into a stroke – but he does not use the dividing slash anywhere else in the MS. If this doesn't simply mean that one of the men was either a Baptist or a Methodist, then he presumably means that he was converted to Methodism, and baptised as one. 'Christian Catholic' may mean 'Catholic Christian', presumably a Roman Catholic.

Page 172 'our army in Egypt': see 'A Note on Dating', and above, p. 92.

Pages 174–8 'the Tithes of the Church': see above, p. 89.

Page 179 'settling a King in Poland': it is most likely that John Pearman is here referring to that period of Polish history that stretched from the last partition of the country in 1797 to the creation of a new Polish kingdom by the Congress of Vienna in 1815. See W. F. Reddaway et al., *The Cambridge History of Poland, 1697–1935*, Cambridge University Press, Cambridge, 1941, pp. 208–310. The loss of men in Italy mentioned is probably a reference to Napoleon's use of the Polish Legion to expel the Hapsburg armies from that country in 1796–7. He made a similar use of these exiled volunteers after the Egyptian Campaign, in 1801. The reference to the Rhine is puzzling. It may be the case that John Pearman was not clear about the geography of central Europe, and was simply here giving a geographical location to the immense Polish involvement in the wars of the three partitioning powers. The Duchy of Warsaw was created in 1807 by the Treaty of Tilsit. It was joined to Saxony under the rule of Frederick Augustus – who was called a king. The Congress of Vienna created a Polish kingdom, with Tsar Alexander I its ruler, represented locally by a Viceroy. There was indeed, an immense loss of Polish life in these various attempts over an 18-year period to 'settle a King in Poland'. The country, and the question of its existence, had been a British radical rallying point from the late eighteenth century.

Page 180 'prayers for our armies in the field': see 'A Note on Dating'.

Page 180–2 This passage on nature has obviously been copied from somewhere; but I have been unable to trace its source.

Pages 183–4 'was Adam & Eve when made': this division of prehistory into states of savagery, barbarism and civility has come down to us so clearly through Engels' transliteration of Morgan's *Ancient Society* of 1877, that there may be a tendency to forget how very old this division is. Perhaps though, John Pearman came across Maine's *Ancient Law*, or an extract from this extremely popular work of the mid-Victorian years. His move here from a discussion of law to the history of civilisation suggests this as a possibility. Henry Sumner Maine, *Ancient Law: its connection with the early history of society and its relation to modern ideas* (1861), John Murray, 1878, pp. 44–112; Lewis Henry Morgan, *Ancient Society*, Macmillan, 1877; Frederick Engels, *The Origin of the Family, Private Property and the State* (1884), Lawrence & Wishart, 1972.

Page 191 'John Company': John Pearman did not serve the East Indian Company: he was in the British army, not the Indian army, though technically, he could be said to have served John Company between 1845 and 1853.

Page 194 'then comes an Oliver Cromwell': I would suggest that this mention of Oliver Cromwell has behind it Pearman's reading of Charles Bradlaugh's *Cromwell and Washington*, C. Watts, 1877, and Bradlaugh's following assessment of his subject: 'Oliver Cromwell is a tyrant, not a Republican; but his heart is, despite the lust of power, a patriot's heart.' (p. 15) Cromwell is presented as a complicated tyrant throughout, and the vocabulary of 'cant' is a feature of its pages. Cromwell is again mentioned on Page 197 of the 'Memoir'.

Page 197 'A True Musselman, not a Mehomitian': see above, p. 50.

Page 198 'The Zulas. . . then again at Burmer. . . Charter in South Africa. . .': see 'A Note on Dating'. See Brian Bond, 'The South African War' in Brian Bond (ed.), *Victorian Military Campaigns*, Hutchinson, 1967, pp. 201–40, and D. M. Schreuder, *The Scramble for Africa*, Cambridge University Press, Cambridge, 1980, pp. 61–112 for British relations with the Zulu nation and settlement with the Boers after the British defeat at Majuba Hill. For British involvement in Burma, see George Bruce, *The Burma Wars, 1824–1886*, Hart-Davis, London, 1973, and for a nineteenth-century radical account of the events leading up to the Third Burma War of 1853, see Richard Cobden, *How Wars Are Got Up in India: the origin of the Burmese War*, Cash, London, 1853. See note 32 (p. 287) for the Maharajah Dulip Singh's similar reaction to these current events.

Page 200 'By Socialism I mean a Just and comparative equal Division of Capital, Property and Labour, and the right of the people to the land.' This distinction between capital and property echoes a central argument of Henry George in *Progress and Poverty*, Kegan Paul Trench, 1881, pp. 15–78.

Page 202 'when Mr Bradlaugh refused to take the oath': for the revival of secularism that resulted from Charles Bradlaugh's attempt to enter Parliament in May 1880 by affirmation rather than oath, see Edward

Royle, *Radicals, Secularists and Republicans: popular freethought in Britain, 1866–1915*, Manchester University Press, Manchester, 1980, pp. 23–34.

Page 213 'eight Children': the ages of the Pearman children in 1882 were 23 years (Rose, b. January 1859), 21 years (John Thomas, b. spring 1861), 19 years (Elizabeth Hannah, b. spring 1863), 17 years (Arthur Robert, b. summer 1865), 15 years (Charlotte Eliza, b. May 1867), 14 years (Charles Ernest, b. summer 1868), 7 years (Florence Ada, b. April 1875), and 5 years (Horace William, b. September 1877). 'my Rose': Rose Pearman was born on 24 January 1859.

Page 216 'my Wife had a baby 4 months old': this was Charlotte Eliza, who had been born on 29 May 1867.

Page 217 'Dr Gooch and Pearle': *Post Office Directory, Buckinghamshire*, for 1869 gives Pearl and Gooch, surgeons, High Street, Eton.

Page 218 'Mr F. Bunce': *Post Office Directory, 1869*, gives Mrs Mary Ann Bunce, *Turk's Head*, 98 High Street, Eton.

Page 223 'that is what they Call Political economy': another possible echo from George, for in *Progress and Poverty*, 'political economy' is not simply explained by its author, but is used as an organising and rhetorical device throughout.

Page 228 'the Popes dreadful curse': John Pearman is evidently copying here, almost certainly, the work of a nineteenth-century Protestant anti-cleric – who has not been traced. The rite of excommunication is contained in the *Pontificale Romanum*, which was last substantially reformed under Clement VIII (1592–1605). The 'Ordo Excommunicandi; et Absolvendi' is not anything like this curse. I am grateful to Sheridan Gilley of the Theology Department, the University of Durham, for helping me over this question. See H. Thurston, *No Popery: Chapters on Anti-Papal Prejudice*, Sheed & Ward, 1930, for a history of popular Protestant anti-clericalism and anti-Catholicism in this period.

Page 232 '85.000': this figure is almost certainly taken from Bradlaugh's pamphlet *The Impeachment of the House of Brunswick* (1873), Freethought Publishing Co., 1881. The first item in Bradlaugh's accounting of 'the actual cost of royalty' is 'Her Majesty the Queen:–Civil List 385,000.0.0.' In all impressions of this work that I have seen, the figure 3 is not tabulated with the other figures in the list. Someone remembering these figures from an earlier reading might well have failed to recall it, or indeed, to have noticed it in the first place. Bradlaugh published again on the cost of royalty in 1882. See Charles Bradlaugh, *The Civil List and the Cost of the Royal Family*, 1882. I am grateful to Edward Royle for this reference.

Page 236 'British Soldiers': the Army Lists show the 2nd Battalion of the Grenadier Guards leaving Windsor for Egypt between August and September 1882. John Pearman probably copied this verse from a newspaper or journal at this time. I have been unable to trace its source.

Page 238 'There is only about 35 pr cent of the people of this earth': see note to Page 248.

Page 242 'Stanleys Game': see 'A Note on Dating'. For British involvement in European colonial involvement in Central Africa, and Henry Stanley's connection with Belgian exploration, see Roger Anstey, *Britain and the Congo in the Nineteenth Century*, Clarendon Press, Oxford, 1962, pp. 57–83, and *passim*.

Page 246 I have been unable to trace the book that John Pearman was reading.

Page 248 'Population of the World': it is possible to see John Pearman combing the geography sections of *Cassell's Popular Educator* and compiling these figures (though the *Popular Educator* could not have been the source for the population of Europe and America); but there probably exists a more direct listing that he copied from, an encyclopedic source that I have not traced. I do not know what 'E.T.C.' stands for. *The Popular Educator* (6 vols), 1880–1884, Cassell, vol. 5, pp. 35–8, 99–101; vol. 6, pp. 119–21, 174–7, 213.

Page 250 'What is a Soldier': I have been unable to find the source for what is obviously a quotation here, direct copying providing for almost faultless spelling. However, I would draw the reader's attention to Richard Carlile's *Character of a Soldier* (1821), of which this passage seems to be a transliteration: 'A Soldier is a machine that privileged rogues work with, a Soldier is a brute, a biped, an erect monster, having the power of locomotion, and a great thirst for human blood:– it hires itself out to slay men. . .'. (Philanthropus) Richard Carlile, *Character of a Soldier*, R. Carlile, 1821, p. 3.

Page 251 James Gilling recorded that the mail arrived just before the Battle of Chilianwala. Pearman's letter was probably written in response to post received then. James Gilling, *The Life of a Lancer in the Wars of the Punjab*, Simpkin Marshall, 1855, p. 134. J. W. Baldwin, a private of the 9th Foot, noted that after the Battle of Ambala his regiment received no mail for five months. *A Narrative of Four Months Campaign in India, Between the Years 1845–6*, Josiah Fletcher, Norwich, 1853.

Page 259 'the Battle of Soo . do . lipore': Sadalapur. Military history calls this an action, not a battle. See note to Page 94.

Page 262 'Genl Wishe army': Lieutenant General Sir William Sampson Wishe (1787–1853), Bengal Artillery. Appointed to the command of the Punjab division at Lahore in 1848. In August, given command of the Multan field force. The Siege of Multan followed, lasting from September 1848 to January 1849. After the surrender of the fort, Wishe marched to meet Lord Gough.

Page 265 Three pages are cut away here.

Page 266 'Names of Men': this list of names demonstrates what a remarkable memory John Pearman had. In the Muster Rolls of the 3rd Light Dragoons, all these men can be traced, enlisting between 1843 and 1846, except for Cumber and Monday, who even, by the most imaginative phonetic transliteration of their names, cannot be found. By this list, John Pearman implies that they were all recruited in 1843, which was actually not the case for over half of them, who appear as recruits in 1844 and 1845. Pearman was, after all, away from the regiment when he deserted, between 30 November 1843 and 26 July 1844. He seems particularly to have remembered men who joined during his absence, as having been recruited with him. Equally indicative of his powers of memory is the confirmation offered by the Muster Rolls of the departure from Gravesend in June 1845: all but four of these names appear on the 'embarked' list in the musters for June 1845. Public Record Office, WO12/590, 591, 592: Monthly Muster Rolls of the Depot of the 3rd Regiment of Light Dragoons for the three months ending 30 September 1843, 30 November 1843, 30 September 1844, 30 June 1845.

Pages 267–8   These pages of notes describe a series of court cases in which John Pearman gave evidence, after the incident of 1869, when Pearman escorted the said Murray to France. Seven years later, in July 1876, at Slough Petty Sessions, one Reginald Temple Grenville Clare Strange Murray – alias Edwardes – was again charged with obtaining £15 under false pretences from Mr Arthur Cockshott, a master at Eton. Murray's solicitor, speaking for his defence, said that 'there was no question as to the insanity of the prisoner, and if the unfortunate man was handed over to him, he would be placed in the custody of those from whom he had escaped. . . he would be moved to Charenton in France'. Murray had been a student at Eton from 1856 to 1863, and since that time had been kept in various forms of custody by his family. The magistrates, not knowing enough as they said, about this 'species of madness', committed him for trial at Quarter Sessions. Pearman gave evidence about the forged cheque. *Bucks Herald*, 8 July 1876. At Buckinghamshire Michaelmas Quarter Sessions on 21 October 1876 his medical history, which included examination by the French psychologist Pinel, was rehearsed. The prisoner received four months' hard labour. *Bucks Herald*, 17 October 1876. I have been unable to trace the next case mentioned by Pearman here.

'To Be Burried': some mystery attaches to this freethinker's vade mecum. Whoever numbered the pages of the 'Memoir' obviously found it between pages 158 and 159, for it is labelled '158a' and '159b'. Gordon Everson photocopied it in this position when he prepared the copy that is now in the British Army Museum. It is no longer with the original manuscript. Its contents suggest that it was written after the 'Memoir' was completed. The radical policeman here reaches the logical position of all his earlier arguments. He was, in fact, buried with pomp and ceremony at Windsor Cemetery in December 1908, the funeral service read by a paid servant of the church. The family requested no flowers, but 'a contingent of the Bucks. Constabulary brought one beautiful wreath, which they afterwards deposited on the coffin. They lined the path as the mourners passed. . .'. *Windsor and Eton Express*, 5 December 1908.

Notes

Introduction

1 Philip Donnellan, 'Gone for a Soldier', BBC production, broadcast 9 March, 1980.

2 Carolyn Steedman, *Policing the Victorian Community: the formation of English provincial police forces, 1856–1880*, Routledge & Kegan Paul, 1984.

3 The Marquess of Anglesey, *Sergeant Pearman's Memoirs*, Cape, 1968.

4 At this date, I only transcribed the second half of the 'Memoir', the part that Anglesey had abridged and substantially edited. There is a photocopy of the complete document deposited in the National Army Museum. MS 8311–11.

5 Margaret Atwood, *The Handmaid's Tale*, Cape, 1986.

6 Virginia Woolf, 'Women and Fiction' (1929), reproduced in Michele Barrett (ed.), *Women and Writing*, Women's Press, 1979, p. 47.

7 For other accounts, see Khushwant Singh, *A History of the Sikhs*, Oxford University Press, Bombay, 2 vols, 1977, vol. 2, pp. 2–97; George Bruce, *Six Battles for India, the Anglo-Sikh Wars, 1845–6, 1848–9*, Arthur Barker, 1969; Byron Farwell, *Queen Victoria's Little Wars*, Allen Lane, 1973, pp. 218–81; E. R. Crawford, 'The Sikh Wars', in Brian Bond (ed.), *Victorian Military Campaigns*, Hutchinson, 1967, pp. 31–68; The Marquess of Anglesey, *A History of the British Cavalry, 1816–1981* (3 vols), vol. 1, 1816–1850, Leo Cooper, 1973, pp. 243–89.

8 H. W. Piper, *The Active Universe: Pantheism and the Concept of Imagination in the English Romantic Poets*, Athlone, 1962, pp. 165–70; Edward Royle, *Victorian Infidels: the Origins of the British Secularist Movement, 1791–1866*, Manchester University Press, Manchester, 1974, pp. 9–31.

9 Philanthropus (Richard Carlile), *Character of a Priest*, Richard Carlile, 1821.

10 My own romance of historical sources has made me return again and again to Gerrard Winstanley, as a possible source for John Pearman's phrase 'animated nature': 'the Earth was made to be a Common Treasury of livelihood for all, without respect of persons, and was not made to be bought and sold: and that mankind, in all his branches, is lord over the beasts, birds, fishes, and the Earth; and was not made to acknowledge any of his own kind to be his Teacher

and Ruler. . . And this being a truth, as it is, then none ought to be lords or landlords over another, but the Earth is free for every son or daughter of mankind to live free upon.' This is certainly what Pearman *meant* by 'animated nature', but Winstanley was not available in print in the nineteenth century until 1899, in an edition from which this quotation is taken. See J. Morrisson Davidson, *Concerning Four Precursors of Henry George, and the Single Tax and also the Land Gospel according to "Winstanley the Digger"*, Labour Leader Publishing Co., 1899, pp. 79–80.

11 David Vincent, *Bread, Knowledge and Freedom: A Study of Nineteenth Century Working Class Autobiography*, Methuen, 1982; John Burnett, *Destiny Obscure, Autobiographies of Childhood, Education and the Family from the 1820s to the 1920s*, Allen Lane, 1982; Dave Morley and Ken Worpole (eds), *The Republic of Letters: working class writing and local publishing*, Comedia, 1982; Julia Swindels, *Victorian Writing and Working Women*, Polity, Oxford, 1985.

12 John Ryder, *Four Years Service in India*, W. H. Burton, Leicester, 1853. Edited and with a preface by James Thompson; Preface, p. vi.

13 Elizabeth Gaskell, *Mary Barton* (1848), Penguin, 1970, pp. 49–50; Richard Hoggart, *The Uses of Literacy*, Chatto & Windus, 1957, pp. 32–5.

14 Steedman, op. cit., pp. 143–7.

15 The phrase is Eli Zaretsky's: *Capitalism, the Family and Personal Life*, Pluto, 1976, pp. 54–5, 27–8.

16 E. G. Pitcher and Ernest Prelinger, *Children Tell Stories: an analysis of fantasy*, International Universities Press, New York, 1963; Carolyn Steedman, *The Tidy House: Little Girls Writing*, Virago, 1982, pp. 85–109.

17 For the PALs regiments, see John Keegan, *Firing Line*, Penguin, 1976, pp. 221–6.

18 As it was for Denise Riley in a 1950s childhood. See Denise Riley, 'Waiting', in Liz Heron (ed.), *Truth, Dare or Promise: Girls Growing Up in the Fifties*, Virago, 1985, pp. 237–8. See page 247: 'It seemed a hideous, unthinkable accident to be born a man, so you would have to become a soldier.'

19 See Lynn Segal, *Is the Future Female?*, Virago, 1987, pp. 162–203 for an argument that denies an inherent masculine tendency towards warfare, and which also briefly outlines a female relationship to nationalism and militarism: 'Wars do not occur because men are eager to fight; on the contrary, military aggression always requires carefully controlled and systematic propaganda. . .'.

20 The literature on this topic is enormous, coming under the headings of language development and developmental linguistics. The reader is referred to a still-useful bibliography in Robin Campbell and Roger Wales, 'The Study of Language Acquisition', in John Lyons

(ed.), *New Horizons in Linguistics*, Penguin, 1970, for a survey of the field since the 1950s. See also Alison Elliot, *Child Language Development*, Cambridge University Press, 1982; Ian Fletcher and Michael Garman (eds), *Language Acquisition: studies in first language acquisition*, Cambridge University Press, Cambridge, 1986, and Catherine Garvey, *Children's Talk*, Fontana, 1984, for more recent bibliographies. These three works also offer a good guide to the conceptual framework of developmental linguistics (though they are not books designed to offer an explication of the discipline to those outside the field). Brian Street, *Literacy in Theory and Practice*, Cambridge University Press, Cambridge, 1984, pp. 19–125 offers a survey of literacy studies, but does not make that survey within a developmental framework. See L. S. Vygotsky, *Thought and Language* (1966), MIT Press, Cambridge, Mass., 1986, and *Mind in Society*, Harvard University Press, Cambridge, Mass., 1978, for the most suggestive indications of how writing may been seen as an aspect of language acquisition and psychological development. See Gunther Kress, *Learning to Write*, Routledge & Kegan Paul, 1982, for a recent theorisation of the role of writing in development.

1   Writers, Editors and Historians

1   Marquess of Anglesey, *Sergeant Pearman's Memoirs*, Cape, 1968, pp. 14–15.
2   For accounts of the Sikh Wars, see note 7, p. 270.
3   Anglesey, op. cit., p. 14.
4   ibid., p. 15.
5   ibid., pp. 17–18.
6   ibid., p. 16.
7   Pearman wrote in the period when the East India Company still governed India, and the military forces – the Indian Army – were directed by the Company's commander-in-chief. Units of Her Majesty's forces – 'the Queen's Army' – served alongside them on different occasions. So John Pearman was not one of the Company's soldiers, though technically, he could be said to have served it in the period 1845–9.
8   See Bibliography, 'Working Class Military Autobiography'.
9   See particularly John Pindar, *Autobiography of a Soldier*, Fife, 1877, and James Gilling, *The Life of a Lancer in the Wars of the Punjab*, Simpkin Marshall, 1855.
10   For further discussion of this point, see below, pp. 40–3.
11   John Keegan, *The Face of Battle*, Penguin, 1978, p. 61.
12   ibid., p. 65.
13   D. H. McKinnon, *Military Service and Adventures in the Far East, including Sketches of the Campaigns against the Afghans in 1839 and the*

Sikhs in 1845–6, By a Cavalry Officer, Charles Oliver, 2 vols, 1847.

14 Linda H. Peterson, *Victorian Autobiography: the tradition of self-interpretation*, Yale University Press, New Haven, 1986, pp. 1–19.

15 *National Reformer*, 26 June 1881. For infidelity (or freethinking) among the officer class in the Indian Army (albeit from a biased source) see H. M. Conran, *Autobiography of an Indian Officer*, Morgan & Clare, 1870, p. 25.

16 See Bibliography, 'Working Class Military Autobiography'.

17 Carolyn Steedman, *Policing the Victorian Community: the formation of English provincial police forces, 1856–1880*, Routledge & Kegan Paul, 1984, pp. 80–130. For the idea of a policeman as a servant, see ibid., pp. 143–7.

18 Robert Blatchford, editor of the socialist *Clarion*, saw the basis of a new collectivism in the experience of soldiering: 'the fact is that the drilling of masses of men together makes for community of thought and feeling; makes a crowd into a regiment, makes a rabble into a nation; develops in men a new faculty of humanism.' Robert Blatchford, *My Life in the Army*, Clarion Press, n.d. (1904), pp. 137–9.

19 Gunther Kress, *Learning to Write*, Routledge & Kegan Paul, 1982, pp. 16–18.

20 Dominick LaCapra, *History and Criticism*, Cornell University Press, 1985, p. 132.

21 L. S. Vygotsky, *Thought and Language* (1966), MIT Press, Cambridge, Mass., 1986, pp. 179–84.

22 E. P. Thompson, *William Morris: Romantic to Revolutionary*, Pantheon, New York, 1971, pp. 299–300.

23 John Gilliland, *Readability*, University of London Press, 1972, pp. 83–109. I have used the SMOG formula used to calculate readability described on p. 94 of Gilliland. In order to apply it, I have had to punctuate John Pearman's text.

24 I have used the readability formula on Book VII, Chapter iv, dealing with 'Private Property in Land Historically Considered', which is a section that Pearman is more likely to have read than others. Henry George, *Progress and Poverty*, Kegan Paul Trench, 1881, pp. 331–45.

25 This argument is not affected by changing fashions in punctuation. A sentence here is taken to mean a unit of written language that is grammatically complete, whether it is closed by a full stop, a semicolon, a comma, or by nothing at all. A late Victorian editor would make different choices about punctuation marks from a mid twentieth-century editor, but this does not alter the fact that John Pearman was composing *in writing* (rather than transcribing what he said, or might have said) and using the syntactic unit of written language called the sentence as his aspiration in composition (though it was an aspiration not always achieved). For a further discussion of

writing as discourse and writing as speech-written-down, see below, pp. 80–2.

26 Dick Leith, *A Social History of English*, Routledge & Kegan Paul, 1983, pp. 32–57.

27 Vowels in English sound much more like each other than do consonants (cannot, in fact, be sounded without an attached consonant) and the symbols that represent vowels are visually similar, in a way that consonant graphemes are not.

28 Phonetic methods of teaching children to read were not used until the end of the nineteenth century. For a description of the syllabic method of instruction that Pearman almost certainly experienced, see Ronald Morris, *Success and Failure in Learning to Read*, Penguin, 1973, pp. 41–6, and *passim*.

29 See below, pp. 71–2.

30 By counting errors in the transcript of the 'Memoir', the reader will not reach these two totals. The transcript presented here is John Pearman's final draft, that is, it reproduces his corrections, rather than the mistakes he made at the earliest stage of composition. See 'A Note on Transcription'.

2 A Working Life

1 Carolyn Steedman, *Policing the Victorian Community: the formation of English provincial police forces, 1856–1880*, Routledge & Kegan Paul, 1984, p. 80.

2 ibid., pp. 124–30.

3 ibid., pp. 132–6.

4 ibid., p. 85.

5 ibid., pp. 137–43.

6 Buckinghamshire Record Office, Constabulary Records, Register of Members of the Force, 1857. He called himself a sawyer again in June 1857, when he got married. See note 14 on p. 280.

7 Steedman, op. cit., pp. 72–3.

8 Edward M. Spiers, *The Army and Society, 1815–1914*, Longman, 1980, pp. 45, 49.

9 Sergeant Major William Taylor thought that all lower ranks preferred service in India: 'Here are no manorial or river rights, the invasion of whose privileges is attended with fine or imprisonment. The soldier may range over hill and dale. . . waging war against all created things, without being called on to tender an account of his actions.' William Taylor, *Life in the Ranks*, Perry Blenkhern, 1847, p. 321. James Gilling noted that 'it is not the least remarkable trait in the character of the aristocratic English officer, that a little of the uphill work of campaigning generally takes down his pride and imperiousness'. James Gilling, *The Life of a Lancer in the Wars of the*

Punjab, or, Seven Years in India, Simpkin Marshall, 1855, p. 155.

10 Steedman, op. cit., pp. 14–15, 19–21.

11 Northamptonshire County Record Office, Constabulary Records, ML 202–12, Journal of Inspector George Williamson.

12 *Police Service Advertiser*, 11 May 1867.

13 David Vincent, *Bread, Knowledge and Freedom: A Study of Nineteenth Century Working Class Autobiography*, Methuen, 1982, p. 36.

14 Steedman, op. cit., p. 113.

15 ibid., pp. 129–30.

16 ibid., p. 121.

17 Select Committee on Police Superannuation, PP 1875, xiii, p. 478. Evidence of Constable James Chambers.

18 Gordon R. Everson, 'Sergeant John Pearman, 3rd Light Dragoons', *The Orders and Medals Research Society*, 20:3 (Autumn 1981), pp. 154–6. Maidstone and its system of training was thought to be particularly nasty by at least one other private soldier, 'hence the frequent desertions from that depot'. Gilling, op. cit., pp. 3–4.

19 *Windsor and Eton Express*, 5 December 1908. But of course theoretically, being a good writer should have helped him to rise. Of the 1830s, when he joined a Scottish regiment, Alexander Somerville remembered that he heard enough from old soldiers to be convinced 'that having a fair education in writing and account keeping, I would have a much better chance in a regiment of English or Irish, where there were few men who could write'. Alexander Somerville, *The Autobiography of a Working Man, by One Who Has Whistled at the Plough*, Charles Gilpin, 1848, p. 188.

3 Soldiers' Stories

1 Edward M. Spiers, *The Army and Society, 1815–1914*, Longman, 1980, pp. 35–71.

2 ibid., pp. 97–117.

3 John Spencer Cooper, *Rough Notes of Seven Campaigns*, John Russell Smith, 1869, pp. 149–50.

4 John Ryder, *Four Years Service in India, By a Private Soldier*, W. H. Burton, Leicester, 1853; James Gilling, *The Life of a Lancer in the Wars of the Punjab*, Simpkin Marshall, 1855; Joseph Donaldson, *Recollections of an Eventful Life*, Richard Griffin, Glasgow, 1856.

5 W. R. Bingham, *The Field of Ferozeshah in Two Cantos, with Other Poems, by a Young Soldier Who Fought in that Glorious Campaign*, Charles Edward Bingham, London, 1848, pp. 45–6.

6 John Keegan, *The Face of Battle*, Penguin, 1978; J. W. Baldwin, *A Narrative of Four Months Campaign in India, Between the Years 1845–1846*, Josiah Fletcher, Norwich, 1853, p. 42; Ryder, op. cit., pp. 35–48.

7 Spiers, op. cit., pp. 59–61. See also The Marquess of Anglesey, *A*

History of the British Cavalry, 1816–1919 (3 vols), vol. 1, 1816–1850, Leo Cooper, 1973, pp. 114–51.

8   Richard Holmes, *Firing Line*, Cape, 1985, p. 191.

9   Gordon R. Everson, 'Sergeant John Pearman, 3rd Light Dragoons', *The Orders and Medals Research Society*, 20:3 (Autumn 1981), pp. 154–6.

10   Spiers, op. cit., p. 60.

11   Keegan, op. cit., p. 268.

12   George Bruce, *Six Battles for India, The Anglo-Sikh Wars, 1845–6, 1848–9*, Arthur Barker, 1969, pp. 321–3, 'Note on Wounds'.

13   See notes to p. 7 of the Introduction.

14   Thomas Quinney, *Sketches of a Soldier's Life in India*, David Robertson, Glasgow, 1853, p. 8.

15   Spiers, op. cit., p. 60. Anglesey, op. cit., pp. 141–2, gives the timetable of a young soldier of the 14th Light Dragoons, in India, 1847: ' "riding school at 6o'clock until 1/2 past 8, stables at 9, carbine drill from 12 till 1 and sword drill in the evening from 1/2 past 4 till 1/2 past 5, and this with the time taken up to clean our accoutrements takes up ther whole of our time".'

16   Holmes, op. cit., p. 106. Horses were long an essential ingredient of war, and their suffering caused grief to men who were inured to human tribulations. See also Anglesey (1973), op. cit., pp. 106–13.

17   Carolyn Steedman, *Policing the Victorian Community: the formation of English provincial police forces, 1856–1880*, Routledge & Kegan Paul, 1984, p. 89. For the marketable skills of ex-cavalry men, see Anglesey (1973), op. cit., p. 149.

18   *Police Service Advertiser*, 7 April 1866.

19   Spiers, op. cit., pp. 35–7. See also Gwyn Harries-Jenkins, *The Army in British Society*, Routledge & Kegan Paul, 1977, pp. 4–5.

20   ibid., pp. 5–6.

21   Holmes, op. cit., p. 16.

22   See above, pp. 7–8 and note 19.

23   Baldwin, op. cit., Preface.

24   Gilling, op. cit., p. 31.

25   ibid.

26   John Ryder's account (see note 4) offers the most intense and painful narrative of desperate marching from well to well.

27   Spencer Cooper, op. cit., p. 6.

28   Alexander Somerville, *Autobiography of a Working Man, by One Who Has Whistled at the Plough*, Charles Gilpin, 1848, pp. 207–9.

29   Holmes, op. cit., pp. 93–108.

30   Holmes, ibid.

31   Baldwin, op. cit., Preface.

32   William Hall, *The Diary of William Hall*, privately printed, Penryn, 1848 (?).

33 T. Gowing, *A Soldier's Experience, or, a Voice from the Ranks Showing the Cost of War in Blood and Treasure*, W. H. Stevens, Norwich, 1884. For the seventeenth-century origins of chapbook literature, see Margaret Spufford, *Small Books and Pleasant Histories: Popular Fiction and Its Readership in Seventeenth Century England*, Cambridge University Press, Cambridge, 1981. See also Richard D. Altick, *The English Common Reader*, University of Chicago Press, Chicago, 1957, pp. 287–8.

34 Bruno Bettelheim, *The Uses of Enchantment: the meaning and importance of fairy tales*, Penguin, 1978, is the most extensive account of this use. See also Jack Zipes, *Fairy Tales and the Art of Subversion*, Heinemann, 1985.

35 Bettelheim, op. cit., pp. 29–31, 124–34.

36 Walter Benjamin, 'The Storyteller', in Hannah Arendt (ed.), *Illuminations*, Schocken, New York, 1969, pp. 83–110; Mick Taussig, 'An Australian Hero', *History Workshop Journal*, 24 (Autumn 1987), pp. 111–33.

37 See Spufford, op. cit., pp. 45–82, 156–93.

38 Isabel Rivers, ' "Strangers and Pilgrims": Sources and Patterns of Methodist Narrative', in J. C. Hilson, M. M. B. Jones and J. R. Watson (eds), *Augustan Worlds*, Leicester University Press, Leicester, 1978, pp. 189–203.

39 John Bunyan, *The Holy War* (1682), Roger Sharrock and James F. Forrest (eds), Clarendon Press, Oxford, 1980, p. 51.

40 See notes 32 and 33.

41 It is important to note that what was evidently some degree of friendship with rural Punjabis was achieved by Pearman in a period when the countryside was under occupation by the British, in the period between the two Sikh Wars, when the British soldiery was intensely unpopular. See Khushwant Singh, *A History of the Sikhs*, Oxford University Press, Bombay, 2 vols, 1977, vol. 2, p. 6.

42 For a brief account of the Sikh nation and religious practice in the early part of the nineteenth century, see W. Owen Cole and Piara Singh Sambhi, *The Sikhs: Their Religious Beliefs and Practices*, Routledge & Kegan Paul, pp. 152–67. For an account of the eighteenth and nineteenth-century background to the Sikh Wars, see Singh, op. cit., vol. 1, pp. 219–96 and vol. 2, pp. 2–39. See also Khushwant Singh, *Ranjit Singh, Maharajah of the Punjab*, Orient Longman, New Delhi, 1985.

43 There is a long account of the two Sikh Wars to be found in Bruce, op. cit., pp. 17–102, but by far the clearest account is to be found in Singh, op. cit., vol. 2, pp. 40–82.

44 Harries-Jenkins, op. cit., p. 184.

45 See 'Memoir', Pages 94f, 104.

46 C. E. Callwell, *Small Wars: their principles and practice*, War Office,

Intelligence Division/Stationery Office, 1896.

47   Marquess of Anglesey, *Sergeant Pearman's Memoirs*, Cape, 1968, pp. 89–90. See also Anglesey (1973), op. cit., pp. 243–9.

48   N. W. Bancroft, *From Recruit to Staff Sergeant* (1885), Ian Henry, Hornchurch, 1979. Introduction by Major-General B. P. Hughes, pp. 5–24.

49   Harries-Jenkins, op. cit., p. 198.

50   Holmes, op. cit., pp. 46–7.

51   See Carolyn Steedman, *The Tidy House: Little Girls Writing*, Virago, 1982, pp. 117–20. A similar moment is recorded by Henry Mayhew. See p. 332, n. 3.

52   Daniel Augustus Sandford, *Leaves from the Journal of a Subaltern during the Campaigns in the Punjab, September 1848 to March 1849*, Blackwood, Edinburgh, 1849, p. 159. See also Harry Dickson, *Six Months in the Ranks, or, The Gentleman Private*, Smith Elder, 1883, p. 194, where Bill Short, an old India hand, is spoken to kindly on Christmas Day by the colonel: 'I never saw a man so much moved by these few kind words. The blood flew to his face, bringing a lump to his throat as if he were going to choke and large tears sprang from his eyes. "God bless you, colonel! God bless you, sir!".'

53   Bancroft, op. cit., p. 59. Quoted in Bruce, op. cit., pp. 154–5.

54   Holmes, op. cit., p. 294.

55   Bancroft, op. cit., p. 59.

56   Holmes, op. cit., p. 294.

57   For the square, ibid., p. 159. Keegan, op. cit., pp. 185–6. See also Anglesey (1973), op. cit., pp. 96–103 for cavalry training, drill and basic field formation in this period.

58   Holmes, op. cit., pp. 290–315.

59   Here, some readers may be reminded of Bunyan's *Holy War*, p. 7. 'In this Country, as I said, it was my lot to travel, and there travel I did, and so long, even till I learned much of their mother-tongue together with the Customs and the manners of them among whom I was. And to speak truth, I was much delighted to see, and hear many things which I saw and heard among them. Yea I had (to be sure) even lived and died a Native among them (so was I taken with them and their doings).' See Page 67 of the 'Memoir' for the conditions under which Pearman achieved this degree of communication with Punjabi villages, and Singh, op. cit., vol. 2, pp. 54, 65 for the unpopularity of the occupying British army. Much public outrage in the Punjab centred on the British slaughter of cattle, which offended Sikh and Hindu religious beliefs. Pearman mentions Muslim prohibitions on the pig in the 'Memoir', but he stole, killed and ate cows on several occasions. He evidently got to know Muslim people much better than he did Hindu or Sikh in this period.

60   D. H. McKinnon, *Military Service and Adventures in the Far East*,

Charles Oliver, 2 vols, 1849, vol. 1, p. 2.

61 John Pindar, *Autobiography of a Private Soldier*, Fife News Office, Cupar, Fife, 1877, p. 27.

62 Baldwin, op. cit., p. 71. For the European officers who were employed to train the Sikh army, see Bruce, op. cit., pp. 47–62, and also Fanja Singh Bajwa, *Military System of the Sikhs During the Period 1799–1849*, Motilal Banarsidass, Delhi, 1964.

63 Edward Royle, *Radicals, Secularists and Republicans: Popular Free-thought in Britain, 1866–1915*, Manchester University Press, Manchester, 1980, pp. 211–12.

64 For Zoroastrianism in India, see Mary Boyce, *Zoroastrians: Their Religious Beliefs and Practices*, Routledge & Kegan Paul, 1979, pp. 192–3, 196–209. There is an altogether fancier explanation of the distinction that John Pearman makes, which is to argue that here, John Pearman was working with a distinction given to him in the 1840s, between Shi'ite and Sunni Muslims, and the Sunni belief in self-government based on the Koran in opposition to the Shi'ite veneration of the Prophet and its recognition of a priestly line. The only recorded veneration of the sun within Indian Islam is that of a philosophical society founded by Akbar the Great (1556–1605), interest in which died with him. All recorded sects in nineteenth-century India were Shi'ite; but away from the centres of orthodox Islam, in the rural Punjab where Pearman did his wandering, Islamic ideas became mixed up with local popular beliefs, and he may have talked to a representative of a small local cult. But if this line of argument is correct, and given his own religious interests and his consistent condemnation of 'priestcraft' in the 'Memoir', the idea that John Pearman was making a distinction between Shi'ite and Sunni Muslims seems a more likely explanation. Aziz Ahmad, *An Intellectual History of Islam*, Edinburgh University Press, Edinburgh, 1969, pp. 44–6; A. S. Tritton, *Islam*, Hutchinson, 1951, pp. 72–88, 123–54. This elaborate explanation of the distinction (one that I adhered to for a very long time) would hold more water if the Indian language that Pearman transcribes phonetically in the 'Memoir' were Punjabi, in which the first syllable of 'sunni' is pronounced like the English word 'sun'; it would then be possible to argue that Pearman confused assertions of Sunni theology with the English word. But he does not show himself speaking Punjabi; in the 'Memoir' he transcribes a rural dialect of Hindustani (Urdu), in which the syllable *sun* is not pronounced in this way. It is fairly certain that using camp-Hindustani, Pearman spoke to a Zoroastrian and tried to work out what his beliefs were by reference to the named religion he knew about, which was Islam.

65 Anglesey, op. cit., pp. 90–7; Bruce, op. cit., pp. 281–96.

66 James Coley, *Journal of the Sutlej Campaign of 1845–6 and also of Lord*

Hardinge's Tour in the Following Winter, Smith Elder, 1856, pp. 52–3.
67　ibid., pp. 55–6.
68　Jim Obelkevitch, *Religion and Rural Society: South Lindsey, 1825–1875*, Clarendon Press, Oxford, 1976, pp. 280–95.

4　'A Low Order of Men'

1　'Many of the police belong to a low order of men. . .'. Select Committee on Penal Servitude, PP 1878–9, xxxvii, p. 337.
2　The County and Borough Police Act, 1856 (19&20 Vict. c.69). See Carolyn Steedman, *Policing the Victorian Community: the formation of English provincial police forces, 1856–1880*, Routledge & Kegan Paul, 1984, pp. 13–21.
3　ibid., p. 25. *Buckinghamshire Advertiser*, 10 January 1857; Hansard, Third Series, 141, p. 139; *The Times*, 21 August 1856.
4　Steedman, op. cit., p. 25.
5　Hansard, Third Series, 140, p. 2130.
6　Steedman, op. cit., pp. 80–91.
7　Edward M. Spiers, *The Army and Society, 1815–1914*, Longman, 1980, pp. 44–5.
8　Steedman, op. cit., p. 161.
9　ibid., p. 93.
10　Buckinghamshire Record Office, Constabulary Records, Register of Members of the Force, 1857. Report by Examiners into Acts of Intimidation. . .by Trade Unionists in Manchester. PP 1867–8, xxxiv, p. 634.
11　Buckinghamshire Record Office, Constabulary Records, Register of Members of the Force, 1857.
12　ibid.
13　George Pearman to the Marquess of Anglesey, 10 February 1968. Letter in the private possession of the Pearman family.
14　Anglesey, op. cit., p. 118, for Lieutenant-Colonel Unett's recommendation of Pearman in his letter of discharge. This letter was used as a reference when he joined the police. Buckinghamshire Record Office, Constabulary Records, Register of Members of the Force. He was recorded as being unmarried in the Register, though Anglesey believed that he married Elizabeth Collins in 1853, when he returned to England. Marquess of Anglesey, *Sergeant Pearman's Memoirs*, Cape, 1968, p. 122. In fact, they got married on 15 June 1857 at Winslow, Bucks. John Pearman had been in the force for three months, and gave his trade as sawyer. See Steedman, op. cit., p. 105 for policemen's tendency to define themselves by trade long after joining the police. When John Pearman registered his first child's birth in April 1859 (Rose Pearman had been born in January), he called himself 'policeman'.

15   County police authorities consistently lauded the virtues of the ploughman turned policeman, and laid out before recruits an almost entirely mythical progress towards the officer class. Yet Buckinghamshire did, in a minor way, fulfil its promise to its constables. John Pearman became an inspector, and Jabez Webb, farm labourer of Newport Pagnell, who joined as a third-class constable in 1857, became deputy chief constable in 1887. He was the ideal-type of county policeman, but in actuality, unique: his is the only instance of such a rise that I found.

16   Alexander Clark, *Reminiscences of a Police Officer in the Granite City Thirty Years Since*, Aberdeen, 1873, p. 33. See also Sean Wilentz, 'Crime, Poverty and the Streets of New York City: the diary of William H. Bell, 1850–51', *History Workshop Journal*, 7 (Spring 1979), pp. 126–55.

17   Steedman, op. cit., pp. 116–23.

18   ibid., pp. 47–53.

19   Carlo Ginzburg, *The Cheese and the Worms*, Routledge & Kegan Paul, 1980; Dominick LaCapra, *History and Criticism*, Cornell University Press, Ithaca, 1985, pp. 45–69.

20   Ginzburg, op. cit., pp. 20–1.

21   LaCapra, op. cit., pp. 66–91.

22   Steedman, op. cit., pp. 69–91.

23   ibid., pp. 162–3.

24   Anthea Trodd, 'The Policeman and the Lady: significant encounters in mid-Victorian fiction', *Victorian Studies*, 27:4 (Summer 1984), pp. 435–60.

25   Steedman, op. cit., pp. 69–91.

26   Jane Gallop, *Feminism and Psychoanalysis*, Macmillan, 1982, pp. 132–50. The phrase 'betwixt and between' is Mary Wollstonecraft's, and describes her feelings about being a governess in Ireland in the 1780s. Ralph M. Wardle, *The Collected Letters of Mary Wollstonecraft*, Cornell University Press, Ithaca, 1979, p. 124. Letter dated 5 November 1786.

27   Steedman, op. cit., pp. 162–3.

28   There are many autobiographies and fictions of detective officers, who were much more romantic figures. See Trodd, op. cit.

29   Steedman, op. cit., pp. 116–23.

30   See note to Pages 163–4 of the 'Memoir'.

31   Steedman, op. cit., pp. 49–52.

32   Among working-class military autobiography that was critical of militarism itself, see John Spencer Cooper, *Rough Notes of Seven Campaigns*, John Russell Smith, 1869; Joseph Donaldson, *Recollections of an Eventful Life*, Richard Griffin, Glasgow, 1856; William Taylor, *Life in the Ranks*, Parry Blenkhern, 1847. See Spiers, op. cit., pp. 72–3, 92–3. See Gwyn Harries-Jenkins, *The Army in Victorian*

Society, Routledge & Kegan Paul, 1977, p. 11.

33   Maureen M. Cain, 'Trends in the Sociology of Police Work', *International Journal of the Sociology of the Law*, 7 (1979), pp. 143–67, especially p. 158.

5   The Practice of Writing

1   Northamptonshire County Record Office, Miscellaneous Records, Police Journals, ML 202–12. Journal of Inspector George Williamson.

2   Sean Wilentz, 'Crime, Poverty and the Streets of New York City: the diary of William H. Bell, 1850–51', *History Workshop Journal*, 7 (Spring 1979), pp. 126–55.

3   See for example the practice in Stratford-upon-Avon, as described in Carolyn Steedman, *Policing the Victorian Community: the formation of English provincial police forces, 1856–1880*, Routledge & Kegan Paul, 1984, pp. 103–5.

4   Jack Goody (ed.), *Literacy in Traditional Societies*, Cambridge University Press, Cambridge, 1968, p. 3.

5   ibid., p. 62.

6   See notes to Pages 267–8 of the 'Memoir'.

7   Warwickshire Record Office, Constabulary Records, CR 908/2; Journal of William Cooper, Constable, Brailes Beat Division.

8   Walter J. Ong, *Orality and Literacy: the technologising of the word*, Methuen, 1982, pp. 147–55.

9   Sylvia Scribner and Michael Cole, *The Psychology of Literacy*, Harvard University Press, Cambridge, Mass., 1981, pp. 7–8.

10   Ong, op. cit., p. 152.

11   For a brief discussion of the debate on industrial time, see Tamara Hareven, *Family Time and Industrial Time*, Cambridge University Press, New York, 1982, pp. 1–8.

12   Steedman, op. cit., pp. 69–91.

13   Scribner and Cole, op. cit., p. 8.

14   See above, pages 56–7, note 19. See also Dave Morley and Ken Worpole, *The Republic of Letters: working class writing and local publishing*, Comedia, 1982, pp. 103–8; Dick Leith, *A Social History of English*, Routledge & Kegan Paul, 1983, pp. 40–57.

15   See Ong, op. cit., pp. 93–6.

16   Gareth Stedman Jones, 'Rethinking Chartism', in *Languages of Class: Studies in English Working Class History, 1832–1982*, Cambridge University Press, Cambridge, 1983, pp. 90–178.

17   ibid., pp. 101–2.

18   ibid., pp. 115–16.

19   Paul A. Pickering, 'Class Without Words: Symbolic Communication in the Chartist Movement', *Past and Present*, 112 (August 1986),

pp. 144–62. Here Pickering also makes the important point that Stedman Jones' analysis relies on the statement of its articulate and published leaders, and assumes that where they spoke or wrote or led, the great mass of Chartists followed.

20 John Burnett, *Destiny Obscure: autobiographies of childhood, education and the family from the 1820s to the 1920s*, Allen Lane, 1982, p. 9. David Vincent, *Bread, Knowledge and Freedom: a study of nineteenth century working class autobiography*, Methuen, 1982, pp. 3–11.

21 ibid., pp. 3, 14.

22 Burnett, op. cit., p. 10.

23 Mary Brigg (ed.), *A Lancashire Weaver's Journal, 1856–1864, 1872–1875*, The Record Society of Lancashire and Cheshire, vol. 122, 1982.

24 Vincent, op. cit., pp. 19, 31.

25 See above, pp. 17–18.

26 Ong, op. cit., pp. 102, 152.

27 Vincent, op. cit., pp. 14–16.

28 See above, pp. 22–3.

29 Carol Chomsky, 'Reading, Writing and Phonology', *Harvard Educational Review*, 40 (1970), pp. 287–309.

30 We cannot assume though, that Pearman retained a Surrey accent throughout his lifetime. Robert Blatchford, writing of soldiering in the 1870s, thought that barrack-room life had a clear effect on the way men spoke. 'I think that, as a rule, soldiers speak more correctly than civilians in their own rank of life, the tendency of barrack life being to assimilate all dialects and slightly to amend the level of merit in grammar and pronunciation – the amendment being due partly to travel and experience and partly to the example of educated officers.' Robert Blatchford, *My Life in the Army*, Clarion Press, n.d. (1904), p. 153. But in the 1840s, it is unlikely that a soldier would come into much contact with officers. See Alexander Somerville, *Autobiography of a Working Man, by One Who Has Whistled at the Plough*, Charles Gilpin, 1848, pp. 214–15.

31 The sociolinguistic history of this particularly difficult aspect of English is to be found in Leith, op. cit., pp. 145–9.

32 See above, p. 23. Phonetic, or phonic, methods of teaching reading depended on the emergence of the phonetic alphabet in the middle years of the nineteenth century, for example, in Alexander Melville Bell's *Visible Speech* (1867), and the establishment of an internationally agreed phonetic notation, in the 1880s and 1890s.

33 See above, pp. 23–4.

34 Mina P. Shaughnessy, *Errors and Expectations*, Oxford University Press, New York, 1977, pp. 91–2.

35 Lev Vygotsky, *Thought and Language* (1966), MIT Press, Cambridge, Mass., 1986, pp. 180–1; Gunther Kress, *Learning to Write*, Routledge

& Kegan Paul, 1982, p. 88, for the sentence as a structure of written language, not spoken language.

36 George Holyoake, *Practical Grammar, with Graduated Exercises* (8th edition), Book Store, 1870, pp. 55–60, on 'Pointing Sentences'. Jonathan Ree, 'Narrative and Identity', in Martin Warner (ed.), *Narrative*, Routledge & Kegan Paul (in preparation), on the need for a history of punctuation and a metaphysics of the quotation mark. Ian Watt gives a brief account of eighteenth-century typographical conventions in his Introduction to Lawrence Sterne, *Tristram Shandy*, Houghton Mifflin, Boston, 1965, pp. xliii–xlv. *Cassell's Popular Educator* is an invaluable guide to the conventions that were being established in the mid-Victorian period: *The Popular Educator* (6 vols), 1872–5, vol. 1. But any history of punctuation would have to distingiush between typographical convention and what got taught to children (and others) in schools.

37 Shaughnessy, op. cit., pp. 206–7.

38 Carolyn Steedman, *The Tidy House: Little Girls Writing*, Virago, 1982, pp. 93–108, and *passim*.

39 He also used brackets more conventionally, to show parenthesis.

40 Shaughnessy, op. cit., pp. 36–7

41 ibid., pp. 226–74.

42 Edward Royle, *Radicals, Secularists and Republicans: popular freethought in Britain, 1866–1915*, Manchester University Press, Manchester, 1980, p. 2.

6 The Propulsion of Experience

1 Royden Harrison, 'The Tenth April of Spencer Walpole: the problem of revolution in relation to reform, 1865–1867', *Before the Socialists*, Routledge & Kegan Paul, 1965, pp. 78–136; for this incident, see pp. 78–96. See also James Hinton, *Labour and Socialism: a history of the British Labour Movement, 1867–1974*, Wheatsheaf, Brighton, 1983, pp. 10–13.

2 ibid., pp. 97–8.

3 Bill Livingstone, then of the Centre for the Study of Social History, University of Warwick, first suggested to me that this combination of personal and public rejection in the summer and autumn of 1867 may have provided for John Pearman's moment of radical revelation in this way.

4 Edward Royle, *Victorian Infidels: the origins of the British secularist movement, 1791–1866*, Manchester University Press, 1974, pp. 114–19. See pp. 22–4 for the idea of philosophical necessity, which 'enabled the idea of regularity in nature to be combined with an exaltation of the powers of reason, and (which) provided a secular system of ethics to match the secularised concept of natural law. . .

In this grand scheme for the perfectability of man the old notions of original sin and salvation found little place.' But John Pearman's text shows with what struggle such ideas might be dealt with by individuals.

5   *Republican*, February 1882. See the cartoon 'Royalty "Raising the Wind" '. I am grateful to Edward Royle for telling me about the royal event of 1882, and for providing me with this reference.

6   Hubert Simmons, *Ernest Struggles; or the comic incidents and anxious moments in connection with the life of a station master, by one who has endured them all*, Hubert Simmons, Reading, 2 vols, 1880. Volume 2 deals with Simmons' life at Windsor. See p. 129 for the primrose story.

7   Quoted in Edward Royle, *Radicals, Republicans and Secularists: popular freethought in Britain, 1866–1915*, Manchester University Press, 1980, p. 126.

8   ibid., pp. 28–34.

9   ibid., p. 29.

10 Charles Bradlaugh, *The Autobiography of Mr Bradlaugh: a page of his life*, Austin, 1873, pp. 7–8.

11 Royle (1980), op. cit., p. 89.

12 Carolyn Steedman, *Policing the Victorian Community: the formation of English provincial police forces, 1856–1880*, Routledge & Kegan Paul, 1984, pp. 125–6, for curtailment of policemen's reading material in this period.

13 F.J. Gould, *The Life Story of a Humanist*, Watts, 1923, p. 38.

14 John Bedford Leno (ed.), *The Anti-Tithe Journal*, 1 (15 November 1881). This is the only copy of the journal that I have been able to find. The ninth edition of the *Encyclopedia Britannica* (vols 1–24), 1878–89, also gives this history.

15 John Bedford Leno, *The Aftermath*, Reeves & Turner, 1892, pp. 28.

16 Raymond South, *Royal Castle, Rebel Town: Puritan Windsor in Civil War and Commonwealth*, Barracuda Books, Buckingham, 1981.

17 Raymond South, *Heights and Depths: Labour in Windsor*, Ray South, Windsor, 1985, p. 8; and personal communication from Raymond South.

18 Richard D. Altick, *The English Common Reader*, University of Chicago Press, Chicago, 1957, p. 197.

19 Percy Bysshe Shelley, *The Complete Poetical Works of Percy Bysshe Shelley* (ed. Thomas Hutchinson), Oxford University Press, 1914. 'Queen Mab', pp. 754–825, lines 168–79. It is at this point that speculation about influences on Pearman could reach the stage of infinite progression: for Percy Bysshe Shelley was a student at Eton between 1804 and 1810, possibly writing stretches of 'Queen Mab' there before he left. Richard Holmes, *Shelley: the Pursuit*, Weidenfeld & Nicolson, 1974, pp. 18–35. Shelley was also living in Windsor in

1813, when 'Queen Mab' was first privately published. See Holmes, p. 224. Did radical Eton and Windsor have a special regard for this poem? Would it have been easier to lay hands on here than in other places? It is very likely that Pearman did read 'Queen Mab', and that the language in which Shelley exposed the unholy trinity of law, church and military, was one that he was able to mobilise for his own argument.

20   ibid., lines 183–6.

21   Philanthropus (Richard Carlile), *Character of a Soldier*, R. Carlile, 1821, p. 5.

22   Royle (1974), op. cit., pp. 22–4.

23   Eileen Yeo, 'Christianity in Chartist Struggle', *Past and Present*, 91 (May 1981). Keith McCleland, 'Radical Politics and the Working Class on Tyneside, 1857–1874', unpublished paper, 1987.

24   See Christopher Hill, 'The Religion of Gerrard Winstanley', *Past and Present*, Supplement 5, 1978, pp. 49–50, for the idea of God as an argument.

25   For the eighteenth-century understanding of natural law theory, see Basil Willey, *The Eighteenth Century Background*, Chatto & Windus, 1946, especially pp. 14–18. Carl L. Becker, *The Heavenly City of the Eighteenth Century Philosophers*, Yale University Press, New Haven, 1963, pp. 33–70. For the philosophical background, see A.P. d'Entreves, *Natural Law*, Hutchinson, 1951. See also Margaret C. Jacob, *The Radical Enlightenment: Pantheists, Freemasons and Republicans*, Allen & Unwin, 1981, pp. 65–86.

26   The figure of God animating creatures with life occurs throughout *Paradise Lost*. See Book ix, line 112: 'of Creatures animate with gradual life.' A direct quotation is to be found in S.T. Coleridge, 'The Aeolian Harp', lines 44–48:

> And what if all of animated nature
> Be but organic harps diversely framed
> That tremble into thought, as o'er them sweeps
> Plastic and vast, one intellectual breeze
> At once the soul of each and God of all?

27   See above, pp. 51–2.

28   Jim Obelkevitch, *Religion and Rural Society: South Lindsey, 1825–1875*, Clarendon Press, Oxford, 1976, pp. 298–9.

29   *Freethinker*, 9 July 1882; *National Reformer*, 9 April 1882. Of course, he may have encountered these ideas long before 1882: secularist tracts were being published in Calcutta in the 1840s; it seems that the *Reasoner* circulated in India; Thomas Cooper lectured in Manchester during the Crimean War, when John Pearman was working in Burnley. Royle (1974), op. cit., pp. 171, 209.

30   Charles Bradlaugh, *The Impeachment of the House of Brunswick* (1873),

Freethought Publishing Co., 1881. *Republican*, November 1881. Another source of these figures may have been Arthur Arnold, *Free Land*, Kegan Paul, 1880, pp. 1–13. See appropriate Note to the 'Memoir'.

31 For the Egyptian crisis and the invasion of the Sudan, see Byron Farwell, *Queen Victoria's Little Wars*, Allen Lane, 1973, pp. 218–81, and M.J. Williams, 'The Egyptian Campaign of 1882', in Brian Bond (ed.), *Victorian Military Campaigns*, Hutchinson, 1967.

32 For the maharajah's letters to *The Times*, and for his connections with Punjabi nationalism in this period, see Michael Alexander and Sushila Anand, *Queen Victoria's Maharajah, Dulip Singh, 1838–93*, Weidenfeld & Nicolson, 1980, pp. 143–66. See *The Times*, 31 August 1882 and 6 September 1882. The connections made by Dulip Singh, in so public a manner, may have helped Pearman make his own. For 'The God of Battles' story, see the *Freethinker*, 1 October 1882, and for a discussion of it, see below, pp. 94–6.

33 John Saville, 'Henry George and the British Labour Movement: a select bibliography with commentary', *Bulletin of the Society for the Study of Labour History*, 5 (Autumn 1962), pp. 18–26.

34 For the uses made by secularists of the ideas of Henry George, see Royle (1980), op. cit., pp. 194–8.

35 This particular issue of the *Freethinker* (1 October 1882) came out under the banner headline, 'Prosecuted for Blasphemy', one that might be especially eye-catching to the irregular reader of it. For the archbishop's prayer, see *The Times*, 7 August 1882.

36 Royle (1974), op. cit., pp. 139–41.

37 Farwell, op. cit., pp. 218–52; D.M. Schreuder, *The Scramble for Africa*, Cambridge University Press, Cambridge, 1980, pp. 61–112; *National Reformer*, 27 March 1881.

38 Schreuder, op. cit., pp. 87–8.

39 *National Reformer*, 8 October 1882.

40 See above, pp. 103–6.

41 Royle (1980), op. cit., p. 212.

42 ibid., pp. 197–8, 207–8.

43 See *National Reformer*, 10 November, 12 December 1878; 14, 21 December 1879.

44 Marquess of Anglesey, *Sergeant Pearman's Memoirs*, Cape, 1968, p. 21. Biographical detail here was taken from the surviving Pearman family.

45 For secularist approaches to the South Africa question, see Royle (1980), pp. 211–12.

46 See above, p. 62.

47 Royle (1974), op. cit., pp. 155, 216; Royle (1980), pp. 71, 168. Note Pearman on Page 10 of the 'Memoir' describing a fellow soldier and his wife as 'Irish but nice people'.

48   Royle (1980), op. cit., pp. 171–3.
49   Royle (1974), op. cit., p. 200; Royle (1980), op. cit., p. 109.
50   *National Reformer*, 9 April 1882.
51   Royle (1980), op. cit., pp. 167–74.
52   Robert Cooper, *Lecture on Original Sin*, Salford, 1838; Royle (1974), op. cit., pp. 108–11.
53   See above, pp. 51–2.
54   See above, note 24.
55   *National Reformer*, 9 April 1882, 'Christianity'.
56   Royle (1980), op. cit., p. 31.
57   For a discussion and a display of his desired trajectory, see William Lamont, 'The Left and its Past: Revisiting the 1650s', *History Workshop Journal*, 23 (Spring 1987), pp. 141–53, and Tony Benn (ed.), *Writings on the Wall: a Radical and Socialist Anthology, 1215–1985*, Faber, 1984, *passim*. Historically, though perhaps not politically, the trajectory does exist. See Jacob, op. cit., pp. 65–86.
58   Royden Harrison, 'The Land and Labour League', *International Institute of Social History Bulletin*, 8 (1953), pp. 169–95.
59   John Vincent, *The Formation of the Liberal Party, 1857–1868*, Constable, 1966, pp. xiii–xxxv, on how 'the really important attitudes [in party formation] had nothing to do with the industrial revolution, much to do with the English Civil war'.
60   The *Republican*'s definition of socialism is in the issue for June 1880; quoted in Royle (1980), op. cit., p. 232. For the *National Reformer*'s discussion of socialism, see the issue for 31 December 1882, 7 January 1883, 4 February 1883 and 4 March 1883. I am extremely grateful to Edward Royle for help on this point.
61   George H. Sabine (ed.), *The Works of Gerrard Winstanley*, Cornell University Press, New York, 1941, p. 355.
62   John Morrisson Davidson, *Concerning Four Precursors of Henry George and the Single Tax, and also the Land Gospel according to 'Winstanley the Digger'*, Labour Leader Publishing Co., 1899. This selection from Winstanley's writing does not include the passage quoted here.
63   See the *National Reformer*, 15 February 1880, 22 February 1880.
64   See Christopher Hill, *The Experience of Defeat*, Faber, 1984, pp. 37, 42 for the endurance of seventeenth-century radicalism.
65   Raymond Williams, *Politics and Letters*, Verso, 1979, pp. 167–8.
66   George Holyoake, *Practical Grammar, with graduated exercises* (8th edition), Book Store, 1870, p. 7.

7 Public and Private

1   David Vincent, *Bread, Knowledge and Freedom: a study of nineteenth century working class autobiography*, Methuen, 1982, pp. 87–107, for an account of this process at work.

2 Roy Pascal, *Design and Truth in Autobiography*, Routledge & Kegan Paul, 1960, pp. 84–94. See Luann Walther, 'The Invention of Childhood in Victorian Autobiography', in George P. Landow (ed.), *Approaches to Victorian Autobiography*, Ohio University Press, Athens, Ohio, 1979, pp. 64–83. Youth replaced childhood in this topography of the personal past towards the end of the century.

3 Most clearly, in Henry Mayhew's encounter with a crippled seller of birds in 1860, and his extraordinary recounting of it. Henry Mayhew, *London Labour and the London Poor* (4 vols, 1861–2), Frank Cass, 1967, vol. 2, pp. 67–9, and for an account of the recounting – though not from this perspective, Carolyn Steedman, 'True Romances', Raphael Samuel (ed.), *Patriotism*, vol. 1, Routledge, in press. For the bird as a female metaphor, see Ellen Moers, *Literary Women*, Women's Press, 1978, pp. 243–64.

4 Richard Holmes, *Firing Line*, Cape, 1985, pp. 136–75; John Keegan, *The Face of Battle*, Penguin, 1976, pp. 128–34.

5 J.W. Baldwin, *A Narrative of Four Months Campaign in India, Between the Years 1845–1846*, Josiah Fletcher, Norwich, 1853, p. 66.

6 James A. Coley, *Journal of the Sutlej Campaign of 1845–1846*, Smith Elder, 1856, p. 10.

7 Robert Blatchford, *My Life in the Army*, Clarion Press, n.d. (1904), pp. 107–8.

8 George Holyoake, *Practical Grammar, with graduated exercises* (8th edition), Book Store, 1870, p. 8.

Bibliography

(The place of publication is London, unless otherwise stated)

Ahmad, Aziz (1969), *An Intellectual History of Islam*, Edinburgh University Press, Edinburgh.

Alexander, Michael and Anand, Sushila (1980), *Queen Victoria's Maharajah, Dulip Singh, 1838–93*, Weidenfeld & Nicolson.

Altick, Richard D. (1957), *The English Common Reader*, University of Chicago Press.

Anglesey, The Marquess of (1968), *Sergeant Pearman's Memoirs*, Cape.

Anglesey, The Marquess of (1973), *A History of the British Cavalry, 1816–1919* (3 vols), vol. 1, 1816–1850, Leo Cooper.

Anstey, Roger (1962), *Britain and the Congo in the Nineteenth Century*, Clarendon Press, Oxford.

Archer, J.H. Lawrence, *Commentaries on the Punjab Campaign, 1848–1849*, W.H. Allen.

Arendt, Hannah (ed.) (1969), *Illuminations*, Schocken, New York.

Atwood, Margaret (1986), *The Handmaid's Tale*, Cape.

Bajwa, Franja Singh (1964), *Military System of the Sikhs During the Period 1799–1849*, Motilal Banarsidass, Delhi.

Baldwin, J.W. (1853), *A Narrative of Four Months Campaign in India, Between the Years 1845–6*, Josiah Fletcher, Norwich.

Bancroft, N.W. (1979), *From Recruit to Staff Sergeant* (1885), Ian Henry, Hornchurch.

Barrett, Michele (ed.) (1979), *Women and Writing*, Women's Press.

Becker, Carl L. (1963), *The Heavenly City of the Eighteenth Century Philosophers*, Yale University Press, New Haven.

Bettelheim, Bruno (1978), *The Uses of Enchantment: the meaning and importance of fairy tales*, Penguin.

Bingham, W.R. (1848), *The Field of Ferozeshah in Two Cantos, by a Young Soldier Who Fought in that Glorious Campaign*, Charles Edward Bingham.

Blatchford, Robert (n.d. [1904]), *My Life in the Army*, Clarion Press.

Bond, Brian (ed.) (1967), *Victorian Military Campaigns*, Hutchinson.

Boyce, Mary (1979), *Zoroastrians: Their Religious Beliefs and Practices*, Routledge & Kegan Paul.

Bradlaugh, Charles (1872), *The Land, the People and the Coming Struggle*, Austin.

Bradlaugh, Charles (1873), *The Autobiography of Mr Bradlaugh: a page of his life*, Austin.

Bradlaugh, Charles (1873), *The Impeachment of the House of Brunswick*, Freethought Publishing Company.

Bradlaugh, Charles (1877), *Cromwell and Washington*, C. Watts.

Brigg, Mary (ed.) (1982), *A Lancashire Weaver's Journal, 1856–1864, 1872–1875*, The Record Society of Lancashire and Cheshire.

Bruce, George (1969), *Six Battles for India, the Anglo-Sikh Wars, 1845–6, 1848–9*, Arthur Barker.

Bruce, George (1973), *The Burma Wars, 1824–1886*, Hart-Davis.

Bunyan, John (1980), *The Holy War* (1682), Clarendon Press, Oxford.

Burnett, John (1982), *Destiny Obscure, Autobiographies of Childhood, Education and the Family from the 1820s to the 1920s*, Allen Lane.

Cain, Maureen M. (1979), 'Trends in the Sociology of Police Work', *International Journal of the Sociology of the Law*, 7, pp. 143–67.

Callwell, C.E. (1896), *Small wars: their principles and practice*, War Office, Intelligence Division/Stationery Office.

Carlile, Richard (1821), *Character of a Priest*, R. Carlile.

Carlile, Richard (1821), *Character of a Soldier*, R. Carlile.

Chomsky, Carol (1970), 'Reading, Writing and Phonology', *Harvard Educational Review*, no. 40, pp. 287–309.

Clark, Alexander (1873), *Reminiscences of a Police Officer in the Granite City Thirty Years Since*, Aberdeen.

Cobden, Richard (1853), *How Wars Are Got Up in India: the origin of the Burmese War*, Cash.

Coley, James (1856), *Journal of the Sutlej Campaign of 1845–6 and also of Lord Hardinge's Tour in the Following Winter*, Smith Elder.

Conran, H.M. (1870), *Autobiography of an Indian Officer*, Morgan & Clare.

Cooper, John Spencer (1869), *Rough Notes of Seven Campaigns*, John Russell Smith.

Cooper, Robert (1838), *Lecture on Original Sin*, Salford.

Dickson, Harry (1883), *Six Months in the Ranks, or, The Gentleman Private*, Smith Elder.

Donaldson, John (1856), *Recollections of an Eventful Life*, Richard Griffin, Glasgow.

Donnellan, Philip (1980), 'Gone for a Soldier', BBC production, March 9, 1980.

Elliott, Alison (1982), *Child Language Development*, Cambridge University Press, Cambridge.

Engels, Frederick (1972), *The Origin of the Family, Private Property and the State* (1884), Lawrence & Wishart.

d'Entreves, A.P. (1951), *Natural Law*, Hutchinson.

Everson, Gordon F. (1981), 'Sergeant John Pearman, 3rd Light Dragoons', *The Orders and Medals Research Society*, vol. 20, no. 3, pp. 154–6.

Farwell, Byron (1973), *Queen Victoria's Little Wars*, Allen Lane.

Fletcher, Ian and Garman, Michael (eds) (1986), *Language Acquisition: studies in first language acquisition*, Cambridge University Press, Cambridge.

Gallop, Jane (1982), *Feminism and Psychoanalysis*, Macmillan.

Garvey, Catherine (1984), *Children's Talk*, Fontana.

Gaskell, Elizabeth (1970), *Mary Barton* (1848), Penguin.

George, Henry (1881), *Progress and Poverty*, Kegan Paul Trench.

Gilliland, John (1972), *Readability*, University of London Press.

Gilling, James (1855), *The Life of a Lancer in the Wars of the Punjab*, Simpkin Marshall.

Ginzburg, Carlo (1980), *The Cheese and the Worms*, Routledge & Kegan Paul.

Goody, Jack (ed.) (1968), *Literacy in Traditional Societies*, Cambridge University Press, Cambridge.

Gould, F.J. (1923), *The Life Story of a Humanist*, Watts.

Gowing, T. (1884), *A Soldier's Experience, or, A Voice from the Ranks Showing the Cost of War in Blood and Treasure*, W.H. Stevens, Norwich.

Hall, William (n.d. [1848]), *The Diary of William Hall*, privately printed, Penryn.

Hareven, Tamara (1982), *Family Time and Industrial Time*, Cambridge University Press, New York.

Harries-Jenkins, Gwyn (1977), *The Army in British Society*, Routledge & Kegan Paul.

Harrison, Royden (1953), 'The Land and Labour League', *International Institute of Social History Bulletin*, no. 8, pp. 169–95.

Harrison, Royden (1965), *Before the Socialists*, Routledge & Kegan Paul.

Heron, Liz (ed.) (1985), *Truth, Dare or Promise: Girls Growing Up in the Fifties*, Virago.

Hill, Christopher (1978), 'The Religion of Gerrard Winstanley', *Past and Present*, Supplement 5.

Hill, Christopher (1984), *The Experience of Defeat*, Faber.

Hilson, J.C., Jones, M.M.B. and Watson, J.R. (1978), *Augustan Worlds*, Leicester University Press, Leicester.

Hinton, James (1983), *Labour and Socialism: a history of the British Labour Movement*, Wheatsheaf, Brighton.

Hoggart, Richard (1957), *The Uses of Literacy*, Chatto & Windus.

Holmes, Richard (1974), *Shelley: The Pursuit*, Weidenfeld & Nicolson.

Holmes, Richard (1985), *Firing Line*, Cape.

Holyoake, George (1870), *Practical Grammar, with Graduated Exercises* (8th Edition), Book Store.

Innes, P.R. (1885), *The History of the Bengal European Regiment now the Royal Munster Fusiliers and How It Helped to Win India*, Simpkin Marshall.

Jacob, Margaret C. (1981), *The Radical Enlightenment: Pantheists, Freemasons and Republicans*, Allen & Unwin.

Keegan, John (1976), *The Face of Battle*, Penguin.

Kress, Gunther (1982), *Learning to Write*, Routledge & Kegan Paul.

LaCapra, Dominick (1985), *History and Criticism*, Cornell University Press, Ithaca.

Lamont, William (1987), 'The Left and Its Past: Revisiting the 1650s', *History Workshop Journal*, 23, pp. 141–53.

Landow, George P. (1979), *Approaches to Victorian Autobiography*, Ohio University Press, Athens, Ohio.

Leith, Dick (1983), *A Social History of English*, Routledge & Kegan Paul.

Leno, John Bedford (1892), *The Aftermath*, Reeves & Turner.

Lyons, John (ed.) (1970), *New Horizons in Linguistics*, Penguin.

McCleland, K. (1987), 'Radical Politics and the Working Class on Tyneside, 1857–1874', unpublished paper.

McKinnon, D.H. (1847), *Military Service and Adventures in the Far East, including Sketches of the Campaigns against the Afghans in 1839 and the Sikhs in 1845–6, By a Cavalry Officer* (2 vols), Charles Oliver.

Maine, Henry Sumner (1878), [1861], *Ancient Law: its connection with the early history of society and its relation to modern ideas*, John Murray.

Marshman, J.C. (1860), *Memoirs of Sir H. Havelock*, Longman Green.

Mather, F.M. (1959), *Public Order in the Age of the Chartists*, Manchester University Press, Manchester.

Mayhew, Henry (1967), *London Labour and the London Poor* (4 vols, 1851–62), Frank Cass.

Moers, Ellen (1978), *Literary Women*, Women's Press.

Moore Smith, G.C., *The Autobiography of Sir Harry Smith*, John Murray.

Morgan, Lewis Henry (1877), *Ancient Society*, Macmillan.

Morley, Dave and Walpole, Ken (eds) (1982), *The Republic of Letters: working class writing and local publishing*, Comedia.

Morris, Ronald (1973), *Success and Failure in Learning to Read*, Penguin.

Morrisson Davidson, J. (1899), *Concerning Four Precursors of Henry George and the Land Gospel according to "Winstanley the Digger"*, Labour Leader Publishing Co.

Obelkevitch, James (1976), *Religion and Rural Society: South Lindsey, 1825–1875*, Clarendon Press, Oxford.

Ong, Walter J. (1982), *Orality and Literacy: the technologising of the word*, Methuen.

Pascal, Roy (1960), *Design and Truth in Autobiography*, Routledge & Kegan Paul.

Peterson, Linda H. (1986), *Victorian Autobiography: the tradition of self interpretation*, Yale University Press, New Haven.

Pickering, Paul A. (1986), 'Class Without Words: Symbolic Communication in the Chartist Movement', *Past and Present*, no. 112, pp. 144–62.

Pindar, John (1877), *Autobiography of a Soldier*, Fife News Office, Cupar, Fife.

Piper, H.W. (1962), *The Active Universe: Pantheism and the Concept of Imagination in the English Romantic Poets*, Athlone.

Pitcher, E.G. and Prelinger, Ernest (1963), *Children Tell Stories: an analysis of fantasy*, International Universities Press, New York.

Police and Constabulary Almanac and Guide (annually, from 1858), Manchester.

Quinney, Thomas (1853), *Sketches of a Soldier's Life in India*, David Robertson, Glasgow.

Reddaway, W.F. et al. (1941), *The Cambridge History of Poland, 1697–1935*, Cambridge University Press, Cambridge.

Roa, G. Subba (1979), *Indian Words in English: a study of Indo-British Cultural and Linguistic Relations*, Clarendon Press, Oxford.

Royle, Edward (1974), *Victorian Infidels: the Origins of the British Secularist Movement, 1791–1866*, Manchester University Press, Manchester.

Royle, Edward (1980), *Radicals, Secularists and Republicans: popular freethought in Britain, 1866–1915*, Manchester University Press, Manchester.

Ryder, John (1853), *Four Years' Service in India*, W.H. Burton, Leicester.

Sabine, George H. (1941), *The Works of Gerrard Winstanley*, Cornell University Press, New York.

Samuel, Raphael (ed.) (in press), *Patriotism*, Routledge.

Sandford, Daniel Augustus (1849), *Leaves from the Journal of a Subaltern during the Campaigns in the Punjab, September 1848 to March 1849*, Blackwood, Edinburgh.

Saville, John (1962), 'Henry George and the British Labour Movement', *Bulletin of the Society for the Study of Labour History*, no. 5, pp. 18–26.

Schreuder, D.M. (1980), *The Scramble for Africa*, Cambridge University Press, Cambridge.

Scribner, Sylvia and Cole, Michael (1981), *The Psychology of Literacy*, Harvard University Press, Cambridge, Mass.

Segal, Lynn (1987), *Is the Future Female?* Virago.

Shaughnessy, Mina P. (1977), *Errors and Expectations*, Oxford University Press, New York.

Shelley, Percy Bysshe (1914), *The Complete Poetical Works*, Oxford University Press.

Simmons, Hubert (1880), *Ernest Struggles: or the comic incidents and anxious moments in connection with the life of a station master, by one who has endured them all*, Hubert Simmons, Reading.

Singh, Khushwant (1977), *A History of the Sikhs* (2 vols), Oxford University Press, Bombay.

Singh, Klushwant (1985), *Ranjit Singh, Maharajah of the Punjab*, Orient Longman, New Delhi.

Somerville, Alexander (1848), *The Autobiography of a Working Man, By One Who Has Whistled at the Plough*, Charles Gilpin.

South, Raymond (1985), *Heights and Depths: Labour in Windsor*, Ray South, Windsor.

Spiers, Edward M. (1980), *The Army and Society, 1815–1914*, Longman.

Spufford, Margaret (1981), *Small Books and Pleasant Histories: Popular Fiction and Its Readership in Seventeenth Century England*, Cambridge University Press, Cambridge.

Stedman Jones, Gareth (1983), *Languages of Class: Studies in English Working Class History, 1832–1982*, Cambridge University Press, Cambridge.

Steedman, Carolyn (1982), *The Tidy House: little girls writing*, Virago.

Steedman, Carolyn (1984), *Policing the Victorian Community: the formation of English provincial police forces, 1856–1880*, Routledge & Kegan Paul.

Street, Brian (1984), *Literacy in Theory and Practice*, Cambridge University Press, Cambridge.

Swindels, Julia (1985), *Victorian Writing and Working Women*, Polity, Oxford.

Taussig, Mick (1987), 'An Australian Hero', *History Workshop Journal*, 24, pp. 110–33.

Taylor, William (1847), *Life in the Ranks*, Parry Blenkhern.

Thackwell, E.J. (1851), *Narrative of the Second Sikh War*, Richard Bentley.

Thompson, E.P. (1971), *William Morris: Romantic to Revolutionary*, Pantheon, New York.

Thurston, Herbert (1930), *No Popery: Chapters on Anti-Papal Prejudice*, Sheed & Ward.

Tritton, A.S. (1951), *Islam*, Hutchinson.

Trodd, Anthea (1984), 'The Policeman and the Lady: significant encounters in mid-Victorian fiction', *Victorian Studies*, vol. 27, no. 4.

Vincent, David (1982), *Bread, Knowledge and Freedom: a Study of Nineteenth Century Working Class Autobiography*, Methuen.

Vincent, John (1966), *The Formation of the Liberal Party, 1857–1868*, Constable.

Vygotsky, L.S. (1978), *Mind in Society*, Harvard University Press, Cambridge, Mass.

Vygotsky, L.S. (1986), *Thought and Language* (1966), MIT Press, Cambridge, Mass.

Wardle, Ralph M. (1979), *The Collected Letters of Mary Wollstonecraft*, Cornell University Press, Ithaca.

Waterfield, Robert, Swinson, A. and Scott, D. (eds) (1968), *The Memoirs of Private Waterfield, 1842–57*, Cassell.

Watkins, Owen Spencer (1906), *Soldiers and Preachers Too, Being the Romantic Story of Methodism in the British Army*, Charles H. Kelley.

Whitworth, G.C. (1885), *An Anglo-Indian Dictionary*, Kegan Paul.

Wilentz, Sean (1979), 'Crime, Poverty and the Streets of New York City: the Diary of William H. Bell, 1850–51', *History Workshop Journal*, 7, pp. 126–55.

Willey, Basil (1946), *The Eighteenth Century Background*, Chatto & Windus.

Williams, Raymond (1979), *Politics and Letters*, Verso.

Yeo, Eileen (1981), 'Christianity in Chartist Struggle', *Past and Present*, no. 91.

Yule, Henry and Burnell, A.C., *Hobson-Jobson: a glossary of colloquial Anglo-Indian Words and Phrases*, John Murray.

Zaretsky, Eli (1976), *Capitalism, the Family and Personal Life*, Pluto.

Zipes, Jack (1985), *Fairy Tales and the Art of Subversion*, Heinemann.

Working-Class Military Autobiography

A Select List

Baldwin, J.W. (1853), *A Narrative of Four Months Campaign in India, Between the Years 1845–6*, Josiah Fletcher, Norwich.
Served with the 9th regiment of Foot.

Bancroft, N.W. (1979), *From Recruit to Staff Sergeant* (1885), Ian Henry, Hornchurch.
Served in the Bengal Horse Artillery.

Blatchford, Robert (n.d. [1904]), *My Life in the Army*, Clarion Press.
Editor of the socialist *Clarion* newspaper, served in the 103rd, later the Dublin Fusiliers.

Cooper, John Spencer (1869), *Rough Notes of Seven Campaigns*, John Russell Smith.
Memories of the Peninsular campaigns. A classically bitter account of the army's treatment of the common soldier.

Donaldson, John (1856), *Recollections of an Eventful Life*, Richard Griffin, Glasgow.
Memories of service in the Peninsular Wars, and in Ireland.

Gilling, James (1855), *The Life of a Lancer in the Wars of the Punjab*, Simpkin Marshall.
Served in the 9th Royal Lancers. Son of a Worksop publican. Had worked as a hairdresser.

Gowing, T. (1884), *A Soldier's Experience, or A Voice from the Ranks Showing the Cost of War in Blood and Treasure*, W.H. Stevens, Norwich.
Son of a Baptist minister from Halesworth, Norwich. Personally embraces the principles of imperialism.

Green, John (1827), *The Vicissitudes of a Soldier's Life, or, a series of reminiscences from 1806–1815*, privately printed, Louth.
Formerly a hawker of books. *Vicissitudes* is notable for its view of battle from the inside, and the extreme conservatism of its author.

Hall, William (n.d. [1848]), *The Diary of William Hall*, privately printed, Penryn.
'A gentleman of this town' suggested that Hall send his 'Diary to the press in the simple form in which I took my notes . . . there has been no attempt to . . . "write a book" '.

Jowett, W. (1856), *Memoir and Diary of Sergt. W. Jowett, Seventh Royal*

Fusiliers, West Kent, privately printed.
Jowett died in the Crimea. This is an edited edition of his journal.
Menzies, John (1883), *Reminiscences of an Old Soldier, with Poems*,
    Crawford & M'Cabe, Edinburgh.
    Memories of enlistment in 1834 in the 45th or 1st Notts Regiment.
    Formerly a ploughman and nurseryman.
Pindar, John (1877), *Autobiography of a Soldier*, Fife News Office, Cupar,
    Fife.
    Formerly a miner of Fife. Enlisted in the 71st regiment of Foot in June
    1858; served in India. Notable for its antagonism towards its
    inhabitants.
Quinney, Thomas (1853), *Sketches of a Soldier's Life in India*, David
    Robertson, Glasgow.
    From an army family near Haddington. Enlisted when very young in
    the Indian army.
Ryder, John (1853), *Four Years' Service in India*, W.H. Burton, Leicester.
    John Ryder also became a policeman, and the foreword to his book
    was written by the Chief Constable of Leicestershire.
Somerville, Alexander (1848), *The Autobiography of a Working Man, By
    One Who Has Whistled at the Plough*, Charles Gilpin.
    Much detail of Somerville's time in the Scotch Greys.
Swanston, Paul (1850), *Memoirs of Sergeant Paul Swanston; being a narative
    of a soldier's life*, B.D. Cousins.
    Memoirs of the Peninsular Wars. The form here is that of an adventure
    story.
Waterfield, Robert, Swinston, Arthur and Scott, Donald (eds) (1968),
    Memoirs of Private Waterfield, 1842–1857, Cassell.

Index

As a great deal of information is conveyed for the first time in the Notes to the transcript of the 'Memoir', this Index makes selective reference to the Notes. Please note that this Index does *not* reproduce John Pearman's spelling when his 'Memoir' is being referred to. Page references to the 'Memoir' itself are in italics.

Abercrombie, Colonel William, *47*, 256
Aberdeen, 56
Alexander the Great, *145, '179*
Alexander, Lieutenant Colonel James Alexander, *31–2, 38, 41*, 254
Aliwal, *40*; *see also* battles
Allahabad, *10, 12*, 251
Amritsar, Treaty of, 262
Anglesey, Marquess of, 4, 13–14, 261–2
'animated nature', 4, 90, *159, 163*, 263
anthropology, 97
Arabi Pasha, *see* Egypt
army: comradeship in, 48; drink, *8, 61–4*, as escape route, 27; *65–6, 69–71, 73, 131, 136, 147–9*; field formations, 48, 252, 253, 256, 257, 260; flogging, *12*; intake, *53*; literacy levels in, 55; mortality rate in, 35; officers, 46; prize agents, *128, 130, 131*; promotion, 37; religion in, *72–1*, 259; soldiering compared with policing, 58–9; welfare reforms in, *70–1*; working conditions, 34, 36; wounding, *36 see also* 'British Soldiers', What Is a Soldier'; *see also* cavalry; *see also* regiments; *see also* soldiers; *see also* Working-Class Military

Autobiography
atheism, 87
Atwood, Margaret (*The Handmaid's Tale*), 2
autobiography, 68, 103: autobiographical models and traditions, 18; military working-class autobiography, 5–6, 7, 17, 18, 20, 34, 37, 105; working-class autobiography, 5, 19, 21, 30, 31–2, 37, 67, 69, 103
Aylesbury, 52, 54, *153, 157, 158*

Badowal, *28, 30, 31*, 254; engagement at (21 January, 1846), 45, *20–5, 42*, 253–4
Baldwin, J.W. (*Narrative of Four Months Campaign in India*), 35, 40, 49, 105
Bancroft, N.W. (*From Recruit to Staff Sergeant*), 45, 47
Barclay, Tom, 22
Bassian, *18*, 252
Bath, *151*
battles, 44, 105: Battle of Aliwal (28 January, 1846), 44, 105, *33–7*, 254; Battle of Chilianwala (13 January, 1849), 44, 45, 50, 110, *101–6*, 261; Battle of Ferozeshah, 44, 47, *42*, 255; Battle of Gujrat (21 February, 1849), 32, 35, 44, 45, 47, 110, *121–6, 173*; Battle of Mudki, 44,

51, *42*, 255; Siege and Battle of Multan, 44; Battle of Ramnagar (22 November, 1848), 45, 85, 105, *80–7*, 260; Battle of Sabraon (10 February, 1846), 45, 105, *44–54*, 255–6; Battle of the Somme (1916), 7

Bell, William (patrolman, New York), 62, 96

Benares (Varanasi), *11*, 251

Benjamin, Walter, 41

Besant, Annie, 95

Bettelheim, Bruno, 41

Bhairowal, Treaty of, 258

Blatchford, Robert, 105

Boer War: First Boer War (1880–1), 15, 92, 94, 109

Bradlaugh, Charles, 19, 88, 89, 92, 100, *202*, 263, 265, 265–6, 266

Brahmaputra River, 251

'British Soldiers' (verse), *236–7*

Bruce, George (*Six Battles for India*), 47

Buckinghamshire Constabulary, 1, 27, 52, *153*, 261

Buddha, *162*

Bunyan, John (*The Holy War*), 42–3

Burma, *198*; Burma War: Third Burma War (1853), 109, 265

Burnett, John (*Destiny Obscure*), 67, 68

Burnley, *152*

Calcutta, *5, 9, 37*

Callwell, Sir Charles (*Small Wars: Their Principles and Practice*), 44

Cambridge, Duke of, 55, *152*, 263

Canterbury, Archbishop of, 109, *172, 173, 174, 180, 201, 250*

Cape of Good Hope, *146*

Carlile, Richard, 5, 91, 267

cast, *69, 170*

cavalry, 35, 36, 48, 253

Cetewayo, *see* Zulus

chapbook fiction, 18, 38, 40

Chartism, 65–6, 89

Chatham, *147, 150*

Cheetham, Harold (Lancashire Constabulary), 54

Chenab River, *76, 77, 78, 91*, 259, 117

Chesham (Buckinghamshire), 54

Chinsura, *6, 9*, 251

cholera, *8, 10, 13*, 251

Christianity, 42, 82, 85, 87, 96, 97, 99

Clark, Alexander (Aberdeen police), 56

Coleridge, S.T. ('Aeolian Harp'), 4

Coley, James, 51, 91, 105

Cooper, John Spencer (*Rough Notes of Seven Campaigns*), 34, 38

Cooper, Robert (*Lecture on Original Sin*), 97–8

Cooper, William (Warwickshire Constabulary), 63

County and Borough Police Act (1856), 52, 53

Crimean War, 17, 26, 34, 52, 53, *150, 151, 152*

Cromwell, Oliver, 100, *194, 197*, 265

Cureton, Brigadier General Sir Charles, 77, *80, 85*, 259

Davidson, John Morrisson (*Four Precursors of Henry George*), 101

Defoe, Daniel, *241*

Dehli, *16*

Diamond Harbour, *5*, 251

Dick, Major General Sir Robert Henry, *47, 48, 49, 50*, 256

Dinapur, *11*, 251

discipline, 18–19, 104, *245*

Donaldson, Joseph, (*Recollections of an Eventful Life*), 34

Donnellan, Philip, 1

Dover, *1, 147*

Duke of Argyll (ship), *146*, 263

East India Company, 15, 48, 51, *191*, 265

Egypt: British occupation of, 15, 92, 94, 109, *172, 173*
English: informal English, 23, 65, 70
English Civil War, 102
English Land Restoration League, 101
error: written errors, 23–4, 70–3
Eton, 13, 29, 54, 86, 87, *158, 214*; Eton College, 61, 89; Master of Eton, 82
Everson, Gordon, 32
Exeter, *151*

fairy-tales, 6, 17, 40–1, *see also* chapbook fiction
Farey, George (Buckinghamshire Constabulary), 54
Field of Ferozeshah in Two Cantos (W.R. Bingham), 34–5
Firozpur: *76, 173,* 259; camp at Ferozepur, 51
Foote, G.W., 88
Foredyce, Colonel John, *114,* 261
Fort William, *6, 6*
Freethinker, 60, 88, 92, 93, 94
freethought, 4, 5, 85, 87, 88, 90, 92, 94, 98–9; freethought press, 60, 89, 91

Galileo, *162*
Ganges River, 38, *1, 195,* 251
Gaskell, Elizabeth (*Mary Barton*), 6
George, Henry (*Progress and Poverty*), 23, 92–3, 263, 265
Gilbert, Major General Sir Walter Raleigh, *47, 48, 49,* 256
Gilling, James (*The Life of a Lancer in the Wars of the Punjab*), 34, 38, 40
Ginsburg, Carlo (*The Cheese and the Worms*), 56–7
'Gone for a Soldier' (BBC broadcast), 1
Gough, Lieutenant Geneal Sir Hugh, 85, *38, 40, 58, 78, 90, 96, 102, 109, 127, 134, 173,* 255

Gould, F.J., 89
Gowing, T. (*A Soldier's Experience*), 40
Gravesend, 1
Great Marlow (Buckinghamshire), *157*
Great Missenden (Buckinghamshire), 89
Great Western Railway, 87–8, *190*
Grenadier Guards, 110, 266–7
Gujerat, 50
Gujrat, *116, 119, 123, 126, 127: see also* battles

Haillah (Helan), *100,* 99
Hall, William (*Diary*), 40, 42
Hardinge, Field Marshal Sir Henry, 47, *58*
Harlow, 54
Harries-Jenkyns, Gwyn, 44
Havelock, Lieutenant Colonel William, *64, 85,* 258
Hindustani (phonetically transcribed), *69, 73, 129,* 258, 259, 261
Hoggart, Richard (*Uses of Literacy*), 6
Holmes, Richard (*Firing Line*), 35, 37, 39, 46, 48, 105
Holyoake, George (*Practical Grammar*), 74, 102, 105
horses, 36, *56*
Hughes, Major General, 45
Hugli River, 251

imperialism, 48–9, 66, 94, 100–2
India, 27, 48, 85, 95
Ireland, 95, *163, 187, 234*: Irish Land Bill (1881), 95; Irish reform, 92
Islam, 50, *182, 197, 235*

Jallunder, 76: Jallunder doab, *138*
Jammu Province, 262
Jelum River, 261
Jesus of Nazareth, *160, 162, 164, 166, 186, 193, 199, 203*

'John Company', *see* East India
   Company
Jugroan, *31*, 254

Kanpur, *13*, 251
Karachi, 146, 263
Karnal, *17, 18*, 252
Kashmir, *92, 138, 139*, 262
Kasur, *56*
Keegan, John (*The Face of Battle*),
   17, 36, 39, 105
King, Lieutenant Colonel, *135*
kingcraft, 174, *239, 249, 250*, 262
Kingston-upon-Thames, 27
Kirkee, *64*, 258
Kunda: Chak Kunda, *56*, 257

LaCapra, Dominick, 21, 56–7
Lahore, *76, 77, 131*: Treaty of, 44,
   58, 257–8
Lancashire, 27, 54
land: land ownership, 24, 59, 89,
   93, 95, *163–4*, 263–4; land
   reform, 91
Land and Labour League, 100
Land Nationalisation League, 101
Land Reform League, 100
language acquisition, 21
law: 60, *226*; natural law, 24, 90–1,
   99
Leno, John Bedford (*Anti-Tithe
   Journal*), 89
Leopold, Prince George Duncan
   Albert (1853–84), 87
Leopold II, King of the Belgians,
   110
letters: as working notes, 14–15,
   68, 84–5; written from Camp
   Gujrat, *251–64*; written to and
   from India, 267; *see also* writing
Levellers, 19, 102
liminality, 56–8
Liverpool, *151*
Lockwood, Colonel Sir George
   Henry, 71, *119*, 258
Long Crendon
   (Buckinghamshire), *153, 157*

Lucknow, *15*
Ludhiana, *20, 22, 38*, 253

McKinnon, D.H. (*Military Service
   and Adventures in the Far East*), 17
Madhumate (Megna) river, 251
magistracy, 56, 59
Maguire, Tom, 22
Mahomet, *162*
Maidstone, *1, 150*
Maine, Henry (*Ancient Law*), 265
Majuba Hill *see* Boer War
Manchester, *151*
Marlborough, Duke of, *179*
marriage, *208–13, 265*
masculinity, 7
Mathias, Captain William, *9, 21,
   31*, 251
Mian Meer, *131, 134*, 257
Methodism, 259: Methodist
   narrative, 41–2
military history, 17
Milton, John, 4
Mohammedanism, *see* Islam
Monghyr, *11*, 251
Monks Risborough
   (Buckinghamshire), 54
Morgan, Lewis Henry (*Ancient
   Society*), 265
Mudki, *76 see also* battles
Multan, Siege of, *74, 116, 130*,
   259, 261
musselman, *see* Islam

Napier, General Sir Charles, *134*
National Army Museum, 5
National Reformer, 60, 87, 89, 92,
   95, 99, 100
National Secular Society, 88, 89
nature, *181*: serenity of nature,
   180; state of nature, *184*; *see also*
   animated nature; *see also* law:
   natural law
necessitarianism, *see* philosophical
   necessity
Newport Pagnell, *155*
North Crawley

(Buckinghamshire), *156*
Northamptonshire Constabulary, 62
Nur-ud-Din, Fakir, *57*, 257

Obelkevitch, Jim, 52
omnipotence, 97, 98, *170, 195, 246*
O'Neal, John (*Lancashire Weaver's Journal*), 67
Ong, Walter (*Orality and Literacy*), 63, 64, 69
Ore, Private (80th Foot), 51–2, 91, 98

PALS regiments, 7
Pearman, Elizabeth, 104, *213*
Pearman, George, 13, 132
Pearman, John (1891–1908), accompanies prisoner to Paris, *267–8*; army career, *270*; children: 86, *208, 209, 210, 211, 213, 214–20*, 266; deserts 3rd Light Dragoons, 32: discharged, 54; during Crimean War: 54–5, *151–3;* family crisis (1867), 16–7, *215–221;* family history, *269;* funeral of, 32: gives instructions for, 91, *248–9;* hospitalised: 35–6, *139–43; marriage, 103–5, 208–13, 280–1;* police career, 25–8, 28–9, 33, 34, 54, 61, *153–8, 214*, 215; writes letter from Camp Gujrat: 14, 84–5, *251–64; see also* battles *see also* Elizabeth Pearman *see also* Sikh Wars
Peninsular Wars, 17, 38, 45, 105
'Peninsular men', 44–5, *120*
pensions, 29, 33, *158, 208, 214*
Phillaur, *37*, 255
philosophical necessity, 4, 90
Pindar, John (*Autobiography of a Soldier*), 49
Plymouth, *151*
Poland, 110, *179*, 264
police: detective work, 56, 58, *153–8;* police distribution, 59;

police mortality rates, 31; police officers, 25, 55; police recruits, 26–7; police turnover, 25–6, 53–4; police working conditions, 27–30, 34; promotion, 28, 37; Select Committee on Police Superannuation (1875), 31; writing in police forces, 62–3; *see also* Buckinghamshire Constabulary; *see also* County and Borough Police Act
Police Service Advertiser, 29, 30, 31
policemen: as servants, 6; *see also* servants
policing, 20; compared with soldiering, 58–9
Policing the Victorian Community (Steedman), 1, 55, 57
Pope, Brigadier, 45
Pretoria Convention (1881), 94, *198*, 265 *see also* Zulus
priesthood, *161, 162, 176*
punctuation, 73–4, 79–80 *see also* writing
Punjab, 43, 44, 102, *56*
Punjab Campaign (Second Sikh War), 252

Quinney, Thomas (*Sketches of a Soldier's Life in India*), 36

radicalism, 66, 99–100
Ramnuggar (Rasulnagar), 77, *78, 86, 91, 98*, 259; *see also* battles
Ravi River, 76, *138*
readability, 22–3
Reading, 89
Reform League, 86–7
regiments: 3rd Light Dragoons, *1, 41, 48, 66*, 250, 266–7; 9th Lancers, *41, 54, 104, 114, 118*; 10th Foot, *47, 117, 119*; 14th Light Dragoons, *64, 65, 66, 85, 104, 118, 119, 131, 132, 134, 135, 136*; 24th Foot, *103, 104, 105, 109, 139*; 16th Lancers, *19, 24, 31, 36, 38, 41, 65*; 29th Foot,

138; 50th Foot, *47*; 53rd Foot, *13, 17, 23, 24, 34, 59*; 62nd Foot, *25, 47*; 75th Foot, *137*; 80th Foot, *47*
Republican, 87, 92, 100
republicanism, 87
Rivers, Isabel, 41
Roman Catholicism, 96; excommunication, *228–31*, 266
Rose, Charles (Buckinghamshire Constabulary), 54, 55
Royle, Edward (*Radicals, Secularists and Republicans*), 85, 88, 90, 95
Ryder, John (*Four Years' Service in India*), 5, 34, 49

Sabraon, *40*; *see also* battles
Sadalapur, *96*: Action at Sadalapur (3 December, 1848), *94–6*, 260, 267
Sandford, Daniel (*Leaves from the Journal of a Subaltern*), 47
Sand Heads, *4*, 250–1
Sandhurst, 27, 54, *152, 210*
Scotland, 95
Scribner, Sylvia and Cole, Michael (*The Psychology of Literacy*), 63–4
Secular Chronicle, 100
secularism *see* freethought
Sergeant Pearman's Memoirs (Anglesey), 13
servants, 1, 58
Shaughnessy, Mina (*Errors and Expectations*), 72–3
Shelley, Percy Bysshe ('Queen Mab'), 4, 89–90
Sherrington (Buckinghamshire), *154, 155*
Sialkot, *138, 139*, 262
Sikh Raj, 43
Sikh Wars (1845–1849), 13, 36, 43–4, 45, 252; *see also* Amritsar, Treaty of; Bhairowal, Treaty of; Lahore, Treaty of
Sikhs, *15, 40, 197*
Simmons, Hubert ('Ernest Struggles'), 87–8

sin, 97, 98–9, *173, 183, 188, 207*, 227
Singh, Maharajah Dulip, 43, 92, *59, 258, 262*
Singh, Maharajah Gulub, *57, 58, 138–9*, 257, 262
Singh, Maharajah Ranjit, 43, *131*
Singh, Rajah Shere, *74, 77, 116*, 259
Smith, Lieutenant General Sir Harry, *19, 26, 47, 48, 49*, 252–3
Smyth, Major General Sir John, *32*, 254
socialism, 82, 100, *199–200, 203*
soldiering *see* army
soldiers: soldier heroes, 40–2; soldiers' stories, 39; *see also* autobiography: military working-class autobiography; *see also* 'British Soldiers'; 'What Is a Soldier'.
Somme, *see* battles
Sommerville, Alexander (*Autobiography of a Working Man*), 38
square formations *see* army; *see also* cavalry
Standring, George, 92
Stanley, Henry, 110; *242*, 242
Steeple Claydon (Buckinghamshire), *153*
Stedman Jones, Gareth (*Languages of Class*), 65–6
Stisted, Lieutenant Thomas Heathcote, *105, 106*, 261
Stockport, 54
Stoke Goldington (Buckinghamshire), *157*
Sunderbans, *9*, 251
Sutlej Campaign (First Sikh War), 252
Sutlej River, *41*, 43, *51, 56, 76, 137*

Tel-el-Kebir, *see* Egypt
Thackwell, Major General Sir Joseph, 32, *13, 78, 94, 114*, 251–2

Thetis (ship) *1*, 251
Thompson, E.P., , 22
ticket-of-leave system, 53
Tiger Isles (Saugaur Sand), *4*,
    250–1
time, 64–5
tithes, 89, *174–8*, 264
transportation, 53
Transvaal, 15
Trodd, Anthea, 58
Turkey, 54

Umbala: camp at Umbala, 51,
    105, *59–74, 136–7*, 262
Unett, Captain Walter, *105, 106*

vagrancy, 53
Vai (Nigeria), *see* writing
Victoria, Queen, 61, *222, 239*:
    income of, 92, *232*
Vincent, David (*Bread, Knowledge
    and Freedom*), 30, 67, 68
Vygotsky, L.S., 73

Waldemarr, Prince Frederick
    William, *38*, 255
Wales, 95, 96, *163, 164, 234*
Wazirabad, 77, *91, 138, 139*, 259
Wellington, Duke of, *54, 179*
'What Is a Soldier' (verse), *250*
White, Lieutenant General Sir
    Michael, *42*, 46, *85, 120, 121*,
    255
Williamson, George

(Northamptonshire
    Constabulary), 28
Windsor, 29, 89, 102: Windsor
    Castle, 13, *37*; 54, 61, 109,
    Windsor and Eton Express, 32
Winkfield (Berkshire), 86, *218,
    220, 221*
Winstanley, Gerrard, 101, 102
Wishe, Lieutenant General Sir
    William, *262*, 267
Woolf, Virginia, 3
Wordsworth, William, 4
writing, 15–16: audience for, 69,
    77; and speech, 65, 66–7, 73, 75,
    76–9, 80–1; as historical
    evidence, 20–1; children's
    writing, 7, 8; cohesion in, 74–5;
    essay form, 83; in police forces,
    62–3; invented writing system
    among the Vai, 63–4; journal-
    keeping, 63, 67; letter-writing,
    67; psychological effects of,
    63–70; relationship to reading,
    22–3; sex-differences in, 3; *see
    also* errors; *see also* punctuation

Yerbury, Lieutenant Colonel John,
    94, 260

Zoroastrianism, 50, *197, 235, 243*
Zulus: 94, *198*, 265: Cetewayo,
    King of the Zulus, 109; defeat at
    Ulundi (1879), 15